OPERATIONS RESEARCH ----------methods and problems

OPERATIONS RESEARCH

New York · John Wiley & Sons, Inc.

London · Sydney

-------------methods and problems

MAURICE SASIENI

Research Associate
Operations Research Group
Case Institute of Technology

ARTHUR YASPAN

Operations Research Division
Lybrand Ross Bros. and Montgomery

LAWRENCE FRIEDMAN

Manager of Operations Research
M & M's Candies

Eleventh Printing, August, 1967

Preface

Most books of a technical nature arise from a specific need in some field of endeavor. In the new and growing field of operations research, students, teachers, and practitioners alike have felt the lack of a textbook containing illustrative problems and exercises. As far as we know, this book makes such material available to the general public for the first time.

Much of the subject matter of this book arose out of a problems course in operations research, designed as a companion course to the general methods course offered at Case Institute of Technology. In developing any new course, according to the familiar law of least effort, one resorts to the techniques of collection, adaptation, and invention in that order. The resulting material will thus not be entirely original; it will, however, express the preference, judgment, and personality of those who do the work.

The book is addressed to readers who have a working knowledge of the differential and integral calculus. Following the introductory material, which includes a problem-centered review of certain basic topics in probability and statistics, each chapter contains (1) the general theory and techniques of a particular problem area in operations research, (2) a number of completely solved problems demonstrating these techniques, and (3) a number of problems for the reader to solve, some with answers. Each of Chapters 4 through 10 is concerned with a separate area in operations research, and is complete in itself as a teaching unit.

v

By following through the examples and solving the problems, a reader of this book can develop skill in formulating and solving mathematical models. He will learn little about such crucial phases of operations research as recognition of a problem, the collection of relevant information, and implementation of a solution. These phases of operations research are perhaps better mastered through practical experience on real problems.

This work can serve as a textbook for a one-semester introductory techniques course, at either the graduate or the advanced undergraduate level. Because of its intermediate mathematical level and wide scope, it could also be used profitably by students majoring in such fields as industrial engineering, statistics, economics, and applied mathematics.

MAURICE SASIENI
ARTHUR YASPAN
LAWRENCE FRIEDMAN

April 1959

Acknowledgments

We are especially indebted to Eliezer Naddor and Russell L. Ackoff. Dr. Naddor, presently at Johns Hopkins University, was one of the originators of the problems course at Case Institute; and many of our examples are based on models which he developed. Dr. Ackoff, the head of the operations research group at Case Institute, has been a constant inspiration; he encouraged the writing of this book and helped obtain the necessary funds for its development.

Other colleagues at Case helped materially with advice and assistance. John D. C. Little contributed some problems, and suggested improvements in certain difficult areas. Others who read parts of the manuscript and offered helpful criticism are E. Leonard Arnoff, John C. Chambers, Richard Cobb, James Fisher, Fred Hanssmann, Sidney Hess, George Summers, and Tibor Fabian.

General reviews of the manuscript as a whole were received from C. West Churchman and Arthur Gould. Richard Bellman and Stuart Dreyfus were kind enough to read and comment on the dynamic programming chapter.

Finally, we are indebted to Betty Keck and Grace White, who took care of typing the manuscript.

M. S.   A. Y.   L. F.

Contents

Contents -- xi

CHAPTER

ONE

Introduction

One of the most remarkable phenomena of this century is the rapid growth in the size and the complexity of human organizations. The mere size of modern business means that administrative decisions can affect vast quantities of capital and large numbers of people. Mistakes can be tremendously costly, and a single wrong decision can require years for rectification. Moreover, the pace of modern business is such that decisions are required more rapidly than ever before; the mere postponement of action can give a decided advantage to a competitor.

It is not surprising that the increase in difficulty of decision making has been followed by efforts to put this activity on a more objective and routine basis. The growing science of operations research, which relies heavily on the methods that have proved so successful in the physical sciences, is one aspect of these efforts.

From the point of view of operations research, a decision is a recommendation that a particular course of action, affecting the system, be carried out. The decision maker attempts to choose that course of action which is expected to yield the "best" results in terms of the larger goals of the organization of which the system is a part. Another way of putting this is to say that the decision maker attempts to render the system more *effective* in furthering the goals of the organization. This notion of effectiveness, which will recur again and again through the book, is a descriptive term applied to the state of a system, much as "health" is a descriptive term applied to the state of a person.

Generally, the decision maker attempts to increase the effectiveness of the system under his control.

Comparison of the effectiveness of different system states is facilitated, though with some abuse to reality, by the choice of a *measure* of effectiveness: i.e. by the choice of some numerical scale for effectiveness. For example, the body temperature of a person is often taken as the measure of his health. The measure of effectiveness usually has characteristic units associated with it (e.g., dollars, dollars per month, defects per thousand items, degrees in the example above); but some commonly used measures are dimensionless, such as the probability of destroying the target in an air attack. Henceforth we shall use the terms "effectiveness" and "measure of effectiveness" interchangeably; and both will refer to the incomplete description of effectiveness that results when we introduce a numerical scale. It is not the purpose of this book to discuss the problems involved in specifying a measure of effectiveness. Notwithstanding this omission, it remains true that a major part of most practical operations research studies consists of identifying the decision makers, discovering their (possibly conflicting) objectives, and translating these objectives into points along compatible scales.

Once the effectiveness scale has been specified, the task becomes one of choosing from the available courses of action the one that maximizes the resulting effectiveness. In the simplest case, the effectiveness is a uniquely determined function of the course of action, and the appropriate course can be chosen by an application of standard mathematical techniques. Usually, however, the situation is more complicated, in that the effectiveness depends not only on the course of action, but also on some list of external variables whose values are beyond the control of the decision maker. These external variables may be continuous or discrete, fixed or probabilistic, accurately known or assignable only by guess. Worse still, in a competitive situation they may be controlled by an opponent who is striving for goals that conflict directly with our own. Whatever the nature of the relevant uncontrollable variables, they have to be included in the mathematical model relating the system effectiveness to the courses of action. After the decision problem has been formulated in this manner, such mathematical tools as enumeration, differentiation, and iteration can be used for the purpose of identifying the best course of action.

In order to clarify the role of mathematical models in operations research, it is helpful to look at the role of such models in the more familiar context of mechanics. The physics student is presented with a series of propositions concerning the behavior of certain ideal systems.

He finds that these propositions, expressed in mathematical symbols, form a model of the real world which can be manipulated far more easily than the real world itself.

Newton's three laws of motion, together with a postulated force called friction which opposes motion, give a mathematical model of the physical world which accounts reasonably well for many observed phenomena. Other phenomena cannot be explained in this simple way; depending on our purpose, we may have to consider air resistance, earth rotation, electrostatic charges, and other factors. Each succeeding variable added to the problem enables us to represent the physical world more closely, at the cost of greater and greater complexity in analysis. How complicated should the model be? This is a matter of personal preference; the fashion is to choose the simplest model that answers the type of questions we wish to ask about the system.

This book has been written in the hope that it will play the same role in the training of the operations research worker as a text on basic physics plays in the training of the engineer. It deals with a selection of the mathematical techniques that have been found useful in operations research. The approach is mainly through the medium of worked examples, against a background furnished by some discussion of the relevant problem area. The problems discussed are simple—many so simple that it is hard to imagine real situations to which they could be applied without drastic refinement. Apart from added complexity, real-life problems differ in another way from those of this book. For ease of presentation, problems are classified in chapters according to the basic function of the system in which they arise. Such a simple classification hardly corresponds to reality; in practice, some sort of synthesis of prototype models is required, with the resulting model adjusted to fit the real situation closely enough to solve the problems under discussion. In this connection, it should be pointed out that mathematical sophistication, though frequently necessary, has no merit per se. Although a great deal of elegant mathematics appears in the literature, far more problems have been solved by the intelligent application of simple arithmetic.

The reader who wishes to get the most out of this book should have some acquaintance with the main concepts and results of the calculus. In particular, he should be familiar with the routines for determining the extreme values of a function of one or more variables, and with the interpretation of a single or multiple integral as the limit of a sum. Occasional allusions are made to the calculus of finite differences; but, as this is less widely taught than ordinary calculus, the portion relevant to our purpose has been treated in an appendix. Finally, a modicum of statistics is assumed, equivalent to that which would be obtained by a student in a one-semester course.

The subject matter proper of this book begins with a brief survey of the elements of probability theory, including the notions of probability of an event, random variable, probability distribution, and conditional probability distribution. This material is basic for an understanding of some of the remaining chapters, and should serve as a good review even for those readers who are already familiar with probability. The succeeding chapter discusses sampling, and gives an introduction to the Monte Carlo method of simulated sampling. Chapters 4 through 10 present various problem areas which have gradually taken distinct shape in operations research: in order, they are inventory, replacement, waiting lines, competitive strategies, allocation, sequencing, and dynamic programming.

REFERENCES

Churchman, C. W., R. L. Ackoff, and E. L. Arnoff, *Introduction to Operations Research*, John Wiley & Sons, New York, 1957.

McCloskey, J. F., and J. M. Coppinger, eds., *Operations Research for Management*, Vol. II, Johns Hopkins Press, Baltimore, 1956.

McCloskey, J. F., and F. N. Trefethen, eds., *Operations Research for Management*, Johns Hopkins Press, Baltimore, 1954.

Morse, P. M., and G. E. Kimball, *Methods of Operations Research*, The Technology Press, Massachusetts Institute of Technology and John Wiley & Sons, New York, 1951.

Probability

Some familiarity with the basic notions of probability is essential for an understanding of the remaining chapters of this book. The information on which decisions are to be based is usually in the form of numbers; and these numbers, as well as the conclusions derived therefrom, are usually doubtful to a greater or lesser extent. The theory of probability furnishes a means for expressing the degree of doubt in mathematical terms.

A rigorous development of probability theory involves logical and mathematical difficulties of high order, and will not be attempted here. Instead, we shall present working definitions of such concepts as "random variable" and "probability distribution," and illustrate their application with examples. The chapter is intended to serve as a brief review for those readers who have an understanding of probability theory, and as a guidepost to further study of the subject for those who come to this book with less preparation. Several good references are given at the end of the chapter.

SIMPLE EVENTS

Suppose that within a particular limited environment the possible states of nature are $E_1, E_2, \cdots, E_n$, and that the environment periodically changes from one state to another in some random fashion. For example, the environment might be a coin lying on the ground with an observer standing beside it; the relevant set of states might be "heads up" and "tails up"; and possible state changes could result from the observer's picking up the coin and flipping it in the air. We shall call the various possible states E_i "simple events" and shall refer to the action precipitating a possible state change as a "trial."

Ignoring the philosophical difficulties involved in such a definition, we shall define the probability of the simple event E_i as "an estimate of the value approached by the ratio

$$\frac{\text{Number of occurrences of } E_i}{\text{Number of trials}}$$

as the number of trials tends to infinity." We will write $P(E_i)$ for the probability of the event E_i.

For definiteness, let us focus attention on the simple event E_1. Clearly $P(E_1)$ is a positive number between 0 and 1. If E_1 is certain to occur at each trial, then the ratio above will be unity at the end of each trial, and we have $P(E_1) = 1$. If the occurrence of E_1 is impossible at each trial, then the ratio will be zero at the end of each trial, and we would have $P(E_1) = 0$. If E_1 is considered more likely to occur than E_2, then our estimate of the number of occurrences of E_1 in a large number of trials should be larger than the estimate of the number of occurrences of E_2; and thus $P(E_1) > P(E_2)$. Also, if our estimating procedure is to be consistent, we must have

$$P(E_1) + P(E_2) + \cdots + P(E_n) = 1$$

since the sum over i of the number of occurrences of E_i in N trials must equal the number of trials.

In some situations, such as in the toss of an unbiased coin or a true die, we might feel that our estimate of the number of times the state E_i will appear in a large number of trials should be the same for each i. In such cases we would have

$$P(E_1) = P(E_2) = \cdots = P(E_n)$$

and, since the sum of the probabilities for the various simple events must be unity as above, we would then have

$$P(E_i) = 1/n \qquad \text{for each } i$$

In tossing an unbiased coin, this would imply that the probability of a head (or a tail) would be assigned the value $1/2$; in the case of a true die, the probability of a 1 (or any other positive integer between 1 and 6) would be taken as $1/6$.

For some purposes it is convenient to construct a geometric model of the situation under discussion, by identifying the realization of the state E_i with a point B_i in some geometric space. The outcome of a trial is then some point in the so-called "sample space" made up of the n points $B_1, B_2, \cdots, B_n$; and the probability associated with any point B_i is defined as the probability of the corresponding simple event E_i. Though we shall not go into the subject very deeply, the idea of a sample space is fundamental in probability theory. The two main properties of a sample space are: (1) each conceivable outcome of a trial is represented by one and only one point in the corresponding sample space, and (2) each point of a sample space has associated with it a non-negative number called the probability of the corresponding simple event, with these probabilities adding to unity.

As an example, suppose that the environment consists of three coins on the ground with an observer beside them, and that a trial consists of tossing all three coins. There are eight possible states, viz.:

H, H, H   T, H, H

H, H, T   T, H, T

H, T, H   T, T, H

H, T, T   T, T, T

(Here, for example, the outcome H, T, H means "heads for coin 1, tails for coin 2, heads for coin 3.") If we have no reason to expect the more frequent appearance of heads than tails in one toss of one coin, then the eight possible states could be regarded as equally likely to occur after a trial, and we would associate the same probability (1/8) with each of the possible simple events. The sample space could be taken as simply eight points $B_1, \cdots, B_8$ strung out along a line; but the symmetric arrangement of Figure 2.1 is perhaps more suggestive.

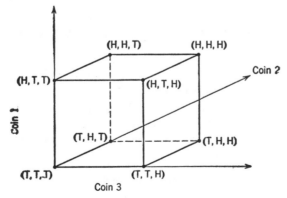

Figure 2.1. Sample space where trial is a toss of three coins.

If a (single) trial consists of the toss of two dice, then each die can show one of the faces 1 through 6; so there are 36 possible outcomes, viz.:

$$
\begin{array}{cccccc}
1\text{--}1 & 2\text{--}1 & 3\text{--}1 & 4\text{--}1 & 5\text{--}1 & 6\text{--}1 \\
1\text{--}2 & 2\text{--}2 & 3\text{--}2 & 4\text{--}2 & 5\text{--}2 & 6\text{--}2 \\
1\text{--}3 & 2\text{--}3 & 3\text{--}3 & 4\text{--}3 & 5\text{--}3 & 6\text{--}3 \\
1\text{--}4 & 2\text{--}4 & 3\text{--}4 & 4\text{--}4 & 5\text{--}4 & 6\text{--}4 \\
1\text{--}5 & 2\text{--}5 & 3\text{--}5 & 4\text{--}5 & 5\text{--}5 & 6\text{--}5 \\
1\text{--}6 & 2\text{--}6 & 3\text{--}6 & 4\text{--}6 & 5\text{--}6 & 6\text{--}6 \\
\end{array}
$$

If the dice are true, all the outcomes are regarded as equally likely, and the probability associated with each would be 1/36. The outcomes can be conveniently represented by the points of a 6-by-6 lattice in two dimensions, as illustrated in Figure 2.2.

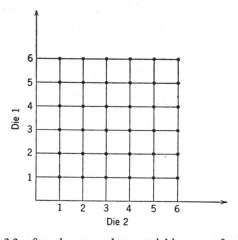

Figure 2.2.   Sample space where a trial is a toss of two dice.

COMPOSITE AND RELATED EVENTS

The simple events discussed in the previous section are the set of mutually exclusive and exhaustive states that could occur as the result of a trial. Our first generalization is the notion of an event G which occurs along with any one of a number of designated simple events. For example, if the trial is a throw of two dice, the event G might be "The sum of the points on the two dice is seven." Then G occurs along with the following six states:

$$1, 6 \quad 2, 5 \quad 3, 4$$

$$4, 3 \quad 5, 2 \quad 6, 1$$

Alternatively, one may say that this event G occurs at the six points along the main diagonal in the sample space of Figure 2.2. The probability of such a derived event is defined in the following way.

The probability $P(G)$ of the event G which occurs at each of a set of points in sample space is defined as the sum of the probabilities of all the points in the set.

Thus the probability of obtaining a "seven" in one throw of two dice is the sum of six probabilities, each of value 1/36, or 1/6. This example illustrates an immediate consequence of the above definition. If all the points in the sample space have the same probability, then the probability of the derived event G is simply the ratio of the number of points at which G occurs to the total number of points.

The next generalization deals with events that are defined (stated) relative to two derived events G and H. There are two basic ways in which this can be done. The event may be defined as the occurrence of both of the events G and H, or it may be defined as the occurrence of at least one of the events G and H. We shall describe events of the former type as the *intersection* of G and H, and write such an event K as

$$K = GH \qquad (G \text{ and } H \text{ occur})$$

Events K of the second type are described as the *union* of G and H, and we write

$$K = G + H \qquad (\text{either } G \text{ or } H \text{ or both occur})$$

The concepts of union and intersection apply equally well to simple events, since a simple event is a special kind of derived event; however, the intersection of two simple events is of little interest since it consists of no sample points whatsoever.

To illustrate, let the trial be a throw of two dice, and let the events G and H be as follows:

G: the sum of the two faces is seven or more.
H: the *first* die shows one of the numbers 2, 3, 4.

Then the event G occurs at points within the triangular-shaped region of Figure 2.3; the event H occurs at points within the rectangular region; the intersection GH occurs at points within the trapezoid; and the union $G+H$ occurs at all the points that lie either in the triangle or in the rectangle or in both. By a count of points, we see that $P(GH) = 9/36$, and $P(G + H) = 30/36$.

The ideas of intersection and union can be extended to more than two events. The intersection of n events is the set of sample points common to all n events; and the union of n events is the set of all those

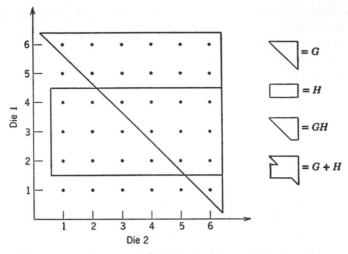

Figure 2.3. Intersection and union of two derived events.

sample points which lie in at least one of the n events. Also, one may speak of intersections and unions of events which are themselves composites of derived events, and so on.

The probability of the event that is the union of two other events G and H is, by definition, the sum of the probabilities of each of the sample points in $G+H$. Conceptually we enumerate all the points that lie in either G or H, being careful to include each point no more than once, and arrive at the formula

$$(2.1) \qquad P(G + H) = P(G) + P(H) - P(GH)$$

If the events G and H have no sample points in common, the events are said to be *mutually exclusive*, and we have the simpler result

$$(2.2) \qquad P(G + H) = P(G) + P(H)$$

In words, the last result says that, if two events are such that the occurrence of one precludes the occurrence of the other, then the probability of occurrence of one or the other is the sum of the individual probabilities of occurrence.

Although equation (2.1) is a useful formula, it does no more than tell us how to compute the probability of the union of two events from the probability of their intersection, and vice versa. For applications, we need a better way of computing the probability of composite events than the complete enumeration of the sample space followed by the count of the relevant sample points. Such a means is furnished by the concept of conditional probability.

The *conditional probability* of the event H, given the occurrence of the event G, is denoted by $P(H|G)$, and is defined as the probability of occurrence of H in the *reduced* sample space obtained from the original sample space in the following manner:

(*a*) The sample points in the new sample space are just the sample points comprising the event G.

(*b*) The new probability associated with each simple event E_k in the new sample space is the original probability $P(E_k)$ divided by $P(G)$. (Then the sum of the new probabilities for the points in the new sample space will be unity as required.)

The only points of H that are in the reduced sample space G are those in the intersection GH, as shown in Figure 2.4. Thus the condi-

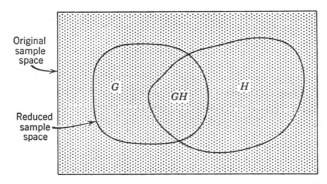

Figure 2.4. Reduced sample space used in defining $P(H/G)$.

tional probability $P(H|G)$ is, by definition, the sum of the new probabilities for points in GH; in other words, it is the sum of the old probabilities for points in GH, divided by $P(G)$. So we have as our formula for conditional probability:

$$(2.3) \quad P(H|G) = \frac{P(GH)}{P(G)} \quad \text{for any two events } G \text{ and } H \text{ with } P(G) > 0$$

This formula is not only useful in its own right, but it also gives us the means for calculating $P(GH)$, namely

$$(2.4) \qquad\qquad P(GH) = P(G)\, P(H|G)$$

Because of the reduction in the sample space, it is usually much easier to calculate $P(H|G)$ first and then use formulas (2.4) and (2.1) than it is to calculate the probabilities of the union and intersection directly from the original sample space.

It may happen that the conditional probability of H, given the occurrence of G, is the same as the original (unconditional) probability of H. If this is true, the event H is said to be *independent* of the event G, and we have the simpler formula

$$P(GH) = P(G)\,P(H) \qquad \text{if } H \text{ is independent of } G$$

If H is independent of G, then it can be easily shown that G is independent of H; so we may speak of the independence of two events G and H without regard to the order. Because of this symmetry, we may write

(2.5) $P(GH) = P(G)\,P(H) \qquad$ for *independent* events G and H

In words, we say that, if two events are independent, then the probability of their simultaneous occurrence is the product of their individual probabilities of occurrence.

The relationships (2.1), (2.2), (2.4), and (2.5) can be generalized to the case of n events. We give the generalizations for (2.2), (2.4), and (2.5), and refer the reader to Chapter 4 of Feller (see references at the end of the chapter) for the general statement of (2.1).

If the events $G_1, G_2, \cdots, G_n$ are mutually exclusive in pairs, then

(2.6) $P(G_1 + G_2 + \cdots + G_n) = P(G_1) + P(G_2) + \cdots + P(G_n)$

For any n events $G_1, G_2, \cdots, G_n$:

(2.7) $P(G_1 G_2 \cdots G_n)$

$$= P(G_1)\,P(G_2|G_1)\,P(G_3|G_1 G_2) \cdots P(G_n|G_1 G_2 \cdots G_{n-1})$$

If the events $G_1, G_2, \cdots, G_n$ are independent (in the sense that the occurrence of a G_k is independent of the occurrence of any of the remaining events, and of any intersection of them), then

(2.8) $P(G_1 G_2 \cdots G_n) = P(G_1)\,P(G_2) \cdots P(G_n)$

From this point on, we shall regard the results (2.1) through (2.8) as valid, regardless of whether the sample space is or can be made explicit. In the examples that follow, the sample space will be enumerated only when that appears to be the most direct way of solving the problem in question.

Example 1

A box contains 25 parts, of which 10 are defective. Two parts are drawn at random from the box. What is the probability

(a) that both are good?
(b) that both are defective?
(c) that one is good and one is defective?

SOLUTION

(a) Let E be the event "the first part drawn is good," and F be the event "the second part drawn is good." Then EF is the event "both are good."

$$P(EF) = P(E) \, P(F \,|\, E) = \tfrac{15}{25} \cdot \tfrac{14}{24} = \tfrac{7}{20}$$

(b) By similar reasoning, the probability that both are defective is found to be $\tfrac{10}{25} \cdot \tfrac{9}{24} = \tfrac{3}{20}$

(c) Let E_1 = event "both are good"
E_2 = event "both are defective"
E_3 = event "one is good and one is defective"

Since at least one of these events must happen,

$$P(E_1 + E_2 + E_3) = 1$$

But, since E_1, E_2, and E_3 are mutually exclusive,

$$P(E_1 + E_2 + E_3) = P(E_1) + P(E_2) + P(E_3)$$

Thus

$$P(E_1) + P(E_2) + P(E_3) = 1$$
$$P(E_3) = 1 - P(E_1) - P(E_2)$$
$$= 1 - \tfrac{7}{20} - \tfrac{3}{20} = \tfrac{1}{2}$$

Another way of arriving at this result is to note that the desired event is $G+H$, where

G = event "first is good and second is defective"
H = event "first is defective and second is good"

$$P(G + H) = P(G) + P(H)$$

since the two events are mutually exclusive

$$= \tfrac{15}{25} \cdot \tfrac{10}{24} + \tfrac{10}{25} \cdot \tfrac{15}{24} = \tfrac{300}{600} = \tfrac{1}{2}$$

Example 2

The ten digits, 0, 1, 2, $\cdots$, 9 are arranged in random order. Find the probability that the digits 3 and 4 are neighbors.

SOLUTION

One way for 3 and 4 to be neighbors is

$$3\,4\,X\,X\,X\,X\,X\,X\,X\,X$$

where the X's represent the remaining numbers; another is

$$X\,3\,4\,X\,X\,X\,X\,X\,X\,X; \text{etc.}$$

One easily sees that there are exactly 18 such possibilities, viz.:

$$3\,4\,X\,X\,X\,X\,X\,X\,X\,X : \text{Event } E_1$$

$$X\,3\,4\,X\,X\,X\,X\,X\,X\,X : \text{Event } E_2$$

$$X\,X\,X\,X\,X\,X\,X\,X\,3\,4 : \text{Event } E_9$$

$$4\,3\,X\,X\,X\,X\,X\,X\,X\,X : \text{Event } E_{10}$$

$$X\,4\,3\,X\,X\,X\,X\,X\,X\,X : \text{Event } E_{11}$$

$$X\,X\,X\,X\,X\,X\,X\,X\,4\,3 : \text{Event } E_{18}$$

$$P(E_1 + E_2 + \cdots + E_{18}) = P(E_1) + P(E_2) + \cdots + P(E_{18})$$

$$\text{since the events are mutually exclusive}$$

$$= 18P(E_1) \qquad \text{since the events are equally likely}$$

$$= 18(\tfrac{1}{10} \cdot \tfrac{1}{9}) = \tfrac{1}{5}$$

Example 3

A series of trials is conducted, where each trial must yield exactly one of the events E_1 and E_2. If the probability that a trial yields E_1 is known to be p, and if the result of a trial is independent of the results of previous trials, find

(a) the probability that n trials yield exactly k E_1's.
(b) the probability that n trials yield at least k E_1's.
(c) the probability that n trials yield at most k E_1's.

SOLUTION

(a) If k is negative, or greater than n, the probability of the event in question is obviously zero.

Let k be some integer of the set 0, 1, 2, $\cdots$, n. We first calculate the probability of the event "the first k trials result in E_1, and the last $n-k$ trials result in E_2." By equation (2.8), the probability of this event is

$$p^k(1 - p)^{n-k}$$

There are many other ways for the desired event to occur; all involve the result E_1 for some set of k trials (not necessarily the first k trials), and the result E_2 for the $n-k$ trials not in this set. There are $C_{n,k}$ such ways, where

$$C_{n,k} = \frac{n!}{k!(n-k)!}$$

and each of these ways is equally likely. Thus the probability $P(k)$ of the event "exactly k E_1's in n trials" is given by

$$P(k) = C_{n,k}p^k(1 - p)^{n-k}$$

(b) The event "at least k E_1's in n trials" may be written as the event $(F_k + F_{k+1} + \cdots + F_n)$, where F_i is the event "exactly i E_1's in n trials."

$$P(F_k + F_{k+1} + \cdots + F_n) = P(F_k) + P(F_{k+1}) + \cdots + P(F_n)$$

since the F_i are mutually exclusive

$$= \sum_{i=k}^{n} P(F_i)$$

$$= \sum_{i=k}^{n} C_{n,i}\, p^i(1 - p)^{n-i} \qquad \text{by part } (a)$$

(c) In a similar fashion, we find that the probability of the event "at most k E_1's in n trials" is

$$\sum_{i=0}^{k} C_{n,i}\, p^i(1 - p)^{n-i}$$

Example 4

Given the information that a family contains two children and that at least one of these two children is a boy, find the probability that both are boys.

SOLUTION

This is a problem in conditional probability, and is solved most directly by considering the sample spaces. The original sample space consists of the four points BB, BG, GB, and GG, each with the probability 1/4. The reduced sample space, comprising the points including at least one boy, consists of the three points BB, BG, and GB, each with the probability 1/3. So the answer to the problem is 1/3.

Note that this is not the same question as: Given that there are two children C and D and that C is a boy, find the probability that D is also a boy. The answer to the latter question is of course 1/2.

Example 5

A, B, and C each fire one shot at a target. The probabilities of each hitting the target are:

A: 0.30.
B: 0.25.
C: 0.10.

If one bullet is found in the target, find the probability that it came from A's gun; from B's gun; from C's gun.

SOLUTION

There are eight possible outcomes to a trial consisting of three shots, one by each of the marksmen. For simplicity, let 1 represent a hit and 0 a miss; then 1–1–0 represents the event "A hits, B hits, C misses," etc. The eight possible outcomes together with their probabilities of occurrence after a trial are:

Outcome	Probability
0–0–0	(.70) (.75) (.90)
0–0–1	(.70) (.75) (.10)
0–1–0	(.70) (.25) (.90)
0–1–1	(.70) (.25) (.10)
1–0–0	(.30) (.75) (.90)
1–0–1	(.30) (.75) (.10)
1–1–0	(.30) (.25) (.90)
1--1–1	(.30) (.25) (.10)

The reduced sample space consists of the points 1–0–0, 0–1–0, and 0–0–1; and the new probabilities are the original probabilities, each divided by the sum of the three probabilities. The conditional probability of 1–0–0, given the occurrence of one of the events 1–0–0, 0–1–0, 0–0–1, is thus

$$\frac{(.30)(.75)(.90)}{(.30)(.75)(.90) + (.70)(.25)(.90) + (.70)(.75)(.10)} = \frac{27}{55}$$

The probability that the bullet lodged in the target should be credited to A is 27/55. The probabilities for B and C are similarly found to be 21/55 and 7/55.

Example 6

A certain popular 5-cent confection comes in two varieties: Plain and Nut. The items are sold exclusively through jobbers. In order to have information on distribution at the retail level, the company investigates a sample of randomly selected retail stores about once a year. Results are tabulated to yield the following three observed probabilities:

a = probability that a store selected at random has Plain in stock
b = probability that a store selected at random has Nut in stock
c = probability that a store selected at random has at least one of the company's products in stock (i.e. either Plain or Nut or both)

$$[c \geq a; \qquad c \geq b; \qquad c \leq a+b]$$

The company wishes to go back through its historical records, and infer the following numbers:

a_1 = probability that a store selected at random *normally* carries Plain (even if out of stock of Plain at the time of observation).
a_2 = probability that a store that normally carries Plain has Plain in stock at a random instant
b_1 = probability that a store selected at random normally carries Nut
b_2 = probability that a store that normally carries Nut has Nut in stock at a random instant

(These four numbers cannot be calculated directly since the original data are unavailable.)

SOLUTION

There are four unknowns a_1, a_2, b_1, b_2, and we attempt to find four relations among them. We first note that a store has a variety in stock if and only if it normally carries the variety and the variety is in stock at the moment of observation. This immediately gives two relations:

(2.9) $$a = a_1 a_2$$

(2.10) $$b = b_1 b_2$$

In order to obtain two more relations, it is necessary to make further assumptions. Plain is the dominant variety of the two, and is the item with which the company is usually identified. The following assumptions are considered plausible:

I. The probability that a store that normally carries Nut is momentarily out of Nut is twice the probability that a store that normally carries Plain is momentarily out of Plain.

II. Any store that normally carries Nut also normally carries Plain

Assumption I gives us our third relation immediately.

$$1 - b_2 = 2(1 - a_2)$$

or

(2.11) $$b_2 = 2a_2 - 1$$

Assumption II permits us to relate c to the other quantities, viz.:

$$c = P \text{ \{a store has either Plain or Nut in stock\}}$$
$$= P \text{ \{a store has Plain\}} + P \text{ \{a store has Nut\}}$$
$$\quad - P \text{ \{a store has both Plain and Nut\}}$$
$$= a + b - P \text{ \{a store has both\}}$$

Now

$$P \text{ \{a store has both\}} = P \text{ \{store normally carries both \textit{and}}$$
$$\text{has both\}}$$
$$= P \text{ \{store normally carries Nut \textit{and}}$$
$$\text{has both\}} \quad \text{by Assumption II}$$
$$= b_1 a_2 b_2$$
$$= a_2 b \quad \text{from (2.10)}$$

The fourth relation is thus

(2.12) $$c = a + b - a_2 b$$

The four simple equations (2.09) through (2.12) yield easily results of the type needed:

$$a_1 = \frac{ab}{a + b - c}$$

$$a_2 = \frac{a + b - c}{b}$$

$$b_1 = \frac{b^2}{2a + b - 2c}$$

$$b_2 = \frac{2a + b - 2c}{b}$$

An idea of the way this works out numerically is given in the table below:

Year	Observed probabilities			Inferred probabilities			
of survey	a	b	c	a_1	a_2	b_1	b_2
1	0.37	0.15	0.40	0.467	0.800	0.250	0.600
2	0.40	0.21	0.43	0.467	0.857	0.294	0.714
3	0.43	0.26	0.45	0.495	0.923	0.307	0.846

PROBLEMS FOR SOLUTION

Set I

1. What is the probability that a bridge hand

    (a) will consist entirely of hearts?   [*Ans.* 1.6×10^{-12}]
    (b) will contain no hearts?   [*Ans.* 0.01]
    (c) will be made up entirely of one suit?   [*Ans.* 6.3×10^{-12}]

[*Hint:* (a) The probability that the first card drawn is a heart is 13/52. The probability that the second card is a heart, given that the first was a heart, is 12/51. Continuing in this manner, we apply equation (2.7) and end up with the product

$$\frac{13}{52} \times \frac{12}{51} \times \frac{11}{50} \times \cdots \times \frac{1}{40}$$

as the answer to part a. Part b is solved in a similar fashion. To solve part c, note that the event "all thirteen cards of one suit" is the union of the four mutually exclusive events "all spades," "all hearts," "all clubs," "all diamonds."]

2. There are 26 people at a cocktail party. What is the probability that at least two of them have the same birthday?   [*Ans.* 0.60]
[*Hint:* First calculate the probability that all 26 birthdays are different, using equation (2.7). Then subtract this probability from unity.]

3. What is the probability of throwing exactly three sevens in six rolls of two dice?   [*Ans.* 0.05]
[*Hint:* Use the result stated in Example 3 of the text.]

4. Find the probability of hitting a ship when one fires five torpedoes, each with the probability 1/4 of scoring a hit.   [*Ans.* 0.76]

5. If I hold two aces in a bridge hand, what is the probability that my partner holds exactly one ace?   [*Ans.* 0.46]

6. A man starts at a certain corner and strolls four blocks. Each time he comes to a corner, he chooses one of the directions north, south, east, and west

with equal probability. What are his chances of ending his walk at the corner where he started? [*Ans.* 9/64]

7. Three players *A*, *B*, and *C* are engaged in a sequence of games in which the winner of each game scores one point. The one that first scores three points will be the final winner. *A* wins the first and third games, whereas *B* wins the second. Find the probability that *C* will be the final winner. [*Ans.* 2/27]

8. You are told that six tosses of a coin yielded four heads and two tails. Assign a probability to the event: "At the end of each toss, the cumulated number of heads exceeded the cumulated number of tails." [*Hint:* Enumerate the sample space. The answer is 1/3.]

DISCRETE DISTRIBUTIONS

In the previous section we developed the idea of a trial resulting in a random appearance of one of a set of states E_1, E_2, $\cdots$, and introduced the notion of sample space as a convenient geometrical model for the outcomes. Here we introduce the concept of a *random variable* defined on points of a sample space. A random variable is simply a set of numbers x_1, x_2, $\cdots$, one for each state, so that the result of a trial is not merely the state E_i but also the number of interest x_i. For example, if the trial is a toss of two dice, a random variable could be defined as the sum of the points shown by the dice. If we denote this random variable by x, then x would have the value 2 for the state (1, 1), 3 for the state (1, 2), 7 for the state (3, 4), and so on. Note that, although there are 36 points in the sample space, there are only 11 possible values for x, namely one of the integers 2, 3, 4, $\cdots$, 12. The

TABLE 1

Random variable x	Frequency function $P(x)$
2	1/36
3	2/36
4	3/36
5	4/36
6	5/36
7	6/36
8	5/36
9	4/36
10	3/36
11	2/36
12	1/36
Total	36/36

event "$x = 2$" occurs at only one point of the sample space; so the probability of the event "$x = 2$" is 1/36. The event "$x = 3$" occurs at the points (1, 2) and (2, 1) and thus has the probability 2/36. The *frequency function* of the random variable x is the complete listing of the values of the random variable, together with their probabilities of occurrence. In this example, the frequency function is defined by Table 1.

The sum of the individual probabilities in any frequency function is 1; this arises from the fact that one and only one of the various outcomes occurs as the result of a trial.

Many random variables can be defined on the same sample space. If the trial is a throw of two dice, we might also define the random variable x as the smaller of the number of points showing on the two dice (or as the common number, in case of a tie). In this case x would have the range 1, 2, 3, 4, 5, 6. The event "$x = 6$" occurs only at the sample point (6, 6), and has a probability of 1/36. The event "$x = 5$" occurs at the three points (5, 6), (6, 5), (5, 5) and has a probability of 3/36; and so on. The complete frequency function for this random variable is given in Table 2.

TABLE 2

Random variable x	Frequency function $P(x)$
1	11/36
2	9/36
3	7/36
4	5/36
5	3/36
6	1/36
Total	36/36

Often the frequency function of a random variable is characterized by two derived numbers: its *mean* and its *variance*. Such a description of a frequency function, though admittedly incomplete, is valuable for many of the applications.

Let x_i ($i = 1, 2, \cdots, n$) be the various possible values that a random variable can assume, and let $P(x_i)$ be the probability that the random variable assumes the value x_i. If we denote the mean by $\bar{x}$ and the variance by Var (x), then we define

(2.13)
$$\bar{x} = \sum_{i=1}^{n} x_i \, P(x_i)$$

$$(2.14) \qquad \text{Var}\,(x) = \sum_{i=1}^{n} (x_i - \bar{x})^2\, P(x_i)$$

For the computation of the variance, it is often more convenient to use the equivalent formula

$$(2.15) \qquad \text{Var}\,(x) = \sum_{i=1}^{n} x_i^2\, P(x_i) - (\bar{x})^2$$

The mean of x is an estimate of the value of x to be expected from a trial, and the variance is a measure of the expected scatter of achieved values of x about this expected value.

Just as in the application of the formulas for the probability of composite events, the underlying sample space need not be explicit in order for the concepts of random variable and probability distribution to be used. A good working definition of a random variable is that it is a chance number turned up by a trial from among the set of numbers $(x_1, x_2, \cdots)$; the frequency function of the random variable is then a set of non-negative numbers

$$P(x_1),\ P(x_2),\ \cdots$$

one for each x_i, such that

$$\sum_{i} P(x_i) = 1$$

With such working definitions, as indeed in any complete treatment of sample spaces, the number of possible values of the random variable x does not have to be finite. An example of a discrete random variable that has an infinite number of potential values is: the number of tosses of a single coin until the appearance of the first head. The event "$x = 1$" is equivalent to the event "first toss is a head," and thus has the probability $1/2$. The event "$x = 2$" occurs along with the event "first toss tails, second toss heads," and has the probability $1/4$, etc. Here the range of x is the totality of positive integers 1, 2, 3, $\cdots$, and the frequency function of x is given by the formula

$$P\{x = n\} = (\tfrac{1}{2})^n$$

for each positive integer n. We might mention that a random variable with an infinite number of potential values must have arisen from a sample space with an infinite number of points, since there is at least one sample point for each possible value of the random variable. However, the probabilities must form a convergent series whose sum is one.

In the above example, by the well-known formula for the sum of a geometric progression,

$$\sum_{1}^{\infty} P\{x = n\} = \sum_{1}^{\infty} (\tfrac{1}{2})^n = 1$$

There are a few discrete probability distributions which recur so often in the applications that they have been given special names, such as "binomial distribution," "Poisson distribution," and so on. These are listed below with a few of their properties.

Binomial Distribution (cf. Example 3)

Range of x: $0, 1, 2, \cdots, n$.

Frequency function: $P(k) = C_{n,k}\, p^k (1 - p)^{n-k}$.

Mean: $\bar{x} = np$.

Variance: $\mathrm{Var}\,(x) = np(1 - p)$.

Poisson Distribution

Range of x: $0, 1, 2, 3, \cdots,$ to ∞.

Frequency function: $P(k) = \dfrac{\lambda^k e^{-\lambda}}{k!}$ where λ is a positive parameter.

Mean: $\bar{x} = \lambda$.

Variance: $\mathrm{Var}\,(x) = \lambda$.

Uniform Distribution

Range of x: $0, 1, 2, \cdots, n$.

Frequency function: $P(k) = \dfrac{1}{n + 1}$.

Mean: $\bar{x} = \dfrac{n}{2}$.

Variance: $\mathrm{Var}\,(x) = \dfrac{n^2}{12} + \dfrac{n}{6}$.

Geometric Distribution

Range of x: $0, 1, 2, \cdots,$ to ∞.

Frequency function: $P(k) = p^k(1 - p)$ where p is a positive parameter less than 1.

$$\text{Mean:} \quad \bar{x} = \frac{p}{1 - p}.$$

$$\text{Variance:} \quad \text{Var} (x) = \frac{p}{(1 - p)^2}.$$

Before proceeding to some examples, we mention the concept of a *cumulative distribution function* for a random variable x. If the range of possible values for x is $(x_1, x_2, \cdots, x_n)$, where the x_i are arranged in increasing order, then the cumulative distribution is defined, for *any* number y, as the probability of the event $\{x \leq y\}$. If we denote the cumulative probabilities by $U(y)$, then it is apparent that if $y < x_1$, $U(y) = 0$, and if $y \geq x_n$, $U(y) = 1$, while

$$(2.16) \qquad U(y) = \sum_{j=1}^{i} P(x_j) \quad \text{for } x_i \leq y < x_{i+1}$$

Example 7

An owner of five overnight cabins is considering buying television sets to rent to cabin occupants. He estimates that about half of his customers would be willing to rent sets. Finally, he buys three sets. Assuming 100% occupancy at all times:

(a) What fraction of the evenings will there be more requests than TV sets?

(b) What is the probability that a customer who requests a television set will receive one?

(c) If the owner's cost per set per day is C, what rental R must he charge in order to break even in the long run?

SOLUTION

(a) The daily number of requests is a random variable, subject to the binomial distribution with $n = 5$ and $p = 1/2$. We want the probability that this random variable assumes the value 4 or 5. This probability is $C_{5,4}(\frac{1}{2})^5 + C_{5,5}(\frac{1}{2})^5 = \frac{6}{32} = 0.188$.

(b) Any one of the following set of mutually exclusive events will result in a given customer's request being satisfied:

1. There are no other requests that night.
2. There is one other request.
3. There are two other requests.
4. There are three other requests, and his precedes at least one of them.

5. There are four other requests, and his precedes at least two of them.

The probabilities of the first three events listed are:

$$P_1 = (\tfrac{1}{2})^4$$

$$P_2 = C_{4,1}(\tfrac{1}{2})^4$$

$$P_3 = C_{4,2}(\tfrac{1}{2})^4$$

Assuming that his request is randomly situated in time with respect to the other requests, the probabilities of events 4 and 5 are:

$$P_4 = \tfrac{3}{4}C_{4,3}(\tfrac{1}{2})^4$$

$$P_5 = \tfrac{3}{5}C_{4,4}(\tfrac{1}{2})^4$$

The probability of the desired event is the sum of these five probabilities, or 73/80.

(c) The daily revenue T is a random variable with the following distribution:

T	Probability
0	$(\tfrac{1}{2})^5 = \tfrac{1}{32}$
R	$5(\tfrac{1}{2})^5 = \tfrac{5}{32}$
$2R$	$10(\tfrac{1}{2})^5 = \tfrac{10}{32}$
$3R$	$10(\tfrac{1}{2})^5 + 5(\tfrac{1}{2})^5 + (\tfrac{1}{2})^5 = \tfrac{16}{32}$

$$\text{Mean } T = \bar{T} = \tfrac{5}{32} \cdot R + \tfrac{10}{32} \cdot 2R + \tfrac{16}{32} \cdot 3R$$
$$= \tfrac{73}{32}R$$

The cost per day is constant at $3C$. The break-even rental is the value of R for which

$$\tfrac{73}{32}R = 3C$$

or

$$R = 1.315C$$

Example 8

Prove that for the uniform distribution, defined by

$$P(k) = \frac{1}{n+1} \qquad k = 0, 1, 2, \cdots, n$$

$$P(k) = 0 \qquad k < 0 \quad \text{or} \quad k > n$$

the mean is $n/2$ and the variance is $n^2/12 + n/6$

SOLUTION

We make use of the following results from elementary algebra:

$$1 + 2 + \cdots + r = \tfrac{1}{2}r(r + 1)$$

$$1^2 + 2^2 + \cdots + r^2 = \tfrac{1}{6}r(r + 1)(2r + 1)$$

Thus

$$\bar{x} = \sum_{i=0}^{n} i \cdot \frac{1}{n + 1} = \frac{1}{n + 1} \sum_{i=1}^{n} i = \frac{1}{n + 1} \cdot \frac{n(n + 1)}{2} = \frac{n}{2}$$

$$\text{Var } (x) = \sum_{i=0}^{n} i^2 \cdot \frac{1}{n + 1} - \left(\frac{n}{2}\right)^2$$

$$= \frac{1}{n + 1} \sum_{i=1}^{n} i^2 - \frac{n^2}{4}$$

$$= \frac{1}{n + 1} \cdot \frac{n(n + 1)(2n + 1)}{6} - \frac{n^2}{4}$$

$$= \frac{n^2}{12} + \frac{n}{6}$$

Example 9

A manufacturing process involves the processing of a part by two machines, machine A and machine B, in that order. The part is subject to breakage in each machine; and, when a part breaks, the machine is out of service temporarily for repairs. If the probability of breakage of a part is p_1 in machine A and p_2 in machine B, find the expected number of parts that will be completely processed before the first breakdown.

SOLUTION

We shall make use of the following elementary algebraic result:

$$y + 2y^2 + 3y^3 + \cdots = \frac{y}{(1 - y)^2} \quad \text{if} \quad -1 < y < 1$$

Let x denote the number of finished pieces at the time the process stops.

The random variable x will take the value 0 if either of these two mutually exclusive events occurs:

1. The first part breaks in machine A.
2. The first part goes through machine A, but breaks in machine B.

Then
$$P\{x=0\} = p_1 + (1 - p_1)p_2 = p_1 + p_2 - p_1p_2$$

For convenience, set $P_0 = p_1 + p_2 - p_1p_2$. Clearly P_0 is also the probability that *any* started part will not go through successfully.

The random variable x will take the value k if both the following events occur:

1. The first k parts go through successfully.
2. The $k+1$st part breaks.

Thus
$$P\{x=k\} = (1 - P_0)^k P_0$$

The mean $\bar{x}$ is obtained, as usual, by

$$\bar{x} = \sum_{k=0}^{\infty} k\, P\{x=k\}$$

$$= \sum_{k=0}^{\infty} k\, P_0(1 - P_0)^k = P_0 \sum_{k=1}^{\infty} k(1 - P_0)^k$$

$$= \frac{1 - P_0}{P_0} \qquad \text{by the above algebraic identity}$$

Thus $\bar{x} = \dfrac{1}{p_1 + p_2 - p_1p_2} - 1$

(This value for the mean can also be obtained by noting that x follows a geometric distribution with parameter $1 - P_0$.)

Up to this point we have considered only situations where a trial results in a value for *one* random variable. In some of the applications, however, a trial can involve two or even more random variables. An example is a trial consisting of the selection of a man from a population and the measurement of his height and weight; another is the selection of a card from a deck and noting its suit and its value. We shall deal specifically only with the bivariate case of two random variables; the extension of the ideas to more than two random variables involves only some expansion of the notation.

If x and y take on only discrete values, with x ranging over the set $(x_1, x_2, \cdots, x_n)$ and y over the set $(y_1, y_2, \cdots, y_s)$, then the result of a "trial" will be one of the ns points (x_i, y_j). The probability distribution of the result of a trial is completely specified by the ns individual probabilities associated with the ns events $\{x = x_i; y = y_j\}$.

In other words, the *joint frequency function* of x and y is given by

$$P(x_i, y_j) = \alpha_{ij} \qquad i = 1, \cdots, n; \qquad j = 1, \cdots, s$$

The values of n, s, and the individual α_{ij} are what serve to distinguish one joint probability distribution from another. For any such joint distribution, $\Sigma\Sigma\alpha_{ij} = 1$.

Even in the bivariate case, it is meaningful to speak of the "frequency function of x"; this is defined conceptually by simply suppressing the value of the second variable in the result of a trial. It can be shown that, in the bivariate case,

$$P\{x = x_i\} = \sum_{j=1}^{s} P(x_i, y_j) \qquad \text{for each } i$$

and similarly that

$$P\{y = y_j\} = \sum_{i=1}^{n} P(x_i, y_j) \qquad \text{for each } j$$

Example 10

Two dice are tossed four times. Find the joint distribution for x, the number of times a 7 is obtained, and y, the number of times an 11 is obtained.

SOLUTION

Here a single trial consists of tossing the dice four times. One approach to the problem might be to regard the sample space as consisting of the 11^4 points $(2, 2, 2, 2)$, $(2, 2, 2, 3)$, $(2, 2, 2, 4)$, $\cdots$, $(12, 12, 12, 12)$, with the corresponding individual probabilities computed by the methods described in the preceding section. Then the joint probability of x and y could be obtained as follows:

(x, y)	$P(x, y)$
$(0, 0)$	Sum of probabilities for those points with no 7's and no 11's
$(0, 1)$	Sum of probabilities for those points with no 7's and one 11
$(0, 2)$	Sum of probabilities for those points with no 7's and two 11's

and similarly for the remaining possible combinations $(0, 3)$, $(0, 4)$, $(1, 0)$, $(1, 1)$, $(1, 2)$, $(1, 3)$, $(2, 0)$, $(2, 1)$, $(2, 2)$, $(3, 0)$, $(3, 1)$, $(4, 0)$. This procedure is lengthy, and so we proceed as below.

Let i and j be two integers between 0 and 4 whose sum does not exceed 4. By the multiplication formula 2.4

$$P\{x = i; y = j\} = P\{x = i\} P\{y = j \,|\, x = i\}$$

From earlier work we know that the probability of a 7 in a toss of two dice is 1/6. Since $P\{x=i\}$ is just the probability of i 7's in four tosses,

$$P\{x=i\} = C_{4,i}(\tfrac{1}{6})^i(\tfrac{5}{6})^{4-i}$$

Now $P\{y=j|x=i\}$ is the probability of j 11's in the remaining $4-i$ tosses. The unconditional probability of 11 in a toss of two dice is 1/18; but the conditional probability of this event, given that the toss is not a 7, is 1/18 divided by 5/6, or 1/15. Then

$$P\{y=j|x=i\} = C_{4-i,j}(\tfrac{1}{15})^j(\tfrac{14}{15})^{4-i-j}$$

Thus the joint frequency function for x and y is

$$P\{x=i; y=j\} = C_{4,i}C_{4-i,j}(\tfrac{1}{6})^i(\tfrac{5}{6})^{4-i}(\tfrac{1}{15})^j(\tfrac{14}{15})^{4-i-j}$$

This may be rewritten as

$$P\{x=i; y=j\} = \frac{4!}{i!j!(4-i-j)!}\left(\frac{1}{6}\right)^i\left(\frac{1}{18}\right)^j\left(\frac{7}{9}\right)^{4-i-j}$$

CONTINUOUS DISTRIBUTIONS

In the preceding section, random variables were discussed, whose possible values were separated or "discrete," such as the number of heads in n tosses of a coin, the number of good apples in a barrel, and so on. Here we turn to random variables which are, more properly and conveniently, regarded as ranging over a continuum of values. Examples are the weight of a carload of coal, the time between clicks of a Geiger counter, the temperature at noon in Miami.

Continuous random variables are defined on sample spaces with a non-denumerable infinity of points. Because of the mathematical difficulties involved, we shall not develop the concept in detail, but retain the notion of a "trial" as a set of operations which result in some single definite (but random) value for x. Then, if a is some particular value on the range of x, the event "the value of x resulting from a trial is less than or equal to a" has a definite probability in the sense of this chapter. We call this probability $P\{x\leq a\}$. Inasmuch as $P\{x\leq a\}$ is defined for each value a on the range of x, it is actually a function of a, which for brevity we shall denote by $U(a)$:

$$U(a) = P\{x\leq a\}$$

The function $U(a)$ corresponding to a continuous random variable x is usually called the "cumulative distribution function of x." Some mathematicians prefer the briefer term "distribution function of x," although "cumulative distribution function" is frequently found in statistical textbooks.

If a and b are two values on the range of x with $a < b$, we may denote by $P\{a<x<b\}$ the probability of the event "the value of x resulting from a trial is more than a but not more than b." We can express $P\{a<x\leq b\}$ in terms of the cumulative distribution function by first noting that

$$P\{x\leq b\} = P\{x\leq a\} + P\{a<x\leq b\} \qquad \text{see (2.2)}$$

Then

$$P\{a<x\leq b\} = U(b) - U(a)$$

In this section we will be concerned only with cumulative distribution functions $U(a)$ that possess derivatives $f(a)$ at all points on the range of x. In such cases $f(a) = U'(a)$, and we have

$$(2.17) \qquad U(a) = \int_{-\infty}^{a} f(x)\, dx; \qquad P\{a<x\leq b\} = \int_{a}^{b} f(x)\, dx$$

The function $f(x)$, defined when the cumulative distribution function is differentiable, is called the "probability density function of x," or more briefly the "density function of x."

Some immediate consequences, for any random variable x with density function $f(x)$, are

(a) $\int_{-\infty}^{\infty} f(x)\, dx = 1.$

(b) If a is a fixed value of x, $P\{x=a\} = 0$.

(c) $f(x)\, dx$ can be regarded as the probability that the random variable takes on a value between x and $x+dx$.

As in the discrete case, the probability distribution of a random variable which ranges over a continuum may be described (incompletely, of course) by its mean $\bar{x}$ and variance Var (x):

$$(2.18) \qquad \bar{x} = \int_{-\infty}^{\infty} x f(x)\, dx$$

$$(2.19) \qquad \text{Var } (x) = \int_{-\infty}^{\infty} (x - \bar{x})^2 f(x)\, dx \qquad \text{definition}$$

$$(2.19') \qquad \text{Var } (x) = \int_{-\infty}^{\infty} x^2 f(x)\, dx - (\bar{x})^2 \qquad \text{in computation}$$

Several familiar examples of probability distributions with x ranging over a continuum are given below, along with the mean and variance for each.

Rectangular Distribution (Figure 2.5)

Range of x: 0 to a.

Density: $f(x) = \dfrac{1}{a}$.

Mean: $\bar{x} = \dfrac{a}{2}$.

Variance: $\text{Var}(x) = \dfrac{a^2}{12}$.

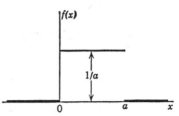

Figure 2.5. Rectangular distribution.

Normal Distribution (Figure 2.6)

Range of x: $-\infty$ to ∞.

Density: $f(x) = \dfrac{1}{\sigma\sqrt{2\pi}} \exp\left[\dfrac{-(x-m)^2}{2\sigma^2}\right]$.

Mean: $\bar{x} = m$.

Variance: $\text{Var}(x) = \sigma^2$.

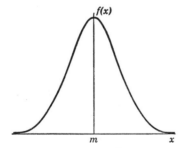

Figure 2.6. Normal distribution.

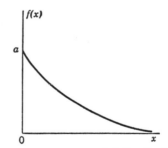

Figure 2.7. Exponential distribution.

Exponential Distribution (Figure 2.7)

Range of x: 0 to ∞.

Density: $f(x) = ae^{-ax}$ where a is a positive parameter.

Mean: $\bar{x} = \dfrac{1}{a}$.

Variance: $\text{Var}(x) = \dfrac{1}{a^2}$.

Gamma Distribution (Figure 2.8)

Range of x: 0 to ∞.

Density: $f(x) = \dfrac{b^{a+1}}{\Gamma(a+1)} x^a e^{-bx}$ where b is a positive param-

eter, and a is a parameter greater than -1. [Here $\Gamma(v)$ denotes the gamma function with argument v.]

Mean: $\bar{x} = \dfrac{a+1}{b}$.

Variance: $\text{Var}(x) = \dfrac{a+1}{b^2}$.

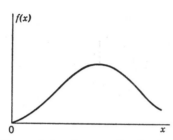

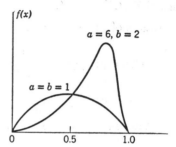

Figure 2.8.   Gamma distribution.   **Figure 2.9.   Beta distribution.**

Beta Distribution (Figure 2.9)

Range of x: 0 to 1.

Density: $f(x) = \dfrac{(a+b+1)!}{a!\,b!} x^a (1-x)^b$ where a and b are

both parameters greater than -1.

Mean: $\bar{x} = \dfrac{a+1}{a+b+2}$.

Variance: $\text{Var}(x) = \left(\dfrac{a+2}{a+b+3}\right)\left(\dfrac{a+1}{a+b+2}\right)$.

(This type of distribution often occurs when the random variable x is a *proportion*.)

If x is a random variable, then any function of x is also a random variable. For instance, the value obtained by squaring the value of a random variable x is a new random variable z, defined by means of the equation $z = x^2$. If $f(x)$ is the density function for x, the density function $g(z)$ for the new random variable $z = z(x)$ may be obtained in two ways:

(1) by use of the relation

$$f(x)\ dx = g(z)\ dz$$

(2) by use of the relation

$$\int_{-\infty}^{x} f(t)\ dt = \int_{-\infty}^{z} g(u)\ du$$

Example 11 *

A hardware store wishes to order Christmas tree lights for sale during the Christmas season. On the basis of past experience, they feel that the demand v for lights can be approximately described by the density function $f(v)$; i.e. $f(v)\ dv$ is the probability that the demand will lie between v and $v+dv$. On each light ordered and sold, they make a profit of a cents; on each light ordered but not sold, they sustain a loss of b cents. Determine the number of lights they should order, to maximize expected profit.

SOLUTION

Let x = number of lights ordered.

The actual profit R is a random variable, which is really a function of both the random variable v and the decision variable x.

Symbolically, the expected profit $E(R)$ for a particular value of x is given by

$$E(R) = \int_{0}^{\infty} R(v, x)\ f(v)\ dv$$

The function $R(v, x)$, by the conditions of the problem, has the form

$$R(v, x) = av - b(x - v) \quad \text{for} \quad v < x$$
$$R(v, x) = ax \qquad\qquad \text{for} \quad v \geq x$$

Then

$$E(R) = \int_{0}^{x} \{av - b(x - v)\}\ f(v)\ dv + \int_{x}^{\infty} ax\ f(v)\ dv$$

We maximize $E(R)$ by differentiating with respect to x and setting the derivative equal to zero: Note that the differentiation problem here is one of differentiating integrals with respect to a parameter. Applying

* This example is a modification of a problem discussed in "Notes from MIT Summer Course in Operations Research," Massachusetts Institute of Technology, 1953.

equation (II.1) of Appendix II, we obtain as the condition for x

$$0 = -b\int_0^x f(v)\, dv + a\int_x^\infty f(v)\, dv$$

If we let
$$U(v) = \int_0^v f(t)\, dt$$

the above equation may be rewritten as

$$-b\, U(x) + a[1 - U(x)] = 0$$

or
$$U(x) = \frac{a}{a+b}$$

The optimal order, then, is the solution x of the equation

(2.20)
$$\int_0^x f(v)\, dv = \frac{a}{a+b}$$

The graphical solution of this equation is suggested in Figure 2.10.

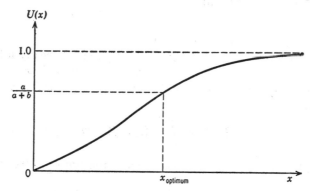

Figure 2.10.   Graphical solution of equation (2.20).

Example 12

A random variable x has range a to b and density $f(x)$. What are the range and density function $g(z)$ of the random variable z, if the value of z is obtained from the value of x by means of

(a) $z = x - a$?
(b) $z = kx$?

SOLUTION

(a) The event $\{z$ between z_0 and $z_0 + dz\}$ occurs when and only when the event $\{x$ between $z_0 + a$ and $z_0 + a + dz\}$ occurs. Thus

$$g(z_0)\, dz = f(z_0 + a)\, dz$$

Canceling dz, and dropping the subscript,

$$g(z) = f(z + a) \qquad 0 \le z \le b - a$$

(b) The event $\{z$ between z_0 and $z_0 + dz\}$ occurs when and only when the event $\{x$ between z_0/k and $z_0/k + dz/k\}$ occurs. Then

$$g(z_0)\, dz = f(z_0/k)(dz/k)$$

or $$g(z) = 1/k\, f(z/k) \qquad ka \le z \le kb$$

Example 13

An extrusion plant is engaged in making up an order for pieces 20 feet long. Inasmuch as the extrusion process creates unusable material at both ends, somewhat more than 20 feet must be extruded. If more than 20 feet of good metal results, the piece is salable; if less than 20 feet of good metal is left, the piece is scrapped. Assume that the extrusion length can be controlled exactly, that the total end scrap per piece is a random variable y with density $f(y)$, and that the extrusion cost is C dollars per foot. Determine the optimum extrusion length if the quantity to be minimized is the extrusion cost per salable piece.

SOLUTION

Let $20 + x =$ extrusion length. The extrusion cost is

$$C(20 + x)$$

and the probability that a piece will be salable is the same as

$$P\{y \le x\}$$

or $$\int_0^x f(y)\, dy$$

Thus the extrusion cost per salable piece is

$$\frac{C(20 + x)}{\displaystyle\int_0^x f(y)\, dy}$$

This has the derivative (with respect to x) equal to

$$C \frac{\displaystyle\int_0^x f(y)\, dy - (x + 20)\, f(x)}{\left[\displaystyle\int_0^x f(y)\, dy\right]^2}$$

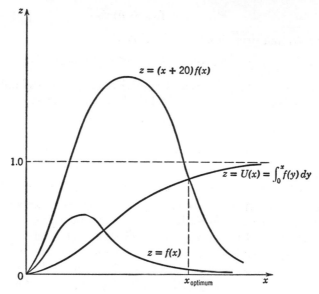

Figure 2.11.   Graphical solution of equation (2.21).

Thus the condition that must be satisfied by the optimal x is

(2.21) $$(x + 20)\, f(x) = \int_0^x f(y)\, dy$$

This equation for x is interpreted graphically in Figure 2.11.

If two random variables x and y both range over a continuum, the joint distribution of x and y is described by assigning probabilities to

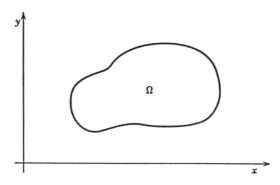

Figure 2.12.   The region Ω (joint probability).

each of the events $\{(x, y)$ lies in $\Omega\}$, where Ω is an arbitrary region of the plane. That is, for any region of the xy plane, there corresponds a definite probability that a "trial" will yield a point within the region. We shall describe these two-dimensional continuous distributions by means of a *joint density function*.

The two random variables x and y are said to have the joint density function $f(x, y)$ if, for every choice of a region Ω in the plane,

$$P\{(x, y) \text{ lies in } \Omega\} = \int\int_\Omega f(x, y) \, dx \, dy$$

Immediate consequences of the definition are:

(a) $\displaystyle\int_{-\infty}^{\infty} \int_{-\infty}^{\infty} f(x, y) \, dx \, dy = 1.$

(b) If x_0 and y_0 are two fixed numbers chosen before the "trial," $P\{x=x_0; y=y_0\} = 0.$

(c) $f(x, y) \, dx \, dy$ is the probability that the point resulting from a "trial" falls within the elementary rectangle with vertices (x, y), $(x+dx, y)$, $(x, y+dy)$, $(x+dx, y+dy)$.

If we are given the joint density function $f(x, y)$ for x and y, the one-dimensional density function for either x or y alone may be obtained simply by integrating out the other variable. Letting $g(x)$ denote the density function for x, and $h(y)$ the density function for y, the explicit formulas are

$$g(x) = \int_{-\infty}^{\infty} f(x, y) \, dy$$

$$h(y) = \int_{-\infty}^{\infty} f(x, y) \, dx$$

Example 14
Given that x and y are two random variables with the joint density function $f(x, y)$, find the distribution of $x+y$ and $x-y$.

SOLUTION
Let $u = x + y$. The probability of the event $\{u < x + y < u + du\}$, for fixed u, is just the probability that the random point will fall

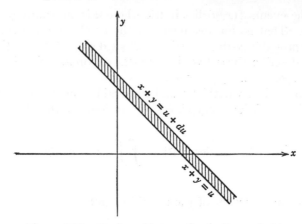

Figure 2.13.   Region of integration in Example 14.

in the shaded area of Figure 2.13.   Thus

$$f(u) \, du = \int \int f(x, y) \, dx \, dy \qquad \text{taken over the shaded area}$$

$$= \int_{-\infty}^{\infty} \int_{u-y}^{u-y+du} f(x, y) \, dx \, dy$$

$$= au \int_{-\infty}^{\infty} f(u-y, y) \, dy$$

Canceling out the du on both sides, we have, for the density of $u = x + y$,

$$f(u) = \int_{-\infty}^{\infty} f(u-y, y) \, dy$$

Similarly, we find, for the density function of $u = x - y$,

$$f(u) = \int_{-\infty}^{\infty} f(u+y, y) \, dy$$

PROBLEMS FOR SOLUTION

Set II

1. Give the (discrete) probability distribution for the sum of two consecutive digits in a random number table. (In such a table, the digit occupying any particular position is a random variable ranging over the integers 0 to 9 with probability 1/10 for each.)

2. Derive the formulas given on page 23 for the mean and variance of a random variable whose distribution is (a) binomial, (b) Poisson.

3. In a sequence of throws with two dice, what is the probability that the first 5 will precede the first 7?

4. Verify the formulas given on pages 31, 32 for the mean and variance of (a) the rectangular distribution, (b) the exponential distribution, (c) the gamma distribution.

5. Prove that the two parameters which appear in the definition of the normal distribution are interpretable as the mean of x and the standard deviation (square root of the variance) of x.

6. Given that x is distributed rectangularly between 0 and 3. Find the distribution of

(a) $2x$.
(b) $x + 2$.
(c) x^2.

7. The density function for the life (operating hours till failure) of a certain type of television tube is

$$f(x) = 0 \qquad x \leq 80$$

$$f(x) = 80/x^2 \qquad x > 80$$

You buy a new set containing three of these tubes. What is

(a) the probability that all three tubes will still be functioning after 120 hours? *[Ans. 8/27]*
(b) the density function of the time till the first tube failure?

8. The useful life u of a light bulb may be regarded as a random variable with density function $h(u)$. If the bulb is observed to be burning at time T, what is the probability that it is still burning at time $T+t$?

REFERENCES

Burington, R. S., and D. C. May, Jr., *Handbook of Probability and Statistics with Tables*, Handbook Publishers, Sandusky, 1953.

Feller, William, *An Introduction to Probability Theory and Its Applications*, Vol. 1, 2nd ed., John Wiley & Sons, New York, 1957.

Fry, Thornton C., *Probability and Its Engineering Uses*, D. Van Nostrand Co., New York, 1928.

Mood, Alexander M., *Introduction to the Theory of Statistics*, Chapters 2 through 6, McGraw-Hill Book Co., New York, 1950.

Moroney, M. J., *Facts from Figures*, Penguin Books, Baltimore, 1951.

CHAPTER

THREE

Sampling

Most operations research studies are concerned, to a greater or lesser degree, with random variables whose means and distributions cannot be known precisely. Though one often assumes a particular value for the mean, in order to test the effect of a change in some controllable variable, this contributes nothing to an understanding of process and is never a strong point in the study. The role of sampling theory in operations research is to systematize, so far as is possible, the assumptions that must be made concerning the means and distributions of relevant random variables.

Inasmuch as the distribution itself is beyond the reach of direct measurement, one must make inferences on the basis of information supplied by "data." The "data" may be regarded as direct measurements of the corresponding individuals in the population which is described by the inaccessible distribution. Such inferences can be defended only if the data are "representative": i.e. if the corresponding individuals can be regarded as having been drawn without bias from the population as a whole. As examples of the false inferences which might be made on the basis of a non-representative sample, we might mention: an estimate of the average age of people in a city based on a sample of 100 interviews at the Old Folks Home; an estimate of average income based on a random sample drawn from a telephone directory, especially in such countries as India; a literacy survey conducted entirely by mail.

The theory of sampling provides guides to the selection of a sample that will be representative, as well as an estimate of the degree of belief in the inferences made on the basis of a representative sample of a given size. In a typical situation, the inference is an estimate of the mean of the theoretical distribution, and the degree of belief in this estimate is expressed as the root-mean-square difference between the estimated mean and the true mean.

This chapter provides a brief introduction to sampling theory. Some attention is also given to the problem of fitting a theoretical distribution to a histogram, and to simulated sampling by the Monte Carlo method.

TYPES OF PHYSICAL SAMPLING

In the simplest type of sampling, we draw a sample of size n in such a way as to insure that each of the N members of the population has the same chance of being included in the sample. A sample selected in this way is called a *simple random* sample. One way of drawing a simple random sample is to number every individual (if the population is finite), put the numbers on slips of paper, and draw lots. A more convenient method is to use a table of random digits. Such tables contain lists of digits so chosen that each digit between 0 and 9 has an equal chance of appearing at a given spot in a single column, and each two-digit number between 00 and 99 has the same chance of appearing at a given spot in a double column, and so on.

Example 1
Using a random number table, show how to draw a simple random sample of ten different individuals from a population with 632 members.

SOLUTION
We number the individuals from 000 to 631, and proceed to read down some three-digit column in a random number table:

346 ✓	686 ✗
248 ✓	905 ✗
232 ✓	358 ✓
383 ✓	221 ✓
640 ✗	507 ✓
366 ✓	232 ✗
353 ✓	137 ✓

We continue to write down three-digit numbers until we have ten *different* numbers lying between 000 and 631. Here our simple random sample includes the members whose tags read: 346, 248, 232, 383, 366, 353, 358, 221, 507, 137.

This procedure obviously guarantees that each number between 000 and 631 has the same chance of being included in the sample.

Another useful type of sampling procedure is called *stratified random sampling*. The members of the population are first assigned to strata or groups, on the basis of some characteristic, and a *simple* random sample is drawn from each stratum. The individuals in all the samples taken together constitute the sample from the population as a whole, viz.:

Stratum	Number in stratum	Number in sample
1	N_1	n_1
2	N_2	n_2
3	N_3	n_3
.	.	.
.	.	.
.	.	.
k	N_k	n_k
Total	N	n

If the component sample sizes n_1, n_2, $\cdots$, n_k are so chosen that

$$\frac{n_1}{N_1} = \frac{n_2}{N_2} = \cdots = \frac{n_k}{N_k} \left(= \frac{n}{N} \right)$$

we have what is known as *proportional* stratified random sampling.

Other important types of sampling procedure, not discussed here, are systematic sampling and cluster sampling.

ESTIMATES FROM SAMPLES AND THEIR PRECISION

Our purpose in sampling is to draw inferences about the parent population; we are usually concerned with estimating parameters of the parent population from the sample. Probably the simplest and most commonly required parameters are the mean and variance, but many others are possible. In order to judge how useful our sampling procedure is, we examine how our estimates would vary if we repeatedly used the same procedure. If the average value of the estimate over all possible samples is the population value, the method of estimation is said to be *unbiased*. If two procedures are both unbiased, we can compare them by considering the variance (over all possible samples) of their estimates.

In general, we choose a sampling procedure which yields unbiased estimates with a variance as low as possible. There may, however, be a few occasions when the cost of avoiding bias is greater than the added value of a bias-free estimate; in such cases we could probably tolerate a small amount of bias.

In what follows we will be thinking of a population (x) of N members, with a mean μ and variance Var (x). Generally sampling will be without replacement; i.e., no member can appear in a particular sample more than once.

If we draw a simple random sample $(x_1, x_2, \cdots, x_n)$ from such a population, it can be shown that the sample mean, $\bar{x} = (1/n) \Sigma x_i$, is an unbiased estimate of the population mean. Thus, if $E(\bar{x})$ denotes the average or "expected" value of $\bar{x}$ over all possible samples, we have

$$(3.1) \qquad\qquad E(\bar{x}) = \mu$$

On the other hand, the sample variance, defined as $\dfrac{1}{n} \displaystyle\sum_{i=1}^{n} (x_i - \bar{x})^2$, is not an unbiased estimate of Var (x). In fact, its expected value is $[(n-1)/n]$ Var (x); we can get an unbiased estimate by multiplying by $n/(n-1)$. That is,

$$\frac{1}{n-1} \sum_{i=1}^{n} (x_i - \bar{x})^2$$

is an unbiased estimate of Var (x).

The sample mean $\bar{x}$ is a random variable whose mean, according to (3.1), is μ. The variance of the sample mean is given (exactly) by

$$(3.2) \qquad\qquad \text{Var}\,(\bar{x}) = \left(1 - \frac{n}{N}\right) \frac{\text{Var}\,(x)}{n}$$

The term $(1 - n/N)$ is called the *finite multiplier*. Some such term can be intuitively justified because, if we sampled the entire population to estimate the mean μ, we would obtain μ every time, and the estimate would have no variance. In this case $n = N$, and (3.2) yields zero for Var $(\bar{x})$. But, when N tends to infinity, we get the simpler form

$$(3.3) \qquad\qquad \text{Var}\,(\bar{x}) = \frac{\text{Var}\,(x)}{n}$$

This result is also true for a finite population when we sample with replacement: i.e., when there is no restriction on the number of times an individual can appear in a particular sample.

In practice, we may be able to use an approximate value of Var (x), obtained from previously collected data, to obtain Var $(\bar{x})$ in advance of our sample; or we may use our sample estimate of Var (x) substituted in (3.2) to obtain an estimate of Var $(\bar{x})$.

In most practical cases the distribution of $\bar{x}$ over many samples can be taken to be normal, provided n is reasonably large (say over 20) and n/N is small.

Example 2

A preliminary series of observations yields the following weights (in pounds) for 20 schoolboys selected at random from a given age group. How many observations would be required if the estimate of the average weight of boys in this age group is to have 95% chance of being correct to $\pm\frac{1}{2}$ pound?

77.3	79.5	72.6	66.1
75.3	80.9	68.1	74.5
82.4	67.5	70.0	68.3
80.1	71.6	75.0	80.2
82.0	81.9	82.0	76.4

SOLUTION

We first compute an unbiased estimate of the variance of an individual observation. We obtain

$$\bar{x} = 75.6, \qquad \Sigma(x - \bar{x})^2 = 579.51, \qquad \tfrac{1}{19}\Sigma(x - \bar{x})^2 = 30.51$$

Hence an unbiased estimate of the variance is 30.51; and the estimated standard deviation is the square root of this, or 5.52.

We now assume that weights of all boys in the age group are distributed with a standard deviation of 5.52 pounds, but with an unknown mean. A sample of n boys will have a mean that is *normally* distributed about the mean of all boys in the age group and that has a standard deviation of

$$\frac{5.52}{\sqrt{n}}$$

From tables we find that 95% of a normal population lies within plus or minus twice the standard deviation of the mean. Since we want a 95% chance of our sample mean lying within half a pound of the population mean, we have

$$2 \times \frac{5.52}{\sqrt{n}} = \frac{1}{2}$$

or

$$n = 488$$

Example 3

Suppose that we have an infinite population of individuals, some of whom possess a certain attribute while the rest do not. Let P be the proportion of individuals in the population that have the attribute. We take a simple random sample of size n, of which m are found to have the attribute. Show that

(3.4) $$\hat{P} = \frac{m}{n}$$

is an unbiased estimate of P, and also that

(3.5) $$\frac{\hat{P}(1 - \hat{P})}{n - 1}$$

is an unbiased estimate of the variance of this estimate.

SOLUTION

The random variable m, by hypothesis, follows the binomial distribution for the number of successes in n trials with success probability P:

$$P(m) = C_{n,m} P^m (1 - P)^{n-m}$$

We know that the expected value $E(m)$ of m may be obtained from the formula $E(m) = nP$. Since n is a constant, we have

$$E(\hat{P}) = E\left(\frac{m}{n}\right) = \frac{1}{n} E(m) = \frac{1}{n} \cdot nP = P$$

This proves that $\hat{P}$ gives an unbiased estimate of P.

The exact value of Var $(\hat{P})$ is given by

$$\text{Var}(\hat{P}) = \text{Var}\left(\frac{m}{n}\right) = E\left\{\frac{m}{n} - E\left(\frac{m}{n}\right)\right\}^2$$

$$= \frac{1}{n^2} E\{m - E(m)\}^2 \qquad \text{since } n \text{ is a constant}$$

$$= \frac{1}{n^2} \text{Var}(m) = \frac{nP(1 - P)}{n^2} = \frac{P(1 - P)}{n}$$

Now

$$E\left[\frac{\hat{P}(1-\hat{P})}{n-1}\right] = \frac{1}{n-1}[E(\hat{P}) - E(\hat{P}^2)]$$

$$= \frac{P}{n-1} - \frac{E(\hat{P}^2)}{n-1}$$

$$= \frac{P}{n-1} - \frac{\text{Var}(\hat{P}) + [E(\hat{P})]^2}{n-1}$$

$$= \frac{P}{n-1} - \frac{P(1-P)}{n(n-1)} - \frac{P^2}{n-1}$$

$$= \frac{P(1-P)}{n} = \text{Var}(\hat{P})$$

Hence (3.5) gives an unbiased estimate of Var $(\hat{P})$.

Example 4

We try to predict the result of a mayoralty election in one of our large cities. Our poll includes interviews with 1000 randomly selected registered voters. Results of the poll are:

> For Candidate A: 532.
> For Candidate B: 468.

On the basis of this information, we publish the prediction of A's election. Election Day comes, and B wins 51.1% of the votes. How unlucky were we?

SOLUTION

In the language of Example 3, the attribute in question is "intention to vote for A." The proportion P of the population possessing the attribute is 0.489; and the estimate $\hat{P}$ from a sample of 1000 is 0.532. The estimate $\hat{P}$ is approximately normally distributed with a mean of 0.489. The variance of $\hat{P}$ need not be estimated in this example, since we know the underlying P; we have as an exact result:

$$\text{Var}(\hat{P}) = \frac{P(1-P)}{1000} = \frac{(0.511)(0.489)}{1000} = 2.499 \times 10^{-4}$$

$$\text{S.D.}(\hat{P}) = 0.0158$$

Our observed result 0.532 differs from the expected result 0.489 by about three standard deviations. The probability of this occurring by chance is less than one in a hundred. We conclude that we were not at all unlucky, but either our "simple random" sample was simply not random, or a sizable proportion of the voters changed their minds between our poll and the election.

We next give estimates of the mean and the corresponding variances for stratified random samples. Recall that the population is subdivided into k strata, of sizes $N_1, N_2, \cdots, N_k$ with $\Sigma N_h = N$. A simple random sample of size n_1 is taken from stratum 1, of size n_2 from stratum 2, etc. with $\Sigma n_h = n$. Let μ be the true mean of the entire population, let μ_h be the true mean of the hth stratum, and let $\bar{x}_h$ be the observed mean of the sample of n_h drawn from the hth stratum. Then it is not hard to show that an unbiased estimate of the true mean μ is given by

$$(3.6) \qquad \hat{\mu} = \frac{1}{N} \sum_{h=1}^{k} N_h \bar{x}_h$$

That is, the estimate of the population mean is the weighted mean of the observed subsample means, where the weight applied to the sub-sample mean $\bar{x}_h$ is N_h/N.

Let x_h be the random variable associated with measurements on *individuals* in the hth stratum. With this notation, the variance of the estimate (3.6) for the population mean μ is given by *

$$(3.7) \qquad \text{Var}\,(\hat{\mu}) = \sum_{h=1}^{k} \left(\frac{N_h}{N}\right)^2 \cdot \frac{N_h - n_h}{N_h} \cdot \frac{\text{Var}\,(x_h)}{n_h}$$

In the special case where the population consists entirely of one stratum, we have $k = 1$, $N_h = N$, $n_h = n$, and the expression for Var $(\hat{\mu})$ becomes, as in (3.2),

$$(3.8) \qquad \text{Var}\,(\hat{\mu}) = \left(1 - \frac{n}{N}\right) \frac{\text{Var}\,(x)}{n}$$

If the sampling procedure is to draw a *proportional* stratified sample, we have

$$\frac{N_h}{N} = \frac{n_h}{n}$$

and (3.6) reduces to

$$(3.9) \qquad \hat{\mu} = \sum_{h} \frac{n_h \bar{x}_h}{n} = \frac{1}{n} [\text{sum of all the values in the sample}]$$

---

* For the derivation of this formula, see W. G. Cochran, *Sampling Techniques*, p. 69, John Wiley & Sons, New York, 1953.

For proportional sampling, equation (3.7) simplifies to

$$(3.10) \qquad \text{Var}(\hat{\mu}) = \left(1 - \frac{n}{N}\right)\frac{1}{nN}\sum_{h=1}^{k} N_h \, \text{Var}(x_h)$$

Example 5

Suppose that the population is divided into k strata with the notation as above, and that the size of the total sample is fixed at n. Determine the optimal sizes n_1, n_2, $\cdots$ of the subsamples from the various strata, if the criterion for optimality is minimum variance for the estimate of μ.

SOLUTION

We start with equation (3.7) for $\text{Var}(\hat{\mu})$. We can ignore the constant factor $1/N^2$, and hence seek to minimize

$$\sum_{h=1}^{k} N_h(N_h - n_h)\frac{\text{Var}(x_h)}{n_h}$$

subject to the constraint

$$\sum_{h=1}^{k} n_h = n$$

We set up the Lagrangian function

$$f(n_1, n_2, \cdots, n_k, \lambda) = \Sigma N_h(N_h - n_h)\frac{\text{Var}(x_h)}{n_h} + \lambda(\Sigma n_h - n)$$

For a minimum, we equate the partial derivatives with respect to $n_1, \cdots, n_k$ and λ to zero:

$$\frac{\partial f}{\partial n_h} = -\frac{N_h^2}{n_h^2}\text{Var}(x_h) + \lambda = 0$$

$$\frac{\partial f}{\partial \lambda} = \sum_{h=1}^{k} n_h - n = 0$$

Hence

$$n_h = \frac{N_h\sqrt{\text{Var}(x_h)}}{\sqrt{\lambda}} = \frac{N_h\sigma_h}{\sqrt{\lambda}} \quad \text{if we set} \quad \sqrt{\text{Var}(x_h)} = \sigma_h$$

From the second equation above, $\sqrt{\lambda}$ has the value

$$\sqrt{\lambda} = \frac{1}{n}\sum_{h=1}^{k} N_h\sigma_h$$

so that we obtain as our final result

$$(3.11) \qquad \frac{n_h}{n} = \frac{N_h\sigma_h}{\sum_{h=1}^{k} N_h\sigma_h}$$

In words, this result says that, for optimal allocation of a sample of given size to strata, the subsample from a stratum should be proportional to the product of the stratum size and the stratum standard deviation.

Example 6

A department store wishes to ascertain the average amount outstanding on its customer accounts. Past experience suggests that the sums outstanding are grouped as shown in Table 1.

TABLE 1

Stratum	Range	Relative frequency	Variance of amount outstanding
1	<5.00	0.20	1
2	5.01– 20.00	0.40	6
3	20.01– 50.00	0.25	20
4	50.01–100.00	0.10	75
5	100.01–250.00	0.03	650
6	>250.00	0.02	2500

Show how to use stratified sampling to minimize the variance of the estimate of the mean amount outstanding for a sample consisting of 5000 accounts.

SOLUTION

For convenience, we rewrite equation (3.11) as follows:

$$n_h = n \frac{(N_h/N)\sigma_h}{\Sigma(N_h/N)\sigma_h}$$

The computations are arranged in Table 2.

TABLE 2

Stratum	Var (x_h)	σ_h	N_h/N	$(N_h/N)\sigma_h$	n_h
1	1	1	0.20	0.20	202
2	6	2.45	0.40	0.98	992
3	20	4.47	0.25	1.12	1133
4	75	8.66	0.10	0.87	881
5	650	25.50	0.03	0.77	779
6	2500	50	0.02	1.00	1015
Totals	—	—	1.00	4.94	5000

It may well happen that the store does not have enough accounts in some strata to take samples of the size indicated in the last column. Suppose, for example, there are 40,000 accounts in all. Then only 800 of them are for amounts in excess of $250 (stratum 6). In this case we would make a complete check of accounts exceeding $250 and re-allocate the remainder of the sample (4200) to the other strata in proportion to the n_h above.

The final results would be:

Stratum	1	2	3	4	5	6
Sample size	213	1,045	1,194	927	821	800
Stratum size	8000	16,000	10,000	4000	1200	800

We compute the variance of the estimated mean from this sample, using equation (3.7):

$$\text{Var }(\hat{\mu}) = (0.20)^2 \cdot \frac{7787}{8000} \cdot \frac{1}{213} + (0.40)^2 \cdot \frac{15,955}{16,000} \cdot \frac{6}{1045}$$

$$+ (0.25)^2 \cdot \frac{8,806}{10,000} \cdot \frac{20}{1194}$$

$$+ (0.10)^2 \cdot \frac{3073}{4000} \cdot \frac{75}{927} + (0.03)^2 \cdot \frac{379}{1200} \cdot \frac{650}{821}$$

$$+ (0.02)^2 \cdot \frac{0}{800} \cdot \frac{2500}{800}$$

$$= 0.00287$$

Example 7

For the population of accounts in Example 6, make a rough estimate of the variance of the sample mean, if the sampling procedure involves taking a simple random sample consisting of 5000 accounts from the entire population.

SOLUTION

Remembering that μ denotes the mean of the population, and μ_h the mean of the hth stratum, and introducing the notation x_{hi} for the value of the ith account in the hth stratum, we have (exactly)

$$N \text{ Var }(x) = \sum_h \sum_i (x_{hi} - \mu)^2 \qquad \text{by definition of the variance}$$

$$= \sum_h \sum_i (x_{hi} - \mu_h + \mu_h - \mu)^2$$

$$= \sum_h \sum_i (x_{hi} - \mu_h)^2 + \sum_h \sum_i (\mu_h - \mu)^2$$

$$+ \text{ a cross-product term which sums to zero}$$

$$= \sum_h N_h \text{ Var } (x_h) + \sum_h N_h(\mu_h - \mu)^2$$

This result may be rewritten:

$$\text{Var } (x) = \sum_h \frac{N_h}{N} [\text{Var } (x_h) + (\mu_h - \mu)^2]$$

To apply this result to the problem at hand, we would have to know the stratum means and the population mean, all of which are unavailable. For a rough estimate, we shall assume that the stratum means lie in the middle of the strata, for the first five strata, and "guess" that the mean of the last stratum is \$400. Then the population mean μ is the weighted mean of these stratum means. We have:

$$\mu_1 = 2.50$$

$$\mu_2 = 12.50$$

$$\mu_3 = 35.00$$

$$\mu_4 = 75.00$$

$$\mu_5 = 175.00$$

$$\mu = \sum_h \frac{N_h}{N} \mu_h = 36.00$$

Using these values, and the figures for Var (x_h) given in the statement of Example 6, we compute

$$\sum_h \frac{N_h}{N} \text{ Var } (x_h) = \quad 84.6$$

$$\sum_h \frac{N_h}{N} (\mu_h - \mu)^2 = 3827.1$$

$$\text{Var } (x) = 3911.7$$

Hence the estimate of the mean account size, if based on a simple random sample of size 5000, will have the variance $3911.7/5000 = 0.782$. Comparing with the result of Example 6, it is seen that there is a tremendous advantage in this situation in using stratified sampling rather than simple sampling. The difference is more dramatic here than in most situations, because the complete sampling of stratum 6 dictated by the optimal stratified procedure eliminated this stratum's contribution to the variance. But, even in the absence of such fortunate circumstances, the precision of the estimate of the mean can usually be improved appreciably through judicious stratification.

PROBLEMS FOR SOLUTION

Set III

1. Use a table of random numbers to obtain a set of 25 three-digit random numbers. Using these as page numbers in your telephone directory, copy down the last three digits of the first number on each page. Find the mean and variance of these 25 three-digit numbers. Are your results compatible with the assumption that the last three digits of a telephone number are uniformly distributed between 000 and 999?

2. An experienced gambler alters his dice so that, in his opinion, the probability of a 7 exceeds 0.30. Before using this equipment, he decides to test it by rolling the dice 100 times and noting the results. How many 7's must he obtain in order to be 99% sure that the probability of a 7 is at least 0.30?
[*Ans.* 41 sevens]

3. A manufacturer wishes to produce electric fuses with no more than 1% defective. He checks quality every so often by taking a sample of 10 fuses from the line; if one or more of the 10 are defective, the manufacturing process is halted, and a search is made for an assignable cause.

(*a*) How often will he fail to halt production when defects are running at 2%? [*Ans.* 82% of the time]
(*b*) How often will he needlessly halt production when defects are running at 0.75%? [*Ans.* 7% of the time]

4. One method of sampling for a proportion is to fix in advance not the sample size n, but the number of observed successes m. If m is fixed, and if P is the relative frequency of the attribute in the population being sampled, determine

(*a*) the probability distribution of the sample size n
(*b*) the expected sample size. [*Ans.* m/P]

5. A machine produces parts which average 1% defective; however, the percentage defective varies from batch to batch. What size batch would insure that only one batch in a hundred would contain more than 2% defectives? [*Ans.* $n \geq 543$]

6. We wish to determine the percentage of boys born in a certain community. It is known that the odds on a given birth being a boy are about 1 in 2. How many birth records should be examined so that there is a 95% chance that the percentage is accurate to within ±1%? [*Ans.* 9604]

7. A sample of five bearings is taken from an automatic grinder, and their diameters are measured. The results are:

$$1.003$$
$$1.001$$
$$0.996$$
$$0.997$$
$$0.998$$

The process is considered to be running satisfactorily if 99% of the output lies in the range 1 ± 0.005. On the basis of this sample, decide whether the grinder needs adjustment. [*Ans.* Yes]

8. A simple random sample of 16 households was drawn from a city area containing 9420 households. The number of persons per household in the sample were as follows:

$$5 \quad 2 \quad 4 \quad 7$$
$$6 \quad 4 \quad 4 \quad 4$$
$$3 \quad 4 \quad 3 \quad 3$$
$$3 \quad 5 \quad 2 \quad 5$$

(*a*) Estimate the total number of people in the area. [*Ans.* 37,680]
(*b*) Approximate the probability that this estimate is between $\pm 10\%$ of the true value. [*Ans.* About 0.75]

9. We wish to estimate the value of farm products in the United States by means of a sample of 1000 farms.* Three different methods of stratification are available to us: by size of farm, type of farm, and type of operator. Using the information shown in Table 3, page 54, and assuming proportional sampling, determine which of the three methods of stratification is most effective. Compare the variance of the resulting sample with that of a simple random sample of 1000 farms.

> [*Ans.* Stratification by farm size yields a sampling variance of 40.21 for the estimated *mean*. This is lower than the variance for the other methods of stratification.]

CURVE FITTING

It is frequently necessary to fit an algebraic function to the observed relationship between two or more variables. Thus, for example, we observe a series of pairs (x_i, y_i) $[i = 1, 2, \cdots, n]$, and we wish to obtain y as a function of x. In order to do this, we must first guess the form of the function in terms of one or more parameters and then estimate the parameters so as to obtain a good fit. We are quite free to decide what we mean by a "good fit." Frequently we agree to mean that the sum of the squares of the errors shall be a minimum. If our formula

---

* This example is taken from Morris H. Hansen, William N. Hurwitz, and William G. Madow, *Sample Survey Methods and Theory*, Vol. I, John Wiley & Sons, New York, 1953.

TABLE 3

Stratum	Number of farms N_h	Variance, est.
A. Size of farm, acres		
Under 10	593,937	17,910
10–29	944,379	12,709
30–49	707,544	13,891
50–69	472,598	15,179
70–99	685,146	16,631
100–139	634,611	24,821
140–179	566,248	33,118
180–219	283,091	51,362
220–259	210,058	63,914
260–499	473,923	97,223
500–999	173,547	180,767
1000 and over	113,807	394,343
All farms	5,858,889	47,393
B. Type of farm		
Not classified by type	106,929	1,125
Fruit and nut	132,873	222,300
Vegetable	93,646	143,303
Horticultural—specialty	14,841	424,325
All other crops	1,860,644	41,571
Dairy	558,667	48,739
Poultry	273,129	69,594
Livestock	809,817	90,392
Forest products	30,645	8,807
General farms	688,807	24,502
Subsistence	1,288,891	146
All farms	5,858,889	47,393
C. Type of operator		
Full owners	3,292,063	35,683
Part owners	661,156	106,153
Managers	47,357	509,610
Tenants—cash	410,091	36,205
share–cash	137,330	48,164
share	682,561	40,052
croppers	446,850	2,696
Other and unknown	181,481	29,438
All farms	5,858,889	47,393

gives $\hat{y}_i = f(a, b, \cdots, k; x_i)$, then we choose $a, b, \cdots, k$ so as to minimize

$$\sum_i (y_i - \hat{y}_i)^2$$

The simplest example is when $f = ax + b$ and we minimize

$$\sum_i (y_i - ax_i - b)^2$$

The details are well known; they may be found in any standard statistics text, and will not be repeated here.

A second problem arises when we have a series of observations $x_i\ [i = 1, \cdots, n]$, and wish to estimate the probability distribution function that fits them best. Again we are free to decide what is meant by a good fit, and here it is more convenient to agree that the best fit is that which makes as many as possible of the observed moments equal to the corresponding moments of the fitted distribution. Let $p(a, b, \cdots, k; x)$ be the distribution we wish to fit, and let $m = m(a, b, \cdots, k)$ be the mean of this distribution. Then, if $\bar{x}$ is the mean of the observations, we determine the parameters $a, b, \cdots, k$ from the simultaneous equations

$$\bar{x} = m\,(a, b, \cdots, k) \qquad \text{first moment (mean)}$$

$$\frac{1}{n} \sum_{i=1}^{n} (x_i - \bar{x})^2 = \int_{-\infty}^{\infty} (x - m)^2\, p(a, b, \cdots, k; x)\, dx \qquad \begin{array}{l} \text{second moment} \\ \text{(variance)} \end{array}$$

$$\frac{1}{n} \sum_{i=1}^{n} (x_i - \bar{x})^3 = \int_{-\infty}^{\infty} (x - m)^3\, p(a, b, \cdots, k; x)\, dx \qquad \text{third moment}$$

and so on, where we use as many equations as there are parameters.

Note that the method requires advance specification of the function $p(a, b, \cdots, k; x)$; it then enables us to find the parameters $a, b, \cdots, k$. We can often guess at the form of p from past experience or, if we have enough data, from the shape of the histogram.

The method works equally well when the theoretical distribution is discrete. We need only replace the integrals by summations.

Example 8

Fit a normal curve to the following series of observations.

15	17	16	5	20	13	11	9	15	21	15	6	5
8	13	10	10	18	15	17	13	20	11	17	21	17
16	13	12	14	13	14	13	11	8	16	15	12	15
25	15	11	14	19	12	10	8	4	20	13	10	9
23	13	12	11	14	19	13	14	6	11	11	15	18

SOLUTION

The normal curve has only two parameters, the mean and standard deviation. Once these are known, the distribution is completely defined. Thus we compute the mean and standard deviation of the observed data, and we have the required normal curve.

The reader can verify that the mean is 13.54 and the standard deviation is 3.67.

The probability density function for the normal distribution with mean m and standard deviation σ is

$$\frac{1}{\sigma\sqrt{2\pi}} \exp\left[\frac{-(x-m)^2}{2\sigma^2}\right]$$

We can use standard tables of the normal distribution to obtain properties of our fitted distribution, remembering that these tables give ordinates and areas for the variable

$$u = \frac{x-m}{\sigma} = \frac{x-13.54}{3.67}$$

Example 9

The gamma distribution, described in Chapter 2, page 32, often furnishes a good fit for observations that are intrinsically non-negative and of fairly wide range. Among other applications, it has proved useful in the analysis of weekly sales data, and in connection with certain inventory models.

Suppose that a metal fabricating company has kept track, over a period of 80 weeks, of its weekly consumption x of a particular kind of alloy, and that the results are as follows:

x	Number of weeks
0– 99	3
100–199	3
200–299	6
300–399	14
400–499	13
500–599	15
600–699	11
700–799	9
800–899	2
900–999	4
	——
	80

Fit a gamma distribution to these data.

SOLUTION

The gamma distribution has the form (apart from a constant factor) $x^a e^{-bx}$, with mean $(a + 1)/b$ and variance $(a + 1)/b^2$. The observed distribution of x has mean 506 and variance 45,200, as the reader may verify. Using the method of moments, we determine the parameters a and b from the equations

$$\frac{a + 1}{b} = 506$$

$$\frac{a + 1}{b^2} = 45{,}200$$

obtaining $a = 4.57$, $b = 0.011$.

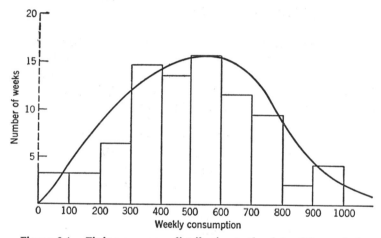

Figure 3.1. Fitting a gamma distribution to the data of Example 9.

Example 10

An owner of five overnight cabins is wondering whether he should build a sixth cabin. His records over the past 100 days show the following occupancy figures:

Nightly occupancy	Number of evenings
0	1
1	3
2	8
3	14
4	18
5	56

Estimate the fraction of evenings that a sixth cabin would be occupied, if built.

SOLUTION

Inasmuch as no records are available for the number of customers turned away, we must settle for the following demand history:

Nightly demand D	Number of evenings $n[D]$	$p(D)$
0	1	0.01
1	3	0.03
2	8	0.08
3	14	0.14
4	18	0.18
5, 6, 7, 8, $\cdots$	56	—

The next step is to fit some theoretical discrete distribution to the observed relative frequencies $p(0), \cdots, p(4)$. The Poisson is a natural first choice to consider. Examining a table of the Poisson distribution, specifically those columns with the mean $\lambda = 2, 3, 4, 5, 6$, we find that the choice $\lambda = 5$ yields an excellent fit, viz.:

D	Observed $f(D)$	Theoretical $f(D)$
0	0.01	0.007
1	0.03	0.034
2	0.08	0.084
3	0.14	0.140
4	0.18	0.175
5	—	0.175
6, 7, 8, $\cdots$	—	0.385

All six cabins will be occupied if the nightly demand exceeds 5. Thus the fraction of evenings with 100% occupancy would be approximately 0.38.

SIMULATED SAMPLING (MONTE CARLO)

Situations frequently arise where some method of sampling is indicated, but where the actual taking of a physical sample is either impossible or too expensive. In such situations, useful information can often be obtained from some type of simulated sampling. Typically, simulated sampling involves replacing the actual universe of items by its theoretical counterpart, a universe described by some assumed probability distribution, and then sampling from this theoretical population by means of a random number table. The methods of taking such a sample, as well as the discussion of decision problems which rely heavily on such sampling methods, are often referred to by the catch-all label of *Monte Carlo Methods*.

To draw an item at random from a universe described by the probability density $f(x)$, one proceeds as follows:

(*a*) Plot the cumulative probability function *

$$y = F(x) = \int_{-\infty}^{x} f(u) \, du$$

(*b*) Choose a random decimal between 0 and 1 (to as many places as desired) by means of a table of random digits.

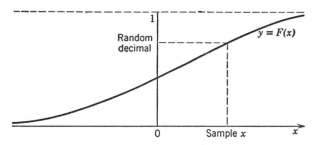

Figure 3.2. Monte Carlo sampling: "Drawing an item" from a population with cumulative distribution function $F(x)$.

(*c*) Project horizontally the point on the y axis corresponding to this random decimal, until the projection line intersects the curve $y = F(x)$.

(*d*) Write down the value of x corresponding to the point of intersection. This value of x is taken as the sample value of x.

In order to justify this procedure, we must show that any item in the population has the same chance of being "measured" as any other item. Equivalently, we want to show that the probability of ending up with a measurement between x_1 and $x_1 + dx$ is proportional to the

---

* The method would work equally well if one plotted the complement $1 - F(x)$.

density $f(x_1)$. Referring to the left-hand diagram of Figure 3.3, we see that

$$P\{x_1 < \text{resulting } x < x_1 + dx\} = dy_1$$

and, from the right-hand diagram, we have

$$dy_1 = f(x_1)\, dx$$

Thus

$$P\{x_1 < \text{resulting } x < x_1 + dx\} \sim f(x_1)\, dx$$

as desired.

The procedure need not be carried through in detail for either the rectangular or the normal distribution, since tables of random deviates

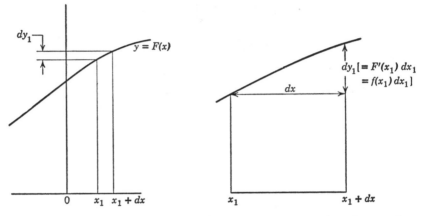

Figure 3.3. **Diagram used in justification of Monte Carlo sampling routine.**

are available for both distributions. For the rectangular distribution, we use tables of random digits, and read a random decimal from an arbitrary spot in the table. This yields a number between 0 and 1. If the distribution in question is rectangular between 12 and 15, say, we multiply the random decimal by 3 and add 12 to the result to obtain our sample value. For the normal distribution, we use tables of random normal deviates, obtained from a population with mean zero and standard deviation unity. The corresponding sample value is obtained by multiplying the random normal deviate by σ, and adding μ.

Example 11

The *range* of a sample is the difference between the largest and smallest observations in the sample. Estimate the mean range in samples of five drawn from a normal distribution.

SOLUTION

We read off a sample of five from the random normal number tables and obtain, e.g.:

$$1.119$$

$$-0.792$$

$$0.063$$

$$0.484$$

$$1.045$$

This sample has range 1.911. Continuing in this way, we obtain ranges of 1.334, 2.633, 3.089, 3.844, 3.013, 3.825, 1.073, 2.488, 1.292, 2.390, 2.796, 2.841, 2.274, 2.827, 1.633, 1.112, 1.730, 3.353, 3.783, 1,433, 2.828, 3.883, 2.621, 2.250. These 25 separate observations of the range have a mean of 2.490.

Thus our estimate of the mean range in samples of five from a normal distribution with standard deviation σ (and any μ) is 2.490σ. This compares with the exact value for the mean range * in samples of five of 2.326σ.

Example 12

A bombing mission is sent to bomb an important factory, which is rectangular in shape and has the dimensions 250 by 500 feet. The bombers will drop 10 bombs altogether, from high altitude, all aimed at the geometric center of the plant. We assume that the bombing run is made parallel to the long dimension of the plant, that the deviation of the impact point from the aiming point is normal with mean zero and standard deviation 200 feet in each dimension, and that these two deviations are independent random variables. Use Monte Carlo sampling to estimate the expected number of bomb hits, and compare your result with the exact value.

SOLUTION

Let x be the horizontal deviation, and y be the vertical deviation, as shown in the diagram. A hit will result if both the following events occur:

$$-250 \le x \le 250$$

$$-125 \le y \le 125$$

Otherwise the bomb will be a miss.

* See A. Hald, *Statistical Tables and Formulas*, p. 60, John Wiley & Sons, New York, 1952.

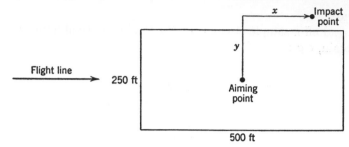

Figure 3.4. Flight line and target area in Example 12.

If we set

$$u = \frac{x}{200}$$

$$v = \frac{y}{200}$$

so that u and v will be the corresponding deviates read from a random normal number table, then the condition for a hit becomes

$$-1.250 \le u \le 1.250$$

$$-0.625 \le v \le 0.625$$

Results of the first three trials are given in Table 4.

These three trials yield 3.33 as the average number of hits per mission. Many more trials should be conducted before one can have any real confidence in the result. One way of estimating how many trials are necessary is to list the *cumulated* mean at the end of each trial, and to stop the trials when the mean seems to have settled down to a stable value. In this example we have

After trial number:	1	2	3
Cumulated mean is:	4	3	3.33

so that more trials are necessary.

In this problem, unlike most Monte Carlo problems, an exact calculation of the answer is much easier than the Monte Carlo calculation. The probability of a hit with a single bomb is just

$$\left\{ \int_{-1.250}^{1.250} f(u)\, du \right\} \times \left\{ \int_{-0.625}^{0.625} f(v)\, dv \right\}$$

$$= 0.789 \times 0.468 \text{ from tables of the normal integral}$$

$$= 0.369$$

TABLE 4

Bomb	u	v	Result
Trial 1, four hits			
1	−0.291	1.221	Miss
2	−2.828	−0.439	Miss
3	0.247	1.291	Miss
4	−0.584	0.541	Hit
5	−0.446	−2.661	Miss
6	−2.127	0.665	Miss
7	−0.656	0.340	Hit
8	1.041	0.008	Hit
9	−0.899	0.110	Hit
10	−1.114	1.297	Miss
Trial 2, two hits			
1	1.119	0.004	Hit
2	−0.792	−1.275	Miss
3	0.063	−1.793	Miss
4	0.484	−0.986	Miss
5	1.045	−1.363	Miss
6	0.084	−0.880	Miss
7	−0.086	−0.158	Hit
8	0.427	−0.831	Miss
9	−0.528	−0.813	Miss
10	−1.433	−1.345	Miss
Trial 3, four hits			
1	−2.015	−0.594	Miss
2	−0.623	−1.047	Miss
3	−0.699	−1.347	Miss
4	0.481	0.996	Miss
5	−0.586	−1.023	Miss
6	−0.579	0.551	Hit
7	−0.120	0.418	Hit
8	0.191	0.074	Hit
9	0.071	0.524	Hit
10	−3.001	0.479	Miss

The mean number of hits in a mission dropping 10 bombs is just 10 times this, or 3.69.

Example 13

A bakery chain delivers fresh pumpernickel bread to one of its retail stores each day. The number of loaves delivered each day is not constant but has the following distribution:

Loaves per day	Probability
10	0.05
11	0.10
12	0.20
13	0.30
14	0.20
15	0.10
16	0.05

The number of customers desiring pumpernickel bread each day has the distribution:

Number of customers	Probability
5	0.10
6	0.15
7	0.20
8	0.40
9	0.10
10	0.05

Finally, the probability that a customer in need of pumpernickel bread wants 1, 2, or 3 loaves is described by:

Loaves to a customer	Probability
1	0.40
2	0.40
3	0.20

Estimate by Monte Carlo methods the average number of loaves of pumpernickel left over per day, and the average number of sales (loaves) lost per day owing to lack of bread. Assume that left-over bread is given away at the end of each day.

SOLUTION

The Monte Carlo sampling routine of the text applies equally well to discrete distributions. The first step is to plot (or visualize) the cumulative distributions for the random variables in question. These are displayed in Figures 3.5, 3.6, and 3.7.

We shall follow through the purchase and sale of bread for 10 days. A larger number of days would, of course, give a more reliable answer. First we compute the number of delivered loaves on each of the 10

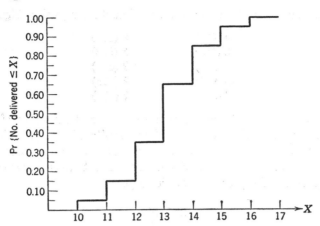

figure 3.5. Cumulative distribution for the daily number of delivered loaves.

days. This is done by taking random numbers from 000 to 999 and applying the Monte Carlo sampling routine, using Figure 3.5. The results are given below; the numbers in parentheses are the random numbers used to determine the sample value of the variable:

13 (608)	10 (022)
15 (861)	10 (048)
12 (215)	10 (029)
13 (380)	12 (333)
14 (775)	14 (844)

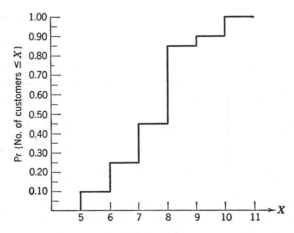

Figure 3.6. Cumulative distribution for the daily number of customers.

Next we compute the daily number of customers, using Figure 3.6:

10 (981)	8 (574)
6 (240)	8 (502)
6 (207)	7 (396)
10 (987)	8 (815)
7 (320)	7 (430)

For each of these 77 customers, we compute the number of loaves wanted by means of Figure 3.7. The results of the procedure are given as the columnar entries in Table 5. The sum for a column gives the demand for that day; and the difference between demand and supply gives the daily surplus or shortage.

TABLE 5

		Day 1	2	3	4	5	6	7	8	9	10
	1	1	1	1	1	1	2	2	3	2	2
	2	2	2	1	2	1	2	1	3	1	2
	3	2	1	1	1	3	2	1	2	1	1
	4	3	3	2	2	1	1	2	2	1	2
Customers within day	5	2	1	2	1	1	2	2	2	3	2
	6	2	2	2	2	1	3	1	1	2	2
	7	1	—	—	1	2	3	2	3	2	2
	8	1	—	—	1	—	3	3	—	1	—
	9	1	—	—	2	—	—	—	—	—	—
	10	2	—	—	1	—	—	—	—	—	—
Daily demand		17	10	9	14	10	18	14	16	13	13
Daily supply		13	15	12	13	14	10	10	10	12	14
Lost sales		4	—	—	1	—	8	4	6	1	—
Leftovers		—	5	3	—	4	—	—	—	—	1

In the 10-day period there were lost sales amounting to 24 loaves, and leftovers amounting to 13 loaves. So the average number of lost sales per day is 2.4 loaves; and the average daily number of left-over loaves is 1.3.

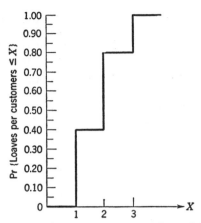

Figure 3.7. **Cumulative distribution for the number of loaves wanted by a customer.**

PROBLEMS FOR SOLUTION

Set IV

1. Estimate the mean range in samples of 10 from a rectangular distribution. Compare your result with the exact value of this parameter. (The distribution of the range in samples from a rectangular distribution can be found in Paul G. Hoel, *Introduction to Mathematical Statistics*, 2nd ed., p. 241, John Wiley & Sons, New York, 1954.)

2. Suppose we are studying the inventory situation in a plant, and are interested in generating possible sales for 30 days. Assuming that the number of sales per day is Poisson with mean 5, generate 30 days of sales by Monte Carlo methods. [*Hint*: Use tables of the cumulative Poisson distribution.]

3. An automobile production line turns out about 100 cars a day, but deviations occur owing to many causes. The production is more accurately described by a probability distribution, viz.:

Production per day	Probability
95	0.03
96	0.05
97	0.07
98	0.10
99	0.15
100	0.20
101	0.15
102	0.10
103	0.07
104	0.05
105	0.03
	———
	1.00

Finished cars are transported across the bay at the end of each day, by ferry. If the ferry has space for only 101 cars, what will be the average number of cars waiting to be shipped, and what will be the average number of empty spaces on the boat?

4. An airline has 15 flights leaving a given base per day, each with one stewardess. The airline has a policy of keeping three reserve stewardesses on call to replace stewardesses scheduled for flights who become sick. The probability distribution for the daily number of sick stewardesses is as follows:

Number sick	Probability
0	0.20
1	0.25
2	0.20
3	0.15
4	0.10
5	0.10
	————
	1.00

Use Monte Carlo methods to estimate the utilization of reserve stewardesses, and also the probability that at least one flight will be canceled because no stewardess is available. Compare with the exact answers.

5. A cab agency finds that the economic life distribution of its cabs is described by the following table:

Months until replacement	Probability
6	0.05
8	0.10
10	0.15
12	0.20
14	0.20
16	0.10
18	0.10
20	0.05
24	0.05
	————
	1.00

If the company maintains a fleet of 20 cars, estimate the number of replacements that will be made in a period of two years.

6. Three points are chosen at random on the circumference of a circle. Estimate the probability that they all lie on the same semicircle, by Monte Carlo methods. [*Ans.* 0.75]

7. A manufacturing company located in Cleveland has three warehouses: one in Los Angeles, one in St. Louis, and one in New York City. The present stock levels in the warehouses are 400, 500, and 600, respectively. The daily

demand at each warehouse follows a Poisson distribution, with means 12, 15, and 20, respectively. A strike at the factory has just occurred, and the factory is to be shut down for an indefinite period. If the factory has 400 items in stock, and will ship 15 times the average daily demand to any warehouse whose stock level drops below 15 times the average daily demand, how long will it take for at least one warehouse to be out of stock?

REFERENCES

Burington, R. S. and D. C. May Jr., *Handbook of Probability and Statistics with Tables*, Handbook Publishers, Sandusky, 1953.

Cochran, William G., *Sampling Techniques*, John Wiley & Sons, New York, 1953.

Churchman, C. W., R. L. Ackoff, and E. L. Arnoff, *Introduction to Operations Research*, John Wiley & Sons, New York, 1957. (Contains brief tables of random numbers and random normal numbers.)

Hansen, M. H., W. N. Hurwitz, and W. G. Madow, *Sample Survey Methods and Theory*, Vol. I (*Methods and Applications*) and Vol. II (*Theory*), John Wiley & Sons, New York, 1953.

Meyer, Herbert A., ed., *Symposium on Monte Carlo Methods*, University of Florida, March 16–18, 1954, John Wiley & Sons, New York, 1956.

Moroney, M. J., *Facts from Figures*, Penguin Books, Baltimore, 1951.

The RAND Corporation, *A Million Random Digits with 100,000 Normal Deviates*, The Free Press, Glencoe, 1955.

CHAPTER

FOUR

Inventory

Inventory is the physical stock of goods that a business keeps on hand in order to promote the smooth and efficient running of its afffairs. It may be held before the production cycle, in the form of raw-material inventory; at an intermediate stage in the production cycle, as in-process inventory; or at the end of the production cycle, as finished-goods inventory. For definiteness, we shall confine our discussion for the most part to finished-goods inventory, but the procedures developed can be adapted with minor changes of wording to other kinds of inventory.

A certain amount of inventory is usually necessary, but a business can function with some degree of efficiency over a fairly wide range of inventory levels. Control over inventory can be exercised by changing the timing of production runs, by changing the size of the runs, and by changes in promotional effort or sales inducements. Here we consider that the marketing activity is either constant or beyond the province of the inventory planner, so that an inventory policy will involve only the timing and amounts of the production runs.

Possible advantages associated with increased inventory are the economies of production with large run sizes, faster shipment of orders to customers, stabilized work loads, and profits from speculation in a market where prices are expected to rise. The disadvantage associated with increased inventory is simply that the holding of inventory costs money (e.g., warehouse rent, depreciation and deterioration, interest on invested capital, physical handling and accounting). Clearly it is desirable to increase inventory only when the resulting savings (or profits) more than outweigh the cost of the increase.

In the examples presented here we will consider only the first two of the advantages mentioned above resulting from increased inventory: namely, production economies with large run sizes, and the reduction of delay in filling customer orders. Although stability of work load and speculation sometimes loom large in the making of inventory policy, no simple theory is available at present for such problems, and a discussion of the attempts at solution would be outside the scope of this book.

KNOWN DEMAND

In this section we consider first a very simple situation in which a contractor has a firm order to supply goods at a uniform rate R per unit time. He starts a production run every t time units, where t is fixed; and his setup cost each time he starts a run is C_3. Production time is negligible; so there will be no delay in fulfilling demand as long as a new run is started whenever inventory is zero. We assume that the contract is such that its terms must be satisfied, and that zero inventory will always be the signal for further production. The cost of holding inventory is assumed to be proportional to both the amount of inventory and the time the inventory is held. Then the cost of holding inventory I for time T may be denoted by $C_1 I T$, where C_1 is the cost of holding one unit in inventory for one time unit. The question to be answered is: How frequently should a production run be made, and what quantity of goods should be produced? We are concerned at this point with balancing the economies of increased run size against the cost of holding inventory.

Figure 4.1 shows the elementary inventory situation we are considering. If a run is to be made at intervals t, an amount Rt must be produced at each run. The shaded area represents

$$\int_0^t I \, dt$$

and has the value $\frac{1}{2} R t^2$. Thus the cost of holding inventory is $\frac{1}{2} C_1 R t^2$ per production run.

The cost of setup is C_3 per production run. Hence the average total cost per unit time is

$$C = \tfrac{1}{2} C_1 R t + \frac{C_3}{t}$$

For a minimum, we differentiate C with respect to t and set the derivative equal to zero, obtaining

(4.1) $$t = \sqrt{2C_3/C_1R}$$

As the reader can verify, the quantity q to be produced at each run becomes

(4.2) $$q = \sqrt{2C_3R/C_1}$$

and the resulting minimum cost has the value $\sqrt{2C_1C_3R}$ per time unit.

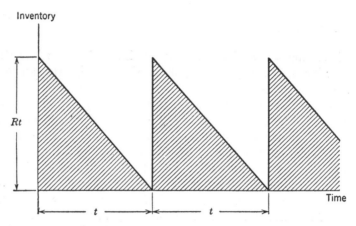

Figure 4.1. Demand constant from month to month, shipment uniform during a month, no shortages permitted.

Equation (4.2) has been termed the "economic lot size formula"; the result was first given by F. W. Harris in 1915. It will be realized that some of the assumptions made are not likely to be satisfied in practice. It seldom happens that customer demand is known exactly or that production time is negligible.

We can generalize the situation somewhat and obtain a similar formula for the optimal lot size. Let us assume that the contract specifies merely some total demand D, to be satisfied during some long time period T, with the proviso that output will be shipped to the customer uniformly between production runs. We decide that each time a production run is made, we will make some fixed quantity q. Figure 4.2 shows the resulting inventory situation.

There will be D/q production runs made during the period T in question. If t_1 is the time interval between run 1 and run 2, and t_2 is the time interval between run 2 and run 3, etc., then the holding costs

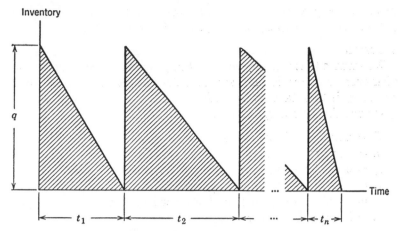

Figure 4.2. Fixed run size and fixed number of runs, with discretion as to scheduling of runs.

for the period T will be

$$\tfrac{1}{2}C_1q(t_1 + t_2 + \cdots + t_n) = \tfrac{1}{2}C_1qT$$

and the setup costs will be

$$\frac{C_3D}{q}$$

Denoting the total cost with a fixed run size q by $C(q)$, we have

$$C(q) = \tfrac{1}{2}C_1qT + \frac{C_3D}{q}$$

The total cost $C(q)$ attains its minimum for a value of q given by

(4.3)
$$q = \sqrt{\frac{2C_3(D/T)}{C_1}}$$

Note that (4.3) is similar to (4.2), except that the fixed demand rate R is replaced by the "average" demand rate D/T.

Other variations are provided in the following examples.

Example 1

A contractor has to supply 10,000 bearings per day to an automobile manufacturer. He finds that, when he starts a production run, he can produce 25,000 bearings per day. The cost of holding a bearing in

stock for one year is 2 cents, and the setup cost of a production run is
$18.00.   How frequently should production runs be made?

SOLUTION

We assume that run sizes are constant, that a new run will be started
whenever inventory is zero, and that the sole reason for producing for
inventory is to obtain lower production costs.
We use the following notation:

R = number of bearings required per day
k = number of bearings produced per day
C_1 = cost of holding one bearing in inventory per day
C_3 = cost of setting up a production run
q = number of bearings produced per run
t = interval between runs

Figure 4.3 gives a sketch of the way inventory varies with time.   In
this figure, the slope of the line NB is the rate of depletion of inventory

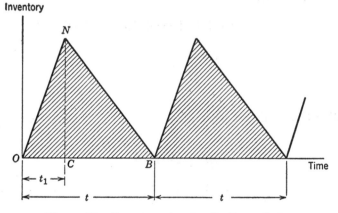

Figure 4.3.   Inventory situation for Example 1.

and has the value $-R$; the slope of ON is the difference between
the rate of production and the rate of depletion, and has the value $k-R$.
Production will continue for a time $t_1 = q/k$, and the period of the
entire inventory cycle has the value $t = q/R$.   The area of triangle
ONB, multiplied by the holding cost of one bearing per day, represents
the inventory holding cost per cycle; this cost, plus the cost of one
setup, gives the total cost per cycle.

To obtain the area of triangle ONB, we first note that its base is t.
The altitude NC is the inventory level at the moment a production run

is completed, or $q - Rt_1 = q(1 - R/k)$. Thus the area of the shaded triangle is $\frac{1}{2}qt(1 - R/k)$, and

$$
\begin{aligned}
\text{Cost per cycle} \quad &= C_3 + \tfrac{1}{2}C_1qt(1 - R/k) \\
F = \text{cost per day} &= C_3/t + \tfrac{1}{2}C_1q(1 - R/k) \\
&= C_3R/q + \tfrac{1}{2}C_1q(1 - R/k)
\end{aligned}
$$

To obtain the optimum run size, we differentiate F with respect to q and set the derivative equal to zero. The result is

$$
q = \sqrt{\frac{2C_3R}{C_1(1 - R/k)}}, \qquad t = \sqrt{\frac{2C_3}{RC_1(1 - R/k)}}
$$

Here $C_1 = 2$ cents per bearing per year $= \$0.000055$ per day
$\quad\;\; C_3 = \$18$
$\quad\;\; R = 10{,}000$ bearings per day
$\quad\;\; k = 25{,}000$ bearings per day

Then

$$
q = \sqrt{\frac{2 \times 18 \times 10^4}{5.5 \times 10^{-5}(1 - \tfrac{10}{25})}} = \sqrt{1.091 \times 10^{10}} = 105{,}000 \text{ bearings}
$$

and

$t = 10.5$ days

In the previous example, the sole objective of holding inventory was to achieve economies of increased run sizes. We assumed implicitly that the costs associated with failure to meet a delivery schedule were so high that such an eventuality would not be allowed to occur. In the rest of the examples of this chapter, we allow the cost of failure to meet a delivery schedule to be finite. It will be seen that there are situations where the total cost can be reduced by deliberately failing to meet some of the scheduled delivery dates.

Example 2

A subcontractor undertakes to supply Diesel engines to a truck manufacturer at the rate of 25 per day. There is a clause in the contract penalizing him $10 per engine per day late for missing the scheduled delivery date. He finds that the cost of holding a completed engine in stock is $16 per month. His production process is such that each month (30 days) he starts a batch of engines through the shops, and all these engines are available for delivery any time after the end of the month. What should his inventory level be at the beginning of each month (i.e., immediately after taking into stock the engines made in the previous month, and then shipping engines to fill unsatisfied demand from the previous month)?

SOLUTION

In this problem we are concerned with balancing the costs of holding inventory against the costs of delayed deliveries to customers. Since the subcontractor has already decided to produce a batch of engines every month, he has fixed the size of each batch at 750 engines, and we may assume that he is no longer concerned with economies in run size.

We shall use the following notation:

C_1 = cost per day of holding an engine in inventory
C_2 = penalty cost per day of failing to deliver one engine on schedule
R = contracted number of engines per day
z = planned inventory level at beginning of a month

Our problem is to find the value of z that minimizes costs.

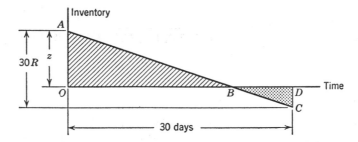

Figure 4.4. Inventory situation for Example 2.

The inventory situation during each month is represented approximately by Figure 4.4. The cross-hatched area represents inventory, and the dotted area represents failure to meet delivery. (Although delivery actually takes place in batches of R engines per day, we are approximating to the actual situation by assuming continuous delivery at the rate of R per day.) With this approximation, the number of "engine-days" of inventory is given by the area of triangle OAB, and the cost of holding inventory is C_1 times this area. By similar triangles $OB/30 = z/30R$, and $OB = z/R$. Therefore the area of triangle OAB is $z^2/2R$, and the cost of holding inventory is $C_1 z^2/2R$.

The number of "engine-days" by which the delivery schedule is missed is given by the area of triangle BDC, easily computed to be

$$(30R - z)^2/(2R)$$

Hence the cost of shortages is $(C_2/2R)(30R - z)^2$.

The total cost $F(z)$ is found by adding these two costs. Therefore

$$F(z) = \frac{C_1 z^2}{2R} + \frac{C_2(30R - z)^2}{2R}$$

For the minimum cost $dF/dz = 0$, and we obtain

$$z = 30R \frac{C_2}{C_1 + C_2}$$

It will be observed that, since $C_2/(C_1 + C_2) < 1$, the optimum inventory level is less than the number of engines to be delivered each month, and we would deliberately plan for a shortage. Here $R = 25$, $C_1 = 16/30$, $C_2 = 10$, so that the best starting inventory is

$$30 \times 25 \times \frac{10}{10 + 16/30} = 712 \text{ engines}$$

It is not difficult to verify that such a policy reduces inventory costs in the ratio $C_2 : (C_1 + C_2)$ as compared with starting each month with an inventory $30R$ and never failing to meet the delivery schedule.

Before reaching a decision to operate with a policy of deliberately missing scheduled delivery dates, careful consideration of the suitability of the model would be required. We have assumed that the cost of missing delivery dates is the \$10 penalty per engine per day late, as specified by the contract. Further analysis might show that this is a considerable underestimate, and that a policy of this type would result in a loss of customer goodwill, with reduced chances of the contract being renewed. If this were so, the true value of C_2 might be much higher than \$10 per engine per day late.

If there are no setup costs associated with starting the production of a batch of engines, the decision to start a batch every month may be correct. However, if setup costs are not zero, there is an interval between setups which will minimize costs for a given starting inventory level. In the next example we will determine the optimal combination of starting inventory level and interval between setups.

Example 3 (modification of previous example)

A contractor undertakes to supply Diesel engines to a truck manufacturer at a rate of 25 per day. He finds that the cost of holding a completed engine in stock is \$16 per month, and there is a clause in the contract penalizing him \$10 per engine per day late for missing the scheduled delivery date. Production of engines is in batches, and each time a new batch is started there are setup costs of \$10,000. How frequently should batches be started, and what should be the initial inventory level (in the sense of the previous example) at the time each batch is completed?

SOLUTION

In these circumstances economies in production costs *per engine* can be achieved by increasing the batch size. Such economies will be offset by the resulting increase in inventory cost; so it is necessary to consider simultaneously the inventory level and the batch size. We will use C_3 to denote the setup cost and t for the interval between starting batches.

Arguing as in Example 2, if z is the planned inventory level on completion of a batch of engines, we can show that the costs of holding inventory together with the penalty costs of missed deliveries will total

$$\frac{C_1 z^2}{2R} + \frac{C_2(tR - z)^2}{2R}$$

over the interval t between batches.

In addition, there is now a setup cost C_3, so that the average cost over time $F(t, z)$ is given by

$$F(t, z) = \frac{1}{t}\left[\frac{C_1 z^2}{2R} + \frac{C_2(tR - z)^2}{2R}\right] + \frac{C_3}{t}$$

(It is necessary to consider average cost, in order to make comparisons between different values of t.) For minimum cost, $\partial F/\partial z = 0$, and $\partial F/\partial t = 0$.

$$\frac{\partial F}{\partial z} = \frac{1}{t}\left[\frac{C_1 z}{R} - \frac{C_2(tR - z)}{R}\right] = 0 \quad \text{or} \quad z = \frac{tRC_2}{C_1 + C_2}$$

$$\frac{\partial F}{\partial t} = -\frac{1}{t^2}\left[\frac{C_1 z^2}{2R} + \frac{C_2(tR - z)^2}{2R} + C_3\right] + \frac{C_2(tR - z)}{t} = 0$$

Substituting for z in the second equation yields, with some rearrangement,

(4.4)
$$t = \sqrt{\frac{2C_3(C_1 + C_2)}{C_1 C_2 R}}$$

and hence

(4.5)
$$z = \sqrt{\frac{2C_2 C_3 R}{C_1(C_1 + C_2)}}$$

Before substituting numerical values in such results, it is advisable to perform a check on the dimensions. The fundamental quantities in the problem are time, which we will denote by $[T]$, numbers of engines, $[N]$, and money, $[\$]$. Since C_1 and C_2 are costs per engine per day, their units are $[\$]/[N][T]$. C_3 is a fixed cost, and the units are simply $[\$]$. R is a number of engines per day; so the units are $[N]/[T]$. z and t are, respectively, numbers of engines, and time with units $[N]$ and $[T]$.

The units of $\dfrac{2C_3(C_1 + C_2)}{C_1 C_2 R}$ are

$$\frac{[\$]\left(\dfrac{[\$]}{[N][T]}\right)}{\left(\dfrac{[\$]}{[N][T]}\right)\left(\dfrac{[\$]}{[N][T]}\right)\left(\dfrac{[N]}{[T]}\right)} = \frac{[\$]^2[N]^2[T]^3}{[\$]^2[N]^2[T]}$$

$$= [T]^2, \text{ which are the units of } t^2$$

The units of $\dfrac{2C_2 C_3 R}{C_1(C_1 + C_2)}$ are

$$\frac{\left(\dfrac{[\$]}{[N][T]}\right)[\$]\left(\dfrac{[N]}{[T]}\right)}{\left(\dfrac{[\$]}{[N][T]}\right)\left(\dfrac{[\$]}{[N][T]}\right)} = \frac{[\$]^2[N]^3[T]^2}{[\$]^2[N][T]^2}$$

$$= [N]^2, \text{ which are the units of } z^2$$

Having satisfied ourselves that the dimensions of equations (4.4) and (4.5) for z and t are correct, we can substitute the numerical values:

$C_1 = \$16/30$ per day per engine
$C_2 = \$10$ per day per engine
$C_3 = \$10,000$
$R = 25$ engines per day

We obtain $t = 40$ days, and $z = 943$ engines.

Thus it would be better to start a new batch approximately every 6 weeks, rather than every month.

The average cost per day is

$$F(t, z) = \frac{1}{t}\left[\frac{C_1 z^2}{2R} + \frac{C_2(Rt - z)^2}{2R} + C_3\right] = \$503$$

with $t = 40$ and $z = 943$. If we start a batch every month, then, from Example 2, z is 712, and the average cost per day is $F(30,712) = \$523$. There is thus a saving of about \$20 a day to be obtained by optimizing z and t simultaneously.

PROBLEMS FOR SOLUTION

Set V

1. An aircraft company uses rivets at an approximately constant rate of 5000 pounds per year. The rivets cost \$2.00 per pound, and the company personnel estimate that it costs \$20.00 to place an order, and that the carrying cost of inventory is 10% per year.

(a) How frequently should orders for rivets be placed, and what quantities should be ordered?

(b) If the actual costs are \$50.00 to place an order and 15% for carrying cost, the optimal policy would change. How much is the company losing per year because of imperfect cost information?

2. A manufacturer receives an order for 6890 items to be delivered over a period of a year as follows:

At end of week 1:   5 items.
At end of week 2:   10 items.
At end of week 3:   15 items.
       etc.

The cost of carrying inventory is \$2.60 per item per year, and the cost of a setup is \$450 per production run.

(a) Compute costs for the following policies:
    (1) Make all 6890 at start of year.   [*Ans.* About \$12,000]
    (2) Make 3445 now and 3445 in 6 months.   [*Ans.* About \$8000]
    (3) Make 1/12 of the order each month.   [*Ans.* About \$9000]
    (4) Make 1/52 of the order each week.   [*Ans.* About \$27,000]
(b) Attempt to devise a more rational policy.

3. A manufacturing concern has a fixed cyclic demand, with a period of one week, as follows:

Monday	9
Tuesday	17
Wednesday	2
Thursday	0
Friday	19
Saturday	9
Sunday	14

Company policy is to maintain constant daily production. The production and shipping departments work seven days a week, and each day's production is available for shipment on the following day.

If a shortage costs four times as much per day as a surplus of the same amount, how much stock should be on hand at the start of business on Monday?

[*Ans.* 10]

4. The weekly production of a given item is normally distributed with mean 10,000 and standard deviation 200. The demand is normally distributed with mean 10,500 and standard deviation 1000. Overtime on Saturday must be scheduled in advance and will produce an average of 500 items normally distributed with standard deviation 20. Each item made in overtime costs an extra $8.00 in production costs. Each item short at the end of the week costs $10.00 (lost sale). Overproduction costs $5.00 per item and cannot be used to fulfill demand in succeeding weeks (e.g., it is immediately sold at a loss). Use Monte Carlo methods to determine whether overtime should be scheduled or not.

PROBABILISTIC DEMAND

As we have already pointed out, practical situations in which we know future demand precisely are somewhat unusual. For this reason the examples already given may appear to be artificial. In this section we assume less information about future demand: we assume that the *probability distribution* of future demand is known, rather than the exact value of the demand itself. The methods used are analogous to those already discussed; and familiarity with the examples already given will aid the reader in following the discussion.

The probability distribution of future demand can often be determined from past experience. Two classes of distribution are distinguishable in theory, although in practice they tend to merge, and either may be used as an approximation to the other when it is convenient. When we are considering goods, such as automobiles, which can only be produced in discrete quantities, we usually think of orders as having a discrete probability distribution. On the other hand, demand for water from a utility company can vary in a continuous manner, and a continuous probability density function might be more appropriate for describing such demand.

However, the manufacturer making thousands of automobiles per year might well decide that one car was such a small unit of his production that for practical purposes the demand could be described by a continuous distribution. Conversely, it might be convenient for the utility company to measure demand in thousands of gallons and to use a discrete probability function.

In situations where future demand is known only in a probabilistic sense, it is not possible to choose policies that will insure the minimization of actual costs. Instead we choose policies that will minimize the *expected* costs. Expected costs are found by taking actual costs co responding to each particular situation that could arise, multiplying by the probability of occurrence of that situation, and then either summing or integrating as is appropriate.

Example 4

An automobile dealer has the option of ordering once every week or once every two weeks. He finds that the cost of holding a car in stock for a week is $6 (insurance, minor deterioration, interest on borrowed capital, etc.). Customers who cannot obtain new cars immediately tend to go to other dealers; and he estimates that for every customer who cannot get immediate delivery he loses an average of $100. For one particular model of car the probabilities of a demand of 0, 1, 2, 3, 4, and 5 cars in a week are 0.05, 0.10, 0.20, 0.30, 0.20, and 0.15, respectively. Every time the dealer places an order, he has fixed costs of $40. How often should he order, and to what level should he bring his stocks? (Assume that there is no time lag between ordering and delivery.)

SOLUTION

We first assume that the dealer orders every week, and that each time he places an order he brings his stock level up to z. We then find z so as to minimize his total expected costs during the week. Similar calculations based on an assumption that he places an order every two weeks will enable us to compare the total expected costs *per week* for the two ordering policies. We can thus decide which policy will result in lower expected costs.

We will require the following notation:

t = interval between orders

n = demand for cars in the time interval t

$p_1(n)$ = probability density of n when t is 1 week
$(n = 0, 1, 2, 3, 4, 5)$

$p_2(n)$ = probability density of n when t is 2 weeks
$(n = 0, 1, 2, \cdots, 9, 10)$

C_1 = holding cost per week for each car in stock

C_2 = cost of failing to deliver a car to a customer on demand

C_3 = cost of placing an order for cars

z = stock level immediately on receipt of a shipment of cars

$F_1(z)$ = expected cost (excluding the ordering cost C_3) associated with a policy of ordering every week to bring the stock level to z

$F_2(z)$ = expected cost (excluding the ordering cost C_3) associated with a policy of ordering every 2 weeks to bring the stock level to z

The inventory situation in a typical interval t, between orders, is shown in Figure 4.5. We will assume that, if there is a demand for n cars in the period t, the demand arises at times

$$\frac{t}{n+1}, \frac{2t}{n+1}, \frac{3t}{n+1}, \ldots, \frac{nt}{n+1}$$

Since we are told that deliveries to the dealer take place immediately on request, each period t starts with an inventory z. Figure 4.5 illus-

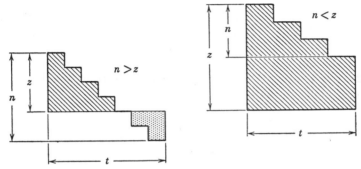

Figure 4.5. Inventory situation for Example 4.

trates the two situations: n greater than z; and n less than z. In both cases the number of automobile-weeks is represented by the cross-hatched area.

For $n > z$, the cross-hatched area is $tz(z + 1)/2(n + 1)$, and thus the cost of holding inventory is $C_1 tz(z + 1)/2(n + 1)$. The dealer will fail to supply $n-z$ customers, and this will cost him $C_2(n-z)$, so that the total cost is

$$\frac{C_1 tz(z + 1)}{2(n + 1)} + C_2(n - z)$$

For $n \le z$, the cost of holding inventory is $C_1 t(z - n/2)$, and all customer demand is satisfied.

The total expected cost $F_t(z)$ for the period t, excluding the ordering cost C_3, is obtained by multiplying the cost associated with demand n by the probability of n, and summing over the appropriate range of n .*

$$F_t(z) = \sum_{n=0}^{z} C_1 t \left(z - \frac{n}{2} \right) p_t(n) + \sum_{n=z+1}^{\infty} \left[\frac{C_1 tz(z + 1)}{2(n + 1)} + C_2(n - z) \right] p_t(n)$$

* The symbol ∞ will be used in summations and integrals to indicate that the range is to extend until all further probabilities are zero.

For the minimum value of $F_t(z)$, we require that z satisfy the relationship

$$(4.6) \qquad \Delta F_t(z-1) < 0 < \Delta F_t(z)$$

where $\Delta F_t(z)$ is the first difference of the function $F_t(z)$, as defined in Appendix I. To obtain $\Delta F_t(z)$ we refer to Appendix I. From the criterion given there we see we can difference under the summation sign, provided it is true that

$$C_1 t \left(z + 1 - \frac{n}{2} \right) p_t(n) = \left(\frac{C_1 t (z+1)(z+2)}{2(n+1)} + C_2(n - z - 1) \right) p_t(n)$$

when n has the value of $z+1$. Since both sides have the value of $(C_1 t/2)(z+1)p(z+1)$, the requirement is satisfied, and we may difference under the summation sign.

$$\Delta F_t(z) = \sum_{n=0}^{z} C_1 t\, p_t(n) + \sum_{n=z+1}^{\infty} \left[\frac{C_1 t(z+1)}{n+1} - C_2 \right] p_t(n)$$

or

$$(4.7)$$

$$\Delta F_t(z) = (C_1 t + C_2) \sum_{n=0}^{z} p_t(n) + C_1 t(z+1) \sum_{n=z+1}^{\infty} \frac{p_t(n)}{n+1} - C_2$$

The calculation of the optimal value of z from equation (4.7) is shown in Table 1. We are given the values of $p_1(n)$ (the distribution of demand corresponding to $t = 1$), and as a preliminary we have to compute $p_2(n)$ (the distribution corresponding to $t = 2$). If it is reasonable to assume that sales in consecutive weeks are mutually independent, then by the methods of Chapter 2, we find that

$$p_2(n) = \sum_{m=0}^{n} p_1(m)\, p_1(n - m)$$

The calculations appear in Table 1.

Thus, if the policy is to order every week, the stock level should be brought up to five cars; if orders are placed every two weeks, the stock level should be eight cars.

To answer the question posed in the statement of the problem, we must compare the total weekly costs associated with the two optimal ordering policies. This could be done from the formula for $F_t(z)$, but it

TABLE 1

A. Order Every Week $[t = 1, C_1 = 6, C_2 = 100]$

n, z	$p_1(n)$	$\dfrac{p_1(n)}{n+1}$	$\sum\limits_{n=0}^{z} p_1(n)$	$\sum\limits_{n=z+1}^{\infty} \dfrac{p_1(n)}{n+1}$	$\Delta F_1(z)$
0	0.05	0.05	0.05	0.2567	−93.15
1	0.10	0.05	0.15	0.2067	−81.62
2	0.20	0.0667	0.35	0.140	−60.48
3	0.30	0.075	0.65	0.065	−29.54
4	0.20	0.04	0.85	0.025	−9.15
5	0.15	0.025	1.00	—	+6

B. Order Every 2 Weeks $[t = 2, C_1 = 6, C_2 = 100]$

n, z	$p_2(n)$	$\dfrac{p_2(n)}{n+1}$	$\sum\limits_{n=0}^{z} p_2(n)$	$\sum\limits_{n=z+1}^{\infty} \dfrac{p_2(n)}{n+1}$	$\Delta F_2(z)$
0	0.0025	0.0025	0.0025	0.1592	−97.81
1	0.0100	0.0050	0.0125	0.1542	−94.90
2	0.0300	0.0100	0.0425	0.1442	−90.05
3	0.0700	0.0175	0.1125	0.1267	−81.32
4	0.1200	0.0240	0.2325	0.1027	−67.80
5	0.1750	0.0292	0.4075	0.0735	−49.07
6	0.2000	0.0286	0.6075	0.0449	−28.19
7	0.1800	0.0225	0.7875	0.0224	−9.65
8	0.1300	0.0144	0.9175	0.0080	+3.62
9	0.0600	0.0060	0.9775	0.0020	+9.72
10	0.0225	0.0020	1.0000	—	+12.00

is probably quicker to compute $F_t(0)$ and then use the first differences already tabulated.

$$F_1(0) = \sum_{n=1}^{\infty} C_2 n \, p_1(n) = 295.00$$

$$F_1(5) = F_1(0) + \sum_{n=0}^{4} \Delta F_1(n)$$

$$= 295 - 273.94 = 21.06$$

$$F_2(0) = \sum_{n=1}^{\infty} C_2 n \, p_2(n) = 590.00$$

$$F_2(8) = F_2(0) + \sum_{n=0}^{7} \Delta F_2(n)$$

$$= 590.00 - 518.79 = 71.21$$

With a policy of ordering every week so as to bring the stock level up to five cars, the weekly cost (exclusive of ordering) is $21.06; thus the total cost per week associated with ordering every week is $21.06 + $40.00, or $61.06. With a policy of ordering every two weeks, so as to bring the stock level up to eight cars, the cost per fortnight (exclusive of ordering) is $71.21; the total cost per fortnight is $111.21, or an average of $55.60 per week. There is thus a saving of $5.46 to be obtained by ordering every two weeks.

Example 5

The raw material for the manufacture of bearings is metal-plated steel strip. Plating is done in a continuous process, and the plating machine is such that there is no setup cost in changing to a strip of the same width but different thickness; there is a setup cost of $9.00 in changing to a strip of a different width. There are just two types of strip which are 6 inches wide: strip type A, and strip type B. Thus there is no setup cost in changing from strip type A to strip type B, but there is a setup cost of $9.00 in changing from any other strip type to either A or B. Knowing this, the manufacturer always runs strip A and strip B consecutively. His problem is how frequently to schedule the production of the 6-inch strip.

Analysis of past sales shows that the weekly requirement (hundreds of feet per week) for strip A is distributed in a Poisson fashion with mean 3, while for strip B the requirement is Poisson with mean 4. The inventory holding cost for strip A or B is 25 cents per hundred feet per week. If plated strip is not available for the next production process when required, scheduled customer delivery dates may be missed, and the sales department estimates that this will cost the company an amount directly proportional to both time and quantity. The cost is $8 per hundred feet per week late, for either A or B. The production process is sufficiently rapid that the time between the setup to produce plated strip and the receipt of strip into inventory can be neglected.

If the period between setups is to be some fixed time interval, how frequently should setups of 6-inch strip be made, and what quantities should be produced?

SOLUTION

The approach here is to compute the minimum cost per week when the interval between production runs is chosen in advance, to use the points thus obtained in order to arrive at a smooth curve representing the variation of minimum cost per week with interval between production runs; then, by interpolation, we may find the best interval between runs and the corresponding run sizes.

We will use the following notation:

λ_1, λ_2 = mean weekly demand (in hundreds of feet) for strip A and strip B, respectively

C_1 = cost per hundred feet per week of holding stocks of A (or B)

C_2 = cost per hundred feet per week of failure to meet demand for A (or B)

$A_t(x)$ = probability of a demand x in time t for A

$\quad = \dfrac{e^{-\lambda_1 t}(\lambda_1 t)^x}{x!}$ since the demand is Poisson

$B_t(x)$ = probability of a demand x in time t for B

$\quad = \dfrac{e^{-\lambda_2 t}(\lambda_2 t)^x}{x!}$ since the demand is Poisson

We will first consider the costs of holding inventory and of shortage during the period t between two production runs. These costs can be considered separately for A and B.

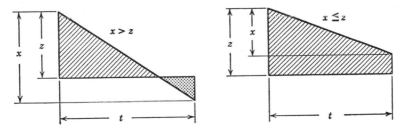

Figure 4.6. Inventory situation for Example 5.

Let $F(z)$ be the expected inventory and shortage costs during t for either A or B alone. There are two possible inventory situations according as the demand x is greater or less than the starting stock, z, as pictured in Figure 4.6. We find, for both A and B,

$$\text{Cost} = \frac{C_1 t z^2}{2x} + \frac{C_2 t (x - z)^2}{2x} \quad \text{if} \quad x > z$$

$$\text{Cost} = C_1 t \left(z - \frac{x}{2} \right) \quad \text{if} \quad x < z$$

The expected cost will not be the same for both A and B, since the probability distribution of x differs for the two strip types. Thus

$$F(z) \text{ for } A = C_1 t \sum_{x=0}^{z} \left(z - \frac{x}{2} \right) A_t(x)$$

$$+ \frac{C_1 t z^2}{2} \sum_{x=z+1}^{\infty} \frac{A_t(x)}{x} + \frac{C_2 t}{2} \sum_{x=z+1}^{\infty} \frac{(x-z)^2 A_t(x)}{x}$$

$$F(z) \text{ for } B = C_1 t \sum_{x=0}^{z} \left(z - \frac{x}{2} \right) B_t(x)$$

$$+ \frac{C_1 t z^2}{2} \sum_{x=z+1}^{\infty} \frac{B_t(x)}{x} + \frac{C_2 t}{2} \sum_{x=z+1}^{\infty} \frac{(x-z)^2 B_t(x)}{x}$$

We apply the criterion of Appendix I, paragraph 6, and find that we may difference both functions under the summation sign. The results are:

$$\Delta F(z) \text{ for } A = (C_1 + C_2) t \left[\sum_{x=0}^{z} A_t(x) + \left(z + \frac{1}{2} \right) \sum_{x=z+1}^{\infty} \frac{A_t(x)}{x} \right] - C_2 t$$

(4.8)

$$\Delta F(z) \text{ for } B = (C_1 + C_2) t \left[\sum_{x=0}^{z} B_t(x) + \left(z + \frac{1}{2} \right) \sum_{x=z+1}^{\infty} \frac{B_t(x)}{x} \right] - C_2 t$$

The criterion for a z that minimizes the cost for product A, which is

$$\Delta F(z - 1) \text{ for } A < 0 < \Delta F(z) \text{ for } A$$

may be restated as: Choose the least value of z that satisfies

$$\sum_{x=0}^{z} A_t(x) + \left(z + \frac{1}{2} \right) \sum_{x=z+1}^{\infty} \frac{A_t(x)}{x} > \frac{C_2}{C_1 + C_2}$$

A similar expression, with $A_t(x)$ replaced by $B_t(x)$, gives the criterion for a z which minimizes the cost for product B.

To obtain the expected cost associated with a particular z, we use

$$F(z) = F(0) + \sum_{x=0}^{z-1} \Delta F(x)$$

Since $\qquad F(0) \text{ for } A = \frac{C_2 t}{2} \sum_{x=1}^{\infty} x A_t(x)$

$$= \frac{C_2 t}{2} E(x \text{ for } A) = \left(\frac{C_2 t}{2} \right) \lambda_1 t$$

we have

$$(4.9) \qquad F(z) \text{ for } A = \frac{C_2 t^2 \lambda_1}{2} + \sum_{u=0}^{z-1} [\Delta F(u) \text{ for } A]$$

Similarly,

$$(4.9') \qquad F(z) \text{ for } B = \frac{C_2 t^2 \lambda_2}{2} + \sum_{u=0}^{z-1} [\Delta F(u) \text{ for } B]$$

The calculations are best tabulated. The tabulation for strip A with $t = 1$ are shown in Table 2, and the results for the remaining cases are presented in Table 3.

TABLE 2. Costs (Excluding Setup) for Strip A—Production Scheduled Every Week

x	$A(x)$	$\dfrac{A(x)}{x}$	$\sum\limits_{i=0}^{x} A(i)$	$\sum\limits_{i=x+1}^{\infty} \dfrac{A(i)}{i}$	$\sum\limits_{i=0}^{x} A(i) + \left(x + \dfrac{1}{2}\right) \sum\limits_{i=x+1}^{\infty} \dfrac{A(i)}{i}$
0	0.05	∞	0.05	0.4114	0.2557
1	0.15	0.15	0.20	0.2614	0.5921
2	0.23	0.115	0.43	0.1464	0.7960
3	0.22	0.0714	0.65	0.075	0.9125
4	0.17	0.0425	0.82	0.0325	0.9663
5	0.10	0.02	0.92	0.0125	0.9888 ←
6	0.05	0.0083	0.97	0.0042	0.9973
7	0.02	0.0029	0.99	0.0013	0.9998
8	0.01	0.0013	1.00	0	1.0000

Since $C_2/(C_1 + C_2) = 0.97$ here, the value of z that minimizes cost if production is scheduled every week is 500 feet. Thus the minimum cost (excluding setups) per week is $F(5)$, which on evaluation turns out to be 1.06. In a similar manner, Table 3 can be derived:

TABLE 3

Interval between production runs, weeks	Optimum stock level Z, ft.		Cost (excluding setup) per run		Cost (including setup) per run, A and B together	Total costs per week, A and B together
	A	B	A	B		
1	500	600	1.06	1.32	11.38	11.38
2	800	1000	3.36	3.43	15.79	7.90
3	1100	1400	6.69	7.94	23.63	7.88

It is seen that the total cost per week is a function of the interval between production runs. We now wish to determine the interval that minimizes this function. A fairly simple method of finding a numerical result is to fit a curve to the values of the function we already know and to interpolate.

Let $h(t)$ be the minimum total costs per week when setups are at intervals of t weeks. We have $h(1) = 11.38$, $h(2) = 7.90$, $h(3) = 7.88$.

Now, as the interval t between setups decreases, the cost of setups *per week* will increase; so it is reasonable to assume that $h(t)$ tends to infinity as t tends to zero.

The simplest curve that will pass through three given points and approach infinity at the origin is $h(t) = A/t + B + Ct$ (see Figure 4.7). By equating coefficients, we find

$$A = 10.4$$

$$B = -0.74$$

$$C = 1.72$$

$$\frac{dh}{dt} = \frac{-A}{t^2} + C = 0$$

for a minimum. Therefore

$$t^2 = \frac{A}{C} = \frac{10.4}{1.72} = 6.04$$

and

$$t = 2.5$$

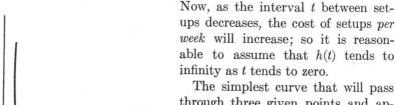

Figure 4.7. Choice of interval t between setups.

Thus the minimum costs would be achieved by scheduling every two and one-half weeks. By a straight-line interpolation in Table 3, we find that 950 feet of A and 1200 feet of B should be scheduled.

Example 6

The situation is the same as for Example 5, except that the inventory levels of the 6-inch strip type are to be reviewed every week. Each week a decision will be made whether or not to produce. If production is to take place, there will be a second decision on the amount. Give decision rules that will minimize expected costs.

SOLUTION

Since inventory is being reviewed every week, it is clear that, once we decide to produce the 6-inch strip, we should bring the inventory of strip A and strip B up to the levels that minimize expected costs to be incurred before the next weekly review. The optimum stock levels, when production runs are made at weekly intervals, are listed in Table 3 of the previous example; they are 500 units for strip A and 600 units for strip B.

If we decide to produce 6-inch strip, the expected cost during the week will be the sum of

(a) the cost for A associated with inventory and shortage when the week starts with an optimal stock level. From Table 3, this cost is 1.06.

(b) the corresponding cost for strip B. From Table 3, this cost is 1.32.

(c) the setup cost of 9.00.

or a total of 11.38 in all.

If we decide not to produce 6-inch strip, we incur expected costs equal to the sum of

(a) the cost for A associated with inventory and shortage when the week starts with the existing stock level.

(b) the cost for B associated with inventory and shortage when the week starts with the existing stock level.

Let y be the existing stock level of A, and z be the existing stock level of B. Denoting expected cost for A associated with an existing stock level of y units by $\alpha(y)$, and the expected cost for B by $\beta(z)$, then we will decide to produce if and only if

$$\alpha(y) + \beta(z) > 11.38$$

In order to use this decision rule, we should have on hand the values $\alpha(u)$ and $\beta(u)$ for the various possible values of u. These values are computed most easily by use of formulas (4.9) of the previous example, where the various first differences are obtained from formulas (4.8) and Table 2. The results are:

u	$\alpha(u)$	$\beta(u)$
0	12.00	16.00
1	6.11	9.34
2	2.99	5.22
3	1.56	2.89
4	1.09	1.76
5	1.06	1.35
6		1.32

Thus, if 'our existing stock level was zero for strip A and 100 feet for strip B, the decision would be: Produce 6-inch strip this week (12.00 +

9.34 > 11.38). But, if we had on hand 300 feet of strip A and 100 feet of strip B, the decision would be: Do not produce 6-inch strip this week.

When the stock levels are not integral multiples of 100 feet, application of the decision rule requires some form of interpolation. A convenient way of making the decision rule "continuous" is by a diagram such as that shown in Figure 4.8. Definite decisions are available for the

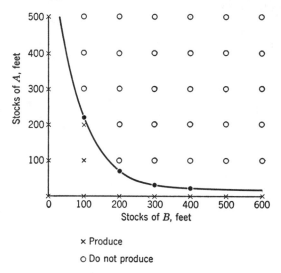

Figure 4.8. **Decision rule without discreteness restriction.**

30 points whose positions are indicated by zeros and crosses. A cross means "Produce" and a zero "Do not produce." The solid dots are obtained by direct interpolation from the table, and the curve drawn through these solid dots divides the yz plane into the two areas "Produce" and "Do not produce."

It could happen that, on starting an inventory policy of this type, initial stocks exceeded the optimum levels. In this case stocks could be reduced to the optimum levels before the scheme started to operate. Once stocks were below optimum levels, they would never again rise above them.

It is obvious that in Examples 5 and 6 we are discussing essentially the same situation. The only difference is in the assumptions made about the way the decision-making process will be organized. Although it is not the purpose of this book to discuss the broader aspects of analysis of management decision processes, the reader is reminded that, in a real situation, much thought might be required before deciding which model most closely approximated to the actual organization. It often happens that it is necessary to analyze two or more models, and to discuss their implications with management before obtaining an answer to a real problem. The student is cautioned that there is no such thing as *the* correct solution to a practical problem; even in textbook discussions there may well be more than one approach which yields a sensible result.

PROBABILISTIC DEMAND WITH PRODUCTION LEAD TIME

In this section we consider the effect of an appreciable lead time between the decision to produce (or order) for inventory and the arrival of goods into inventory. The main difference between the calculations of this and the previous section is that here we have to consider the depletion of inventory between the date at which a decision is made and the start of the period for which costs will be affected by the decision.

Example 7

An airline runs a school for air hostesses each month; it takes two months to assemble a group of girls and to train them. Past records of turnover in hostesses show that the probability of requiring x new trained hostesses in any one month is $g(x)$ [$x = 0, 1, 2, \cdots$], and the probability of requiring y new hostesses in any two-month period is $h(y)$. In the event that a trained hostess is not required for flying duties, the airline still has to pay her salary at the rate of C_1 per month. If insufficient hostesses are available, there is a cost of C_2 per girl short per month. Show how to determine decision rules for the size of classes.

SOLUTION

Suppose that it is the end of a month and the personnel manager has to decide how many new girls should be trained so that they become available for flying duties in two months' time. He will have the following information on which to make his decision:

(*a*) the number of girls surplus to requirements, as at the end of the month (possible negative).

(*b*) the number of girls presently in training who will be available for flying duties on the first of the following month.

(*c*) the number of girls presently in training who will be available for flying duties on the first of the second month hence.

Let z = the sum of (a), (b), and (c) plus the number of girls he schedules to start training. Then, if there were no staff losses, z girls would be surplus to requirements in two months' time. The personnel manager has to make a decision about the size of z which will minimize, in some sense, the expected cost of surplus staff (including negative surplus, or shortage).

His decision cannot affect the situation in the next two months, because the existing surplus and trainees are not affected by his deci-

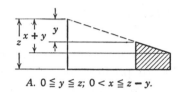

A. $0 \leqq y \leqq z;\ 0 < x \leqq z - y$.

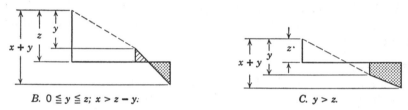

B. $0 \leqq y \leqq z;\ x > z - y$. ⠀⠀⠀⠀⠀⠀⠀⠀⠀⠀ C. $y > z$.

Figure 4.9. Inventory situation for Example 7.

sion, and none of the new trainees can be surplus in the next two months. The new trainees will affect the situation in the third month, but the costs during the fourth month will depend on the decision to be made a month hence. Thus the present decision should be aimed at minimizing costs during the third month.

Figure 4.9 shows possible inventory situations during the third month. In that figure, x represents personnel losses during the third month, y represents personnel losses in the first two months, and z is the decision variable as defined above. There are three possible situations, depending on the relative values of x, y, and z. In all three cases the cross-hatched area represents "inventory months" and the dotted area represents "shortage months." We are assuming that demand for new girls arises uniformly during the month.

In situation A, the third month starts with an inventory $z - y$, and ends with an inventory $z - y - x$, so that the total (actual) cost is

$$\frac{C_1}{2}\left[(z - y) + (z - y - x)\right] = C_1\left(z - y - \frac{x}{2}\right)$$

In situation B, the third month starts with an inventory $z-y$ and ends with a shortage $x+y-z$. As in Example 5, the area representing inventory cost is $(1/2x)(z-y)^2$, and the area representing shortage cost is $(1/2x)(x+y-z)^2$. The total cost is

$$\frac{1}{2x}[C_1(z-y)^2 + C_2(x+y-z)^2]$$

In situation C, the third month starts with a shortage $y-z$ and ends with a shortage $x+y-z$, so that the cost is

$$\frac{C_2}{2}\{(y-z) + (x+y-z)\} = C_2\left(\frac{x}{2}+y-z\right)$$

We now multiply by the joint probability of demands for y girls during the lead time (first two months), and x girls during the third month, and sum over the range of x and y. Assuming that the random variables x and y are independent, the joint probability density function is $g(x)\,h(y)$.

Let $F(z)$ denote the total expected cost corresponding to a particular z. Then

$$F(z) = \sum_{y=0}^{z} \sum_{x=0}^{z-y} C_1\left(z-y-\frac{x}{2}\right) g(x)\,h(y)$$

$$+ \sum_{y=0}^{z} \sum_{x=z-y+1}^{\infty} \frac{1}{2x}[C_1(z-y)^2 + C_2(x+y-z)^2]\,g(x)\,h(y)$$

$$+ \sum_{y=z+1}^{\infty} \sum_{x=0}^{\infty} C_2\left(\frac{x}{2}+y-z\right) g(x)\,h(y)$$

In order to find the value of z that minimizes $F(z)$, we require $\Delta F(z)$. The first difference of this function $F(z)$ is worked out in Appendix I, paragraph 6, as an illustrative example. The result given there, with slight changes in notation and form, is

$$\Delta F(z) = \sum_{y=0}^{z} \sum_{x=0}^{z-y} C_1\, g(x)\,h(y)$$

$$+ \sum_{y=0}^{z} \sum_{x=z-y+1}^{\infty} \frac{1}{2x}[C_1(2z - 2y + 1)$$

$$+ C_2(2z - 2x - 2y + 1)]\,g(x)\,h(y)$$

$$- \sum_{y=z+1}^{\infty} \sum_{x=0}^{\infty} C_2\, g(x)\,h(y)$$

This result can be simplified considerably by the use of the relations

$$\sum_{x=0}^{\infty} g(x) = 1, \qquad \sum_{y=0}^{\infty} h(y) = 1$$

which hold because $g(x)$ and $h(y)$ are probability densities. After simplification, $\Delta F(z)$ has the form

$$\Delta F(z) = (C_1 + C_2) \sum_{y=0}^{z} h(y) \left[\sum_{x=0}^{z-y} g(x) + \left(z - y + \frac{1}{2} \right) \sum_{x=z-y+1}^{\infty} \frac{g(x)}{x} \right] - C_2$$

The minimum value of $F(z)$ will be given by the smallest value of z for which $\Delta F(z) \geq 0$: i.e. by the smallest value of z for which

$$\sum_{y=0}^{z} h(y) \left[\sum_{x=0}^{z-y} g(x) + \left(z - y + \frac{1}{2} \right) \sum_{x=z-y+1}^{\infty} \frac{g(x)}{x} \right] \geq \frac{C_2}{C_1 + C_2}$$

The number of girls to be called for training is then this value of z minus the sum of the quantities (a), (b), and (c) defined in the first paragraph of the solution.

Example 8

A dealer in industrial solvents has one product which is made especially for him. He places orders for supplies every month and receives delivery one month later. In the event that his tank capacity is insufficient to hold all the quantity ordered at the time of delivery, the balance of the order is wasted at a cost of k per gallon wasted.

Customer demand for one month can be represented by the probability density function $p(x)$; and demand in one month is independent of demand in any other month. The cost of storing the solvent is C_1 per gallon per month, and the cost of a shortage is C_2 per gallon per month. In addition, there is a fixed cost per month of KZ, where Z is his total storage capacity.

If the criterion is minimum expected total cost, discuss the determination of

(a) the amount to be ordered each month with present storage capacity.

(b) the best value for total storage capacity.

SOLUTION

Let Z be the storage capacity, and z the amount in the tanks plus the amount on order immediately after an order is placed.

Suppose that there is a demand y in the first month following the order and a demand x in the second month. As in the airline hostess problem the decision about z will affect costs only in the second month following the order.

We have to consider the following possibilities.

(1) $z - y > Z$. In this case an amount $z - y - Z$ will be wasted, and the second month will start with Z in storage.

(2) $0 \leq z - y \leq Z$. In this case there will be no waste, and the second month will start with $z - y$ in storage.

(3) $z - y < 0$. In this case there will be no waste, but the second month will start with a shortage left from the previous month.

The costs of inventory and shortage can be derived by reasoning very similar to that used in the airline hostess problem. In case 1 the costs are

$$C_1\left(Z - \frac{x}{2}\right) + k(z - y - Z) \qquad \text{if} \quad x \leq Z$$

$$\frac{C_1 Z^2}{2x} + \frac{C_2(x - Z)^2}{2x} + k(z - y - Z) \quad \text{if} \quad x > Z$$

In case 2 the costs are

$$C_1\left(z - y - \frac{x}{2}\right) \qquad\qquad \text{if} \quad x \leq z - y$$

$$\frac{C_1}{2x}(z - y)^2 + \frac{C_2}{2x}(x + y - z)^2 \quad \text{if} \quad x > z - y$$

In case 3 the costs are

$$C_2\left(\frac{x}{2} + y - z\right)$$

In order to obtain the total expected costs, we multiply by the appropriate probability density functions and integrate with respect to x and y. We must also add the fixed storage cost KZ.

We will use $F(z, Z)$ to denote the result.

$$F(z, Z) = \int_{y=0}^{z-Z} \int_{x=0}^{Z} p(x)\, p(y) \left[C_1 \left(Z - \frac{x}{2} \right) + k(z - y - Z) \right] dx\, dy$$

$$+ \int_{y=0}^{z-Z} \int_{x=Z}^{\infty} p(x)\, p(y) \left\{ \frac{1}{2x} [C_1 Z^2 + C_2(x - Z)^2] \right.$$

$$\left. + k(z - y - Z) \right\} dx\, dy$$

$$+ \int_{y=z-Z}^{z} \int_{x=0}^{z-y} p(x)\, p(y) \left[C_1 \left(z - y - \frac{x}{2} \right) \right] dx\, dy$$

$$+ \int_{y=z-Z}^{z} \int_{x=z-y}^{\infty} p(x)\, p(y) \left\{ \frac{1}{2x} [C_1 (z - y)^2 \right.$$

$$\left. + C_2(x + y - z)^2] \right\} dx\, dy$$

$$+ \int_{y=z}^{\infty} \int_{x=0}^{\infty} p(x)\, p(y) \left[C_2 \left(\frac{x}{2} + y - z \right) \right] dx\, dy$$

$$+ KZ$$

If the storage capacity Z is held at its present level, $F(z, Z)$ is a function only of the quantity z. Call this function $G(z)$. In order to minimize this function, we require the derivative dG/dz.

Appendix II discusses differentiation under the integral sign. Application of equations (II.6), (II.7), and (II.8) of Appendix II and some manipulation yields

(4.10) $$\frac{dG}{dz} = (C_2 + k)\, A(z - Z) - C_2$$

$$+ (C_1 + C_2) \int_{z-Z}^{z} p(y)\, [A(z - y) + B(z - y)]\, dy$$

where we define

$$A(u) = \int_{0}^{u} p(v)\, dv$$

$$B(u) = u \int_{u}^{\infty} \frac{p(v)}{v}\, dv$$

In order to obtain the optimal value of z, we set the right-hand side of (4.10) equal to zero and attempt to solve the resulting equation for z. Trial-and-error methods using numerical integration would give usable results for the decision variable z.

If the storage capacity Z is also considered to be a decision variable, $F(z, Z)$ is a function of two variables z and Z. After differentiating $F(z, Z)$ and simplifying as above, we end up with two equations to be solved numerically for z and Z:

$$\frac{\partial F}{\partial z} = (C_2 + k) A(z - Z) - C_2 + (C_1 + C_2) \int_{z-Z}^{z} p(y)[A(z - y)$$
$$+ B(z - y)] \, dy = 0$$
$$\frac{\partial F}{\partial Z} = K + \{(C_1 + C_2)[A(Z) + B(Z)] - (C_2 + k)\}A(z - Z) = 0$$

PROBLEMS FOR SOLUTION

Set VI

1. A baking company sells cake by the pound. It makes a profit of 50 cents a pound on every pound sold on the day it is baked. It disposes of all cake not sold on the date it is baked at a loss of 12 cents a pound. If demand is known to be rectangular between 2000 and 3000 pounds, determine the optimal daily amount baked. [*Ans.* 2807 pounds]

2. The probability distribution of monthly sales of a certain item is as follows:

Monthly sales	Probability
0	0.02
1	0.05
2	0.30
3	0.27
4	0.20
5	0.10
6	0.06
	1.00

The cost of carrying inventory is $10 per unit per month. The current policy is to maintain a stock of four items at the beginning of each month. Assuming that the cost of shortage is proportional to both time and quantity short, obtain the imputed cost of a shortage of one item for one time unit. (Because the problem is stated in discrete units, the answer will consist of a range of values for the imputed cost.)

3. A newspaper boy buys papers for 3 cents each and sells them for 7 cents each. He cannot return unsold newspapers. Daily demand has the following distribution:

No. of customers	23	24	25	26	27	28	29	30	31	32
Probability	.01	.03	.06	.10	.20	.25	.15	.10	.05	.05

If each day's demand is independent of the previous day's, how many papers should he order each day?

4. A manufacturer of a perishable commodity is limited, because he takes advantage of bulk transportation, to one shipment a month from factory to warehouse. This shipment takes place on the first of each month, and includes all the previous month's production. There is one production run a month, which starts at the beginning of the month and continues at the rate of k units per day until the monthly production quota of q units is finished. (Here k is fixed, and q is a decision variable.) Production costs C per unit.

Goods are sold only from the warehouse. The probability of a demand on the warehouse for a quantity n during the month is $p(n)$; it may be assumed that the demand on the warehouse is spread uniformly over the month. Storage, either at the warehouse or at the factory, costs C_1 per unit per month. Any warehouse surplus at the end of the month is considered stale, inasmuch as it is over a month old, and is disposed of through outlets which will take an unlimited amount of stale goods, but at a price P' (less than C) per unit. The sales price of fresh goods (i.e. goods received at the warehouse on the first of the current month) is P per unit.

Find the expected profit per month as a function of the monthly production quota q, and, by differencing this function, determine the condition for optimal q.

5. Discuss the problem of the automobile dealer (Example 4 of the text) if the assumption of immediate delivery from the factory is replaced by an assumption that delivery takes place two weeks after the dealer places an order.

6. A company owns two warehouses X and Y. Shipments from the factory are made on the first of each month to bring the stock at X up to S_1 and the stock at Y up to S_2. Demand during the month is uniform at each warehouse, with a density function $f(x)$ at X and $g(y)$ at Y, and with x and y independent. Inventory holding costs are C_1 per unit per month and shortage costs are C_2 per unit per month, at either warehouse. In the event of a shortage at one warehouse, deliveries are made from the other warehouse, but only provided the latter is certain that its own orders for the month can be taken care of out of the stock that remains. However, it costs an extra amount k per unit to make a delivery from X to a customer of Y, and vice versa. It may be assumed that, by the time one warehouse has run out of stock, the other warehouse can predict its total demand for the month exactly.

Show how to find values of S_1 and S_2 which will minimize the total expected cost.

Hint: The achieved total cost is a function of the realized values of x and y.

The form of the function is different in different areas of the xy plane. There are six such areas, viz.:

$$
\begin{array}{lll}
A: & 0 \leq x \leq S_1, & 0 \leq y \leq S_2 \\
B: & x \geq S_1, & 0 \leq y \leq S_1 + S_2 - x \\
C: & y \geq S_2, & 0 \leq x \leq S_1 + S_2 - y \\
D: & 0 \leq x \leq S_1, & y \geq S_1 + S_2 - x \\
E: & x \geq S_1, & y \geq S_2 \\
F: & 0 \leq y \leq S_2, & x \geq S_1 + S_2 - y
\end{array}
$$

Find the functional form in each area, multiply by the joint density function of x and y, and integrate to obtain the total expected cost as a function of S_1 and S_2.]

7. This problem is identical with problem 6, except that the trans-shipment assumption is revised to read as follows: In the event of a shortage at one warehouse, deliveries are made from the other warehouse until such time as both warehouses are out of stock.

REFERENCES

Arrow, K. T., S. Karlin, and H. Scarf, *Studies in the Mathematical Theory of Inventory and Production*, Stanford University Press, Stanford, 1958.

Bowman, E. H., and R. B. Fetter, *Analysis for Production Management*, Richard D. Irwin, Inc., Homowood, Ill., 1957.

Churchman, C. W., R. L. Ackoff, and E. L. Arnoff, *Introduction to Operations Research*, John Wiley & Sons, New York, 1957.

Magee, John F., *Production Planning and Inventory Control*, McGraw-Hill Book Co., New York, 1958.

Vazsonyi, Andrew, *Scientific Programming in Business and Industry*, John Wiley & Sons, New York, 1958.

Whitin, T. M., *The Theory of Inventory Management*, Princeton University Press, Princeton, 1953.

CHAPTER

FIVE

Replacement

Replacement theory is concerned with situations in which efficiency tends to worsen in time, and in which it can be restored to a previous level by some kind of remedial action. The problem is to determine the times at which such remedial action should be taken, in order to minimize some appropriate measure of effectiveness.

In this chapter we consider in turn the replacement of capital equipment that deteriorates with time, group replacement of items such as light bulbs which fail completely, some problems in mortality and staffing, and finally some examples of replacement situations which do not fit into these three categories.

CAPITAL EQUIPMENT THAT DETERIORATES WITH TIME

A typical example of such replacement situations is the problem of when a fleet owner should replace a truck. A truck wears out with age, and the problem is to discover the "best" time at which to purchase a replacement. Before we attempt to analyze such situations, let us first consider the truck owner and find out why he possesses a truck. We may suppose that one reason is to transport goods as cheaply as possible, but there may be other reasons. Thus the owner might feel that a new truck lends prestige to his business.

If we concentrate on the cheapness of transportation, we could begin by examining the way in which costs increase with the age of the truck. With a fixed mileage every month we might obtain a graph as in Figure 5.1.

In addition to running costs there are the capital costs of purchasing the truck. These can be expressed as average costs per month, and the average monthly cost will decrease, the longer a replacement is postponed. However, there comes a point at which the rate of increase of

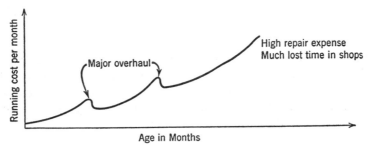

Figure 5.1.   Monthly running costs for a truck.

running costs more than offsets the savings in average capital costs. At this point replacement is justified.

Example 1

A fleet owner finds from his past records that the costs per year of running a truck whose purchase price is $6000 are as given below:

Year	1	2	3	4	5	6	7	8
Running costs	1000	1200	1400	1800	2300	2800	3400	4000
Resale price	3000	1500	750	375	200	200	200	200

At what age is a replacement due?

SOLUTION

We first compute a table (Table 1) showing the average cost per year during the life of the truck. The third column of the table gives the difference between the purchase price and the resale price at the end of the year in question.

We conclude that the truck should be replaced at the end of the fifth year. If the truck is not replaced at this time, the average cost per year will start to increase.

TABLE 1. COSTS OF OWNING AND OPERATING A TRUCK

Replace at end of year	Total running costs	Total capital costs	Total costs	Average cost per year
1	1,000	3000	4,000	4000
2	2,200	4500	6,700	3350
3	3,600	5250	8,850	2950
4	5,400	5625	11,025	2756
5	7,700	5800	13,500	2700
6	10,500	5800	16,300	2717

Example 2

The truck owner of the previous example has three trucks, two of which are two years old and the third one year old. He is considering a new type of truck with 50% more capacity than one of the old ones at a unit price of $8000. He estimates that the running costs and resale price for the new truck will be as follows:

Year	1	2	3	4	5	6	7	8
Running costs	1200	1500	1800	2400	3100	4000	5000	6100
Resale price	4000	2000	1000	500	300	300	300	300

Assuming that the loss of flexibility due to fewer trucks is of no importance, and that he will continue to have sufficient work for three of the old trucks, what should his policy be?

SOLUTION

As in Example 1, we can show that the lowest average annual cost can be achieved by replacing one of the larger trucks every five years. With such a policy the average annual cost would be $3540 per truck. This is equivalent to $2360 per payload of the smaller trucks. Since this is less than the minimum average annual cost for one of the smaller trucks, the latter will be replaced by the new larger trucks.

Having decided to replace the old-type trucks with the larger trucks, we still must decide when the new trucks should be purchased. We assume that for uniformity the replacement will involve two new trucks and all three of the old trucks. The new trucks will be purchased when the cost for the next year of running the three old trucks exceeds the average yearly cost for two new-type trucks.

Examination of Table 1 shows that the total yearly cost for one smaller truck is $4000 in the first year, and $2700, $2150, $2175, $2475, $2800 in years 2, 3, 4, 5, and 6, respectively. Hence the total costs next year for two smaller trucks aged two years and one smaller truck aged one year will be

$$2 \times 2150 + 2700 = 7000$$

In subsequent years the costs will be \$6500, \$7125, and \$8075 for years 2, 3, and 4. The average annual cost for two larger trucks will be \$7080, so that the costs for the old trucks will not exceed those for the larger trucks until the third year hence. Thus all three trucks should be replaced two years from now.

Note that the old trucks will be replaced before any of them reaches the normal replacement age.

In these two examples we have made the simplest possible analysis of the costs involved. In practice, we usually wish to consider not only the amounts of expenditures but the points in time at which they occur. We now give an example to illustrate how this can be done.

Example 3

A manufacturer is offered two machines A and B. A is priced at \$5000, and running costs are estimated at \$800 for each of the first five years, increasing by \$200 per year in the sixth and subsequent years. Machine B, which has the same capacity as A, costs \$2500 but will have running costs of \$1200 per year for six years, increasing by \$200 per year thereafter. If money is worth 10% per year, which machine should be purchased? (Assume that the machines will eventually be sold for scrap at a negligible price.)

Solution

We can regard the statement that money is worth 10% per year in two ways. First, we may suppose that any spare cash now available could be made to produce 10% return in a year, and so spending \$100 today would be equivalent to spending \$110 in a year's time. (If we plan to spend \$110 a year from now, we could spend \$100 today on an investment which would be worth \$110 next year.)

Alternatively, we might suppose that expenditures are made by borrowing money at 10% per annum. Again expenditure of \$110 in a year's time is equivalent to \$100 today. If we spent \$100 today, at the end of a year we would have to pay \$110 to liquidate the debt. Viewed either way, \$100 today is equivalent to \$110 a year from now.

Similarly, one dollar a year from now is equivalent to $(1.1)^{-1}$ dollars today, and one dollar r years from now is equivalent to $(1.1)^{-r}$ dollars today. This quantity $(1.1)^{-r}$ is called the *present value* or *present worth* of one dollar spent r years from now.

In order to compare A and B, we have to compare the present worth of the expenditure on the two machines. Instead of going through the arithmetic twice, it will be simpler to establish an algebraic formula for the present worth and to substitute numerical values later.

Let C be the purchase price, and let R_n be the running cost in year n. Let i = rate of interest so that $v = 1/(1 + i)$ is the present worth of a unit to be spent a year hence. (v is known as the *discount rate*.) Suppose the machine is to be replaced after r years. Then assuming that expenditure can be considered to take place at the beginning of each year,* the present worth of the expenditure, which we will denote by $P(r)$, is given by

$$(5.1) \qquad P(r) = C + R_1 + vR_2 + v^2R_3 + v^3R_4 + \cdots + v^{r-1}R_r$$

Now $P(r)$ increases as r increases; so the present worth, if we replace after $(r+1)$ years, is greater than if we replace after r years. For the extra money we get an extra year's service, and we wish to compare some function of the replacement interval which allows for this.

In order to do this, let us suppose that replacement occurs in r years, and that the manufacturer sets up a fund $P(r)$ to be invested at interest i, from which all expenditure on the machine will be made. Suppose that he obtains the sum $P(r)$ by borrowing funds at the same rate i, and he repays the loan by fixed annual payments throughout the life of the machine. In this way the variable payments actually made can be translated into fixed annual payments. We can use these fixed payments as a basis for comparing replacement at the end of different periods. (In the previous examples we did much the same thing when comparing the average costs per year, ignoring interest.)

The present worth of fixed annual payments x for r years is

$$x + vx + v^2x + \cdots + v^{r-1}x = \frac{x(1 - v^r)}{1 - v}$$

Since this is to be the sum borrowed we see that

$$(5.2) \qquad\qquad x = \frac{1 - v}{1 - v^r} P(r)$$

Thus the best period at which to replace the machine is the period r which minimizes $P(r)(1 - v)/(1 - v^r)$. We can simplify this criterion somewhat by noting that the function to be minimized is a positive constant times the function $F(r) = P(r)/(1 - v^r)$. The period at which to replace the machine is the period r which minimizes $F(r)$.

---

* If this is unrealistic, the results still follow, provided R_n is modified to mean expenditure during the year discounted to the beginning of the year.

Since the possible values of r are discrete, we employ the methods of finite differences to calculate the optimal r. According to Appendix I, the condition on r for $F(r)$ to be a minimum is

$$(5.3) \qquad \Delta F(r-1) < 0 < \Delta F(r)$$

subject to the usual checks on whether the resulting value of r actually provides an absolute minimum. We next evaluate $\Delta F(r)$:

$$\Delta F(r) = \Delta \left[\frac{P(r)}{1 - v^r} \right] = \frac{P(r+1)}{1 - v^{r+1}} - \frac{P(r)}{1 - v^r}$$

$$= \frac{P(r+1) - P(r) + v^{r+1}P(r) - v^r\, P(r+1)}{(1 - v^r)(1 - v^{r+1})}$$

$$= \frac{v^r R_{r+1} + (v^{r+1} - v^r)C + (v^{r+1} - v^r) \sum\limits_{j=1}^{r} v^{j-1}R_j - v^{2r}R_{r+1}}{(1 - v^r)(1 - v^{r+1})}$$

$$= \frac{v^r R_{r+1}}{1 - v^{r+1}} + \frac{(v^{r+1} - v^r)\, P(r)}{(1 - v^r)(1 - v^{r+1})}$$

Thus we have

$$(5.4) \qquad \Delta F(r) = \frac{v^r}{1 - v^{r+1}} \left(R_{r+1} - \frac{1 - v}{1 - v^i} P_r \right)$$

Since $v^r/[1 - v^{r+1}]$ is always positive for $|v| < 1$, $\Delta F(r)$ has the same sign as the quantity in brackets, and the condition (5.3) for the optimal replacement interval r becomes

$$(5.5) \qquad \frac{1 - v^{r-1}}{1 - v} R_r - P_{r-1} < 0 < \frac{1 - v^r}{1 - v} R_{r+1} - P_r$$

Returning now to the numerical values of the problem, we tabulate the results for machine A (Table 2).

TABLE 2. REPLACEMENT COSTS FOR MACHINE A

Year r	Running cost R_r	v^{r-1}	$v^{r-1}R_r$	$P(r)$	$[(1-v^r)/(1-v)]R_{r+1}$
1	800	1.0000	800	5,800	800
2	800	0.9091	727	6,527	1,528
3	800	0.8264	661	7,188	2,189
4	800	0.7513	601	7,789	2,790
5	800	0.6830	546	8,335	4,170
6	1000	0.6209	621	8,956	5,749
7	1200	0.5645	677	9,633	7,497
8	1400	0.5132	718	10,351	9,390
9	1600	0.4665	746	11,097	11,403
10	1800	0.4241	763	11,860	

Thus it would be best to replace machine A after nine years. In a similar fashion, the reader can verify that machine B is best replaced after eight years. The equivalent fixed annual charge, computed from (5.2), is \$1752 for machine A and \$1680 for machine B. We conclude that it would be better to purchase machine B. (The average of the *actual* payments is \$1578 for A and \$1588 for B.)

In practice, there is a further complication in this type of replacement problem. The tax situation of a business is considerably affected by its capital equipment replacement policies. A discussion of tax law is outside the scope of this book, but in any real problem the incidence of tax cannot be ignored.

It is of interest to compare the corrected annual payment x as given by (5.2) with the actual annual cost, for a situation where the interest rate approaches zero. When the interest rate i tends to zero, the discount rate v tends to one. The limit of x in (5.2), when v tends to one, is found by l'Hôpital's rule to be $P(r)/r$. This is just the average annual cost; so the method of Examples 1 and 2 is a limiting case of the method of Example 3.

ITEMS THAT FAIL COMPLETELY

We now turn to the second type of replacement problem, where we are concerned with items that either work or fail completely; that is, loss of usefulness is sudden and complete. The principles used in analyzing this type of situation have been largely developed by the actuarial profession in connection with human lives, and we will use their terminology and notation as is convenient.

Example 4

The following mortality rates have been observed for a certain type of light bulb.

Week	1	2	3	4	5
Percent failing by end of week	10	25	50	80	100

There are 1000 bulbs in use, and it costs \$1.00 to replace an individual bulb which has burnt out. If all bulbs were replaced simultaneously, it would cost 25 cents per bulb. It is proposed to replace all bulbs at fixed intervals, whether or not they have burnt out, and to continue replacing burnt-out bulbs as they fail. At what intervals should all the bulbs be replaced?

SOLUTION

We first compute the probability that a new bulb fails in successive weeks (no group replacement policy in operation). Let p_i denote the probability that a bulb, which was new when installed, fails during the ith week of its life. This probability is clearly the difference between the proportion "alive" at the beginning of the ith week and the proportion alive at the end of the ith week. We obtain the following table:

Week (i)	Probability that a new bulb installed at time zero fails during week i (p_i)
1	0.10
2	0.15
3	0.25
4	0.30
5	0.20
	1.00

Note that no installed bulb survives more than five weeks. Thus a bulb that has already lasted four weeks is *sure* to fail during the fifth week. However, the unconditional probability of failure during the fifth week, for a new bulb installed at time zero, is what we are denoting by p_5 and has the value 0.20.

With two simplifying assumptions, we can compute the number of replacements due to failure in successive weeks, under a policy of no group replacement. We assume

(a) that bulbs that fail during a week are replaced just before the end of that week.

(b) that the actual percentage of failures during a week for a subpopulation of bulbs with the same age is the same as the expected percentage of failures during the week for that subpopulation.

Let n_i denote the number of replacements made at the end of the ith week, if all 1000 bulbs are new initially. Then, under our assumptions we immediately obtain:

$$
\begin{aligned}
n_0 &= n_0 & &= 1000 \\
n_1 &= n_0 p_1 & &= 100 \\
n_2 &= n_0 p_2 + n_1 p_1 & = 150 + 10 & = 160 \\
n_3 &= n_0 p_3 + n_1 p_2 + n_2 p_1 & = 250 + 15 + 16 & = 281 \\
n_4 &= n_0 p_4 + n_1 p_3 + n_2 p_2 + n_3 p_1 & &= 377 \\
n_5 &= n_0 p_5 + n_1 p_4 + n_2 p_3 + n_3 p_2 + n_4 p_1 & &= 350 \\
n_6 &= \quad\quad n_1 p_5 + n_2 p_4 + n_3 p_3 + n_4 p_2 + n_5 p_1 & &= 230 \\
n_7 &= \quad\quad\quad\quad\quad n_2 p_5 + n_3 p_4 + n_4 p_3 + n_5 p_2 + n_6 p_1 & &= 286
\end{aligned}
$$

It will be noticed that the number of bulbs failing each week increases until week 4 and then decreases. It can be shown the number will later start to increase, and it will continue to oscillate until ultimately the system settles down to a steady state in which the proportion of bulbs failing each week is the reciprocal of their average life. The average life is $1 \times 0.10 + 2 \times 0.15 + 3 \times 0.25 + 4 \times 0.30 + 5 \times 0.20 = 3.35$. In the steady state, the number of failures each week will be $1000/3.35 = 299$. Thus the present policy of replacing bulbs only on failure costs $299 a week.

If all bulbs were replaced at the end of the first week, the cost would be $250 plus the cost of replacing failures during the week; i.e. $250 + 100 = 350$. If all bulbs were replaced every two weeks, the cost during two weeks would be $250 + 100 + 160 = 510$ dollars. This is an average of $255 per week. Replacement at the end of three weeks would cost $250 + 100 + 160 + 281 = 791$ dollars every three weeks, or an average of $264 per week. Thus it would be cheapest to replace all the bulbs every two weeks.

Example 5

A large population is subject to a given mortality curve for a very long period of time. All deaths are immediately replaced by births, and there are no other entries or exits. Show that the age distribution ultimately becomes stable and that the number of deaths per unit time becomes constant.

SOLUTION

The reader who associates the wording of this problem with human populations will probably realize that no group of people ever existed under these conditions. The problem is stated in this way because the analysis was first done with hypothetical human populations in mind. However, it is only necessary to translate the problem into industry, where death is equivalent to a part failure, and birth to replacement, and we have a fairly common situation.

In order to simplify the problem, we will assume that each death occurs just before some time $t = k$, where k is an integer, and that no individual survives longer than $\omega + 1$ time units.

Let $f(t)$ be the number of births (replacements) at time t, and let $p(x)$ be the probability of a member dying just before age $x+1$. At time t, the survivors of the $f(t-x)$ births at time $t-x$ are aged x, so that their a priori probability of dying just before time $t+1$ is $p(x)$, and the number of deaths of such survivors just before time $t+1$ is $p(x) f(t-x)$.

Hence, the total number of deaths just before time $t+1$ will be

$$\sum_{x=0}^{\omega} f(t - x)\, p(x) \qquad t = \omega,\, \omega + 1,\, \omega + 2, \cdots$$

Since deaths are replaced by births, this quantity equals the births at time $t+1$:

$$(5.6) \qquad f(t + 1) = \sum_{x=0}^{\omega} f(t - x)\, p(x)$$

This is a difference equation in t, and may be solved by substituting $f(t) = A\alpha^t$:

$$A\alpha^{t+1} = A \sum_{x=0}^{\omega} p(x)\alpha^{t-x}$$

We divide by $A\alpha^{t-\omega}$ and obtain

$$(5.7) \quad \alpha^{\omega+1} - [\alpha^\omega\, p(0) + \alpha^{\omega-1}\, p(1) + \cdots + \alpha\, p(\omega - 1) + p(\omega)] = 0$$

This is a polynomial equation in α. We note that, since $\sum_{0}^{\omega} p_x = 1$, one solution is $\alpha = 1$. It can be shown that the modulus of all the remaining roots is less than unity. Let us denote the remaining roots by $\alpha_1, \alpha_2, \cdots, \alpha_\omega$. A little reflection will show that the general solution to (5.6) has the form

$$f(t) = A_0 + A_1\alpha_1{}^t + A_2\alpha_2{}^t + \cdots + A_\omega\alpha_\omega{}^t$$

where $A_0, A_1, \cdots, A_\omega$ are constants which could be determined from a knowledge of the age distribution at some given point in time. Since each $|\alpha_i| < 1$, we see that, for large t, $f(t) = A_0$. That is, the number of deaths per unit time (as well as the number of births) is constant at A_0. The probability of surviving longer than x time units is $1 - p(0) - p(1) - \cdots - p(x - 1)$. We will use $P(x)$ to denote this probability, and interpret $P(0)$ as unity. The number of survivors aged x at any fixed point in time is the number of births at an instant x time units earlier, multiplied by $P(x)$. Hence, once births and deaths have settled down to a constant rate A_0, the number of survivors aged x is stable at $A_0 P(x)$.

Since the number of births always equals the number of deaths, the size N of the total population remains constant, and we have

$$N = A_0 \sum_{x=0}^{\omega} P(x)$$

or

$$(5.8) \qquad A_0 = \frac{N}{\sum\limits_{x=0}^{\omega} P(x)}$$

Once A_0 has been computed by means of (5.8), the limiting age distribution may be computed by the rule given at the end of the previous paragraph; namely, the number of survivors aged zero is A_0, the number of survivors aged 1 is $A_0 P(1)$, the number of survivors aged 2 is $A_0 P(2)$, and so on.

Finally, we show that the denominator in (5.8) may be interpreted as the mean age at death. We first write

$$\sum_{x=0}^{\omega} P(x) \qquad \text{as} \qquad \sum_{x=0}^{\omega} P(x) \, \Delta(x)$$

which is permissible since the first difference of x is unity. Then upon applying equation (I-17) of Appendix I, we obtain

$$\sum_{x=0}^{\omega} P(x) = (\omega + 1) \, P(\omega + 1) - [0] \, P(0) - \sum_{x=0}^{\omega} (x + 1) \, \Delta P(x)$$

But $P(\omega + 1) = 0$ and $\Delta P(x) = -p(x)$. Hence

$$\sum_{x=0}^{\omega} P(x) = \sum_{x=0}^{\omega} (x + 1) \, p(x)$$

$$= \sum_{y=1}^{\omega+1} y \, P\{\text{age at death is } y\}$$

$$= \text{mean age at death}$$

Therefore, the ultimate rate of deaths can be obtained by dividing the size of the population by the mean age at death.

STAFFING PROBLEMS

Problems connected with recruitment and promotion of staff sometimes lend themselves to analysis similar to that used in industrial replacement. We give two examples which will illustrate the principles.

Example 6

An airline requires 200 assistant hostesses, 300 hostesses, and 50 supervisors. Girls are recruited at age 21 and, if still in service, retire at age 60. Given the "life" table (Table 3), determine

1. How many girls should be recruited each year.
2. At what ages should promotions take place.

(Assume that all withdrawals and promotions take place on the anniversary of entry.)

TABLE 3.   "LIFE TABLE" FOR AIRLINE HOSTESSES

x	λ_x	d_x	p_x	q_x	x	λ_x	d_x	p_x	q_x
21	1000	400	0.600	0.400	41	119	6	0.952	0.048
22	600	120	.800	.200	42	113	7	.947	.053
23	480	96	.800	.200	43	106	7	.942	.058
24	384	77	.800	.200	44	99	6	.936	.064
25	307	46	.800	.200	45	93	7	.930	.070
26	261	33	.850	.150	46	87	7	.923	.077
27	228	22	.875	.125	47	80	7	.915	.085
28	206	16	.900	.100	48	73	7	.906	.094
29	190	9	.925	.075	49	66	7	.896	.104
30	181	8	.950	.050	50	59	6	.885	.115
31	173	6	.958	.042	51	53	7	.873	.127
32	167	6	.962	.038	52	46	7	.860	.140
33	161	6	.965	.035	53	39	6	.846	.154
34	155	5	.967	.033	54	33	6	.831	.169
35	150	4	.968	.032	55	27	5	.815	.185
36	146	5	.968	.032	56	22	4	.798	.202
37	141	5	.968	.032	57	18	4	.780	.220
38	136	5	.965	.035	58	14	3	.761	.239
39	131	6	.961	.039	59	11	3	.741	.259
40	125	6	.957	.043					

Notation

λ_x = number of girls out of original 1000 still in service at age x

d_x = withdrawals between ages x and $x+1$

p_x = probability that a girl in service at age x will still be in service at age $x+1$

q_x = probability that a girl in service at age x will withdraw before age $x+1$

$$\left[d_x = \lambda_x - \lambda_{x+1} = -\Delta\lambda_x; \quad p_x = \frac{\lambda_{x+1}}{\lambda_x}; \quad q_x = \frac{d_x}{\lambda_x}; \quad p_x + q_x = 1 \right]$$

SOLUTION

Let z, which is a constant to be determined, be the number of girls recruited each year. If 1000 girls had been recruited each year for the past 39 years, there would be λ_x now in service at each age x. Hence the total number in service will be

$$\sum_{x=21}^{59} \lambda_x = 6480$$

By proportion, if z girls are recruited each year, the total number in the system will be $6480(z/1000)$. We require 550. Hence

$$6480(z/1000) = 550$$

$$z = 85$$

Suppose that promotion from assistant hostess to hostess occurs at age x_1. We always have in the system $(85/1000)\lambda_x$ girls of age x. The number of assistant hostesses in the system is thus $0.085\Sigma\lambda_x$, where the summation goes from $x = 21$ to $x = x_1-1$. We require 200 assistant hostesses. Hence the condition on x_1 is

$$0.085 \sum_{x=21}^{x_1-1} \lambda_x = 200$$

or

$$\sum_{x=21}^{x_1-1} \lambda_x = 2532$$

From the λ_x column of the life table, we find that $x_1 = 25$, to the nearest integer.

Similarly, if promotion from hostess to supervisor takes place at age x_2 we obtain the condition

$$\sum_{x=25}^{x_2-1} \lambda_x = \frac{300}{0.085} = 3529$$

whence $x_2 = 48$.

Thus 85 assistant hostesses of age 21 will be recruited each year, and promotions to hostess and supervisor will occur at ages 25 and 48, respectively.

In staffing problems of this type, with fixed total staff and fixed size of staff groups, the proportion of staff in each group determines the age at promotion, and conversely. In practice, "career prospects" are often considerably improved by the possibility of expansion.

Before leaving this problem, we will indicate briefly how a life table can be obtained. From past experience, we compute the observed percentages p'_x for each age x. More specifically, p'_x is the observed percentage of survivals at the end of a year of a group aged x at the beginning of the year. [In obtaining these p'_x, it may be necessary to lump some ages together because of sparsity of data.] Starting with any convenient number (here, 1000) for λ_z at the youngest age z, we compute successively

$$\lambda'_{z+1} = p'_z\lambda_z, \qquad \lambda'_{z+2} = p'_{z+1}\lambda'_{z+1}, \qquad \text{etc.}$$

These values λ'_x are then plotted against x, and a smooth curve is drawn passing as close as possible to the points. From the curve, values of λ_x are read off for each age x and the results entered in the table. The remainder of the table can then be computed from the λ_x column.

Of course, a great deal more sophistication can be used. Allowances might have to be made for entrants during the year, and mathematical methods might be used in curve fitting, but in many problems simple methods of the sort described here often suffice.

Example 7

An airline, whose staff are subject to the same survival rates as in Example 6, presently has a staff whose ages are distributed as in Table 4. It is estimated that for the next two years staff requirements will increase by 10% per year. If girls are to be recruited at age 21, how many should be recruited for next year and at what age will promotions take place? How many should be recruited for the following year, and at what age will promotions take place?

TABLE 4. PRESENT STAFF AGE DISTRIBUTION

Assistants		Hostesses		Supervisors	
Age	Number	Age	Number	Age	Number
21	90	26	40	42	5
22	50	27	35	43	4
23	30	28	35	44	5
24	20	29	30	45	3
25	10	30	28	46	3
	—	31	26	47	3
	200	32	20	48	6
		33	18	49	2
		34	16	50	—
		35	12	51	—
		36	10	52	4
		37	8	53	3
		38	—	54	5
		39	8	55	—
		40	8	56	3
		41	6	57	2
			—	58	—
			300	59	2
					—
					50

SOLUTION

We multiply the number of staff at each age by the probability p_x that they will remain in service for one year, thus obtaining the age distribution one year later.

For example, the number of supervisors in one year's time will be:

5 × 0.947	=	4.735		Aged 43
4 × 0.942	=	3.768		44
5 × 0.936	=	4.68		45
3 × 0.930	=	2.79		46
3 × 0.923	=	2.769		47
3 × 0.915	=	2.745		48
6 × 0.906	=	5.436		49
2 × 0.896	=	1.792		50
0 × 0.885	=	0		51
0 × 0.873	=	0		52
4 × 0.860	=	3.44		53
3 × 0.846	=	2.538		54
5 × 0.831	=	4.155		55
0 × 0.815	=	0		56
3 × 0.798	=	2.394		57
2 × 0.780	=	1.56		58
0 × 0.761	=	0		59
2 × 0	=	0		60 *

Total 42.802

* All those aged 60 retire.

Thus, in a year's time there will be 43 remaining supervisors. Since a total of 55 will be required, 12 girls have to be promoted from the hostess group. Assuming that promotion is based solely on age, the oldest 12 hostesses will be promoted. In a year's time, there will be

$$6 \times 0.952 = 5.712 \text{ hostesses aged 42}$$

$$8 \times 0.957 = 7.656 \text{ hostesses aged 41}$$

Thus, these two age groups together (13.368) will more than suffice to fill the vacancies for supervisors. One hostess aged 41 will not be promoted. (Computations are carried out to three decimal places to avoid errors in summation. Of course, policies must be expressed in integral numbers of girls.)

In a similar fashion, we can compute the number of remaining hostesses and thus obtain the number of assistants to be promoted. Finally, we obtain the number of assistants remaining and deduce the number of recruits required by subtraction.

The results of the calculations are shown in Table 5. From the table, we see that the number of 21-year-old recruits should be 143 next year, and 168 the year after that. Next year girls aged 24 and over will be promoted to hostess, and 17 girls aged 23 will be promoted. In the year after that, promotion will be at age 23, and in addition 12 girls aged 22 will be promoted. Next year all but one of the girls aged 41 and over will be supervisors. In the year after that, all girls aged 40 and over and 3 girls aged 39 will be supervisors.

TABLE 5. NUMBER OF GIRLS IN SERVICE AT THE START OF EACH YEAR

x	Present year	Next year	Following year	x	Present year	Next year	Following year
21	90	143	168	41	6	7.656 §	7.357
22	50	54	85.8 *	42	5	5.712	7.289
23	30	40 †	43.2	43	4	4.735	5.409
24	20	24	32	44	5	3.768	4.460
25	10	16	19.2	45	3	4.68	3.527
26	40	8	12.8	46	3	2.79	4.352
27	35	34	6.8	47	3	2.769	2.575
28	35	30.625	29.75	48	6	2.745	2.534
29	30	31.5	27.563	49	2	5.436	2.487
30	28	27.75	26.363	50	—	1.792	4.871
31	26	26.6	26.363	51	—	—	1.586
32	20	24.908	25.483	52	4	—	—
33	18	19.24	23.961	53	3	3.44	—
34	16	17.37	18.567	54	5	2.538	2.910
35	12	15.472	16.797	55	—	4.155	2.109
36	10	11.616	14.977	56	3	—	3.386
37	8	9.68	11.244	57	2	2.394	—
38	—	7.744	9.370	58	—	1.56	1.867
39	8	7.72	7.473 ‡	59	2	—	1.187
40	8	7.688	7.419				
				Total	550	605.363	666.390

* 12 girls aged 22 will be promoted hostesses.
† 17 girls aged 23 will be promoted hostesses.
‡ 3 girls aged 39 will be promoted supervisors.
§ 6 girls aged 41 will be promoted supervisors.

	Present	Next	Following
Total required	550	605	666
Supervisors	50	55	61
Hostesses	300	330	363
Assistants	200	220	242

MISCELLANEOUS REPLACEMENT PROBLEMS

There are many replacement situations that cannot be classified as neatly as those in the examples so far. Apart from problems about capital equipment which deteriorates with age, the determination of replacement policies usually requires probability theory. We conclude this chapter with two general examples.

Example 8

A company manufactures automobile batteries at a factory cost of $10 each. Battery life is subject to mortality as in Table 6. The company has a guarantee policy under which, if a battery fails during the first month after purchase, a refund of the full price of a new battery is made; if it fails during the second month, a refund of 29/30 of the full price is given; during the third month, 28/30, and so on until the 30th month after purchase, at which time a refund of 1/30 of the full price is made. At what unit price should batteries be sold so that on average the company will break even? (Assume battery age is zero at time of purchase.)

TABLE 6. BATTERY LIFE MORTALITY

Age in months	Probability of failure in next month	Age in months	Probability of failure in next month
0	0.05	16	0.00
1	0.00	17	0.01
2	0.00	18	0.01
3	0.00	19	0.01
4	0.00	20	0.01
5	0.00	21	0.01
6	0.00	22	0.01
7	0.00	23	0.015
8	0.00	24	0.015
9	0.00	25	0.020
10	0.00	26	0.025
11	0.00	27	0.030
12	0.00	28	0.035
13	0.00	29	0.040
14	0.00	30 and over	0.71
15	0.00		
		Total	1.00

SOLUTION

Let K be the break-even price, and let p_i be the probability that a new battery will fail during the $i + 1$st month after purchase.

The average refund on batteries that fail will be

$$\sum_{i=0}^{29} \frac{30 - i}{30} Kp_i = 0.0908K$$

The break-even price K is the sum of the factory cost and the expected refund. Thus

$$K = 10 + 0.0908K$$

yielding $\qquad\qquad K = \$11.00$

Example 9

A certain piece of equipment is extremely difficult to adjust. During a period when no adjustment is made, the running cost increases

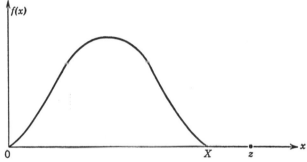

Figure 5.2. Density function for running cost after an adjustment (Range of x: 0 to X).

linearly with time, at a rate of b dollars per hour each hour. The running cost immediately after an adjustment is not known precisely until the adjustment has been made. Before the adjustment, the resulting running cost x is deemed to be a random variable x with density function $f(x)$, as shown in Figure 5.2. If each adjustment costs k dollars, when should adjustments be made?

SOLUTION

We assume a policy of making an adjustment every time the running cost reaches a certain rate z, and wish to determine that value of z for which the expectation of the average cost per hour over some long period of time is a minimum.

The optimal z will first be derived on the assumption that $z > X$, where X (see Figure 5.2) is the highest running cost that can result immediately after an adjustment.

Suppose that an adjustment has just been made at time $t = 0$, resulting in running costs at a rate x. The next adjustment will occur when running costs have climbed back to z, at time $t = (z - x)/b$. The total cost for this cycle from one adjustment to another will be the cost of an adjustment k, plus the integral from $t = 0$ to $t = (z - x)/b$ of the running cost $x + bt$. We obtain

$$(5.9) \qquad \text{Cost for this cycle} = k + \frac{z^2 - x^2}{2b}$$

The cost per hour for the cycle is the cycle cost divided by the cycle time $(z - x)/b$. We obtain

$$\text{Cost per hour for the cycle} = \frac{bk}{z - x} + \frac{z + x}{2}$$

The expected cost per hour for the cycle, which is seen to be the expected cost per hour for the time that this policy is in operation, will be our measure of effectiveness for the decision variable z. Denoting this expected cost per hour by $h(z)$, we have

$$(5.10) \qquad h(z) = \int_0^X f(x) \left[\frac{bk}{z - x} + \frac{z + x}{2} \right] dx$$

To minimize $h(z)$, we differentiate the right-hand side with respect to z, in the manner explained in Appendix II. The result is

$$\frac{dh}{dz} = \int_0^X f(x) \left[\frac{1}{2} - \frac{bk}{(z - x)^2} \right] dx = \frac{1}{2} - bk \int_0^X \frac{f(x)}{(z - x)^2} dx$$

$$= 0 \text{ for a minimum}$$

This condition on z can be rewritten as

$$(5.11) \qquad \int_0^X \frac{f(x)}{(z - x)^2} dx = \frac{1}{2kb}$$

The solution $z = z_0$ of this equation will be the best value for the decision variable z, at least in the range $z > X$.

We now show that the minimum cannot occur for $z < X$. If $z < X$, repeated adjustments may be necessary at time $t = 0$ before the cycle can begin. Consider the running cost x which results from the adjustment made just before $t = 0$: i.e. at the end of the previous cycle. The probability that no further adjustment is necessary at $t = 0$ is the same as the probability of the event $\{x < z\}$. If we use the notation

$$F(z) = \int_z^X f(x)\, dx$$

we have

$$P\,\{\text{no further adjustment at } t = 0\} = 1 - F(z)$$

Similarly, we observe that

$$P\,\{r \text{ further adjustments at } t = 0\} = [F(z)]^r[1 - F(z)]$$

Each such adjustment will cost k dollars. The expected cost of these further adjustments at $t = 0$ is

$$[1 - F(z)]\sum_{r=1}^{\infty} kr\,[F(z)]^r = \frac{k\,F(z)}{1 - F(z)}$$

Once all needed adjustments have been made, so that costs are running at a rate x, less than z, the remainder of the cycle cost will be as in (5.9). Adding (5.9) to the expected adjustment cost gives

$$\text{Cost for cycle} = \frac{k}{1 - F(z)} + \frac{z^2 - x^2}{2b}$$

The cycle time is still $[z - x]/b$; so we have

$$\text{Cost per hour for the cycle} = \frac{kb}{(z - x)[1 - F(z)]} + \frac{z + x}{2}$$

In calculating the expected cost per hour, the density used for x is no longer $f(x)$, but the conditional density $f(x\,|\,x < z) = [1 - F(z)]^{-1} f(x)$. Denoting as before the expected cost per hour by $h(z)$, we have

$$(5.12) \quad h(z) = \frac{kb}{[1 - F(z)]^2}\int_0^z \frac{f(x)}{z - x}\, dx + \frac{1}{2[1 - F(z)]}\int_0^z (z + x)\, f(x)$$

Inasmuch as z is definitely less than X in this calculation, $f(x)$ will exceed some fixed positive number in some neighborhood of z, at least for density functions of the type shown in Figure 5.2. The first integral in (5.12) is therefore of the order of $\displaystyle\int_0^z \frac{dx}{z - x}$, which is itself infinite. The interpretation is that the expected hourly cost $h(z)$ is infinite for any z chosen less than X. Since $h(z_0)$ as given by (5.11) and (5.10) is obviously finite, we conclude that the value z_0 previously obtained is the optimal value for the decision variable z.

PROBLEMS FOR SOLUTION

Set VII

1. (a) Machine A costs $9000. Annual operating costs are $200 for the first year, and they increase by $2000 every year (e.g. in the fourth year operating costs are $6200). Determine the best age at which to replace the machine. If the optimum replacement policy is followed, what will be the average yearly cost of owning and operating the machine? (Assume that the machine has no resale value when replaced, and that future costs are not discounted.)

(b) Machine B costs $10,000. Annual operating costs are $400 for the first year, and they increase by $800 every year. You now have a machine of type A which is one year old. Should you replace it with B, and if so, when?

(c) Suppose you are just ready to replace machine A with another machine of the same type, when you hear that machine B will become available in a year. What should you do?

2. Machine C costs $10,000. Operating costs are $500 per year for the first five years. In the sixth and succeeding years operating costs increase $100

TABLE 7. TRUCK TIRE MORTALITY

Age of tire at failure, miles	Percentage of tires
0	0
0– 1,000	0
1,001– 2,000	0
.	.
.	.
.	.
9,001–10,000	0
10,001–11,000	0.010
11,001–12,000	0.010
12,001–13,000	0.015
13,001–14,000	0.020
14,001–15,000	0.027
15,001–16,000	0.036
16,001–17,000	0.040
17,001–18,000	0.060
18,001–19,000	0.090
19,001–20,000	0.130
20,001–21,000	0.180
21,001–22,000	0.165
22,001–23,000	0.125
23,001–24,000	0.080
24,001–25,000	0.012
	1.000

each year. Assuming a 10% cost of money per year, find the optimum length of time to hold the machine before replacing it.

3. Truck tires which fail in service can cause expensive accidents. It is estimated that a failure in service results in an average cost of $250, exclusive of the cost of replacing the blown tire. New tires cost $100 each, and are subject to mortality as in Table 7. If the measure of effectiveness for a replacement policy is the average cost per mile, and if tires are to be replaced after a certain fixed mileage or on failure (whichever occurs first), determine the optimum replacement policy.

[*Hint:* Assume that failures take place at the exact ages 10,500; 11,500; 12,500; etc. Compute average useful life per tire for various replacement ages, and the expected cost of failures for various replacement ages.]

[*Ans.* Replace at 15,000 miles; average cost 0.812 cent per mile]

4. The following failure rates have been observed for a certain type of light bulb.

End of week	Probability of failure to date
1	0.05
2	0.13
3	0.25
4	0.43
5	0.68
6	0.88
7	0.96
8	1.00

The cost of replacing an individual failed bulb is $1.25. The decision is made to replace all bulbs simultaneously at fixed intervals, and also to replace individual bulbs as they fail in service. If the cost of group replacement is 30 cents per bulb, what is the best interval between group replacements? At what group replacement price per bulb would a policy of strictly individual replacement become preferable to the adopted policy?

5. A computing machine has a large number of electronic tubes, each of which has a life normally distributed about a mean of 1200 hours with a standard deviation of 150 hours. If all tubes were to be replaced at fixed intervals on the night shift (when the computer is not normally used), the only costs would be the costs of labor and parts, which average about $3.00 a tube. Replacement of individual tubes which fail in service costs about $8.00 for labor and parts, plus the cost of computer down time which runs about $80.00 for an average tube failure. How frequently should all tubes be replaced? [*Hint:* The average working life of a tube is 1200/16, or 75 days. Consider the costs of policies involving group replacement at the end of 50 days, at the end of 55 days, etc.]

6. At time zero, all items in a certain system are new. Each item has a probability p of failing immediately before the end of the first month of life, and a probability $q = 1 - p$ of failing immediately before the end of the second month (i.e. all items fail by the end of the second month). If all items are replaced as they fail, show that the expected number of failures $f(x)$ at the

end of month x is given by

$$f(x) = \frac{N}{1 + q}\left[1 - (-q)^{x+1}\right]$$

where N is the number of items in the system.

If the cost per item of individual replacements is C_1, and the cost per item of group replacement is C_2, find the conditions under which

(a) A group replacement policy at the end of each month is the most profitable.

(b) A group replacement policy at the end of every other month is the most profitable.

(c) No group replacement policy is better than a policy of pure individual replacement.

7. A piece of equipment either can fail completely, so that it has to be scrapped (no salvage value), or may suffer a minor defect which can be repaired. The probability that it will not have to be scrapped before age t is $f(t)$. The conditional probability that it will need a repair in the interval t to $t+dt$, given that it is in running order at age t, is $r(t)\,dt$. The probability of a repair or complete failure is dependent only on the age of the equipment, and not on the previous repair history.

Each repair costs C, and complete replacement costs K. For some considerable time the policy has been to replace only on failure.

(a) Derive a formula for the expected cost per unit time of the present policy of replacing only on failure.

(b) It has been suggested that it might be cheaper to scrap equipment at some fixed age T, thus avoiding the higher risk of repairs with advancing age. Show that the expected cost per unit time of such a policy is

$$\frac{C\int_0^T f(u)\,r(u)\,du + K}{\int_0^T f(u)\,du}$$

(c) By differentiating this expression, find a condition to be satisfied by T for minimum cost.

REFERENCES

Churchman, C. W., R. L. Ackoff, and E. L. Arnoff, *Introduction to Operations Research*, John Wiley & Sons, New York, 1957.

Feller, William, *An Introduction to Probability Theory and Its Applications*, Vol. 1, 2nd ed., Chapters 11 through 13, John Wiley & Sons, New York, 1957.

Terborgh, B., *Dynamic Equipment Policy*, McGraw-Hill Book Co., New York, 1949.

SIX

Waiting lines

Decision situations frequently arise in which units arriving for service must wait before they can be serviced. If the laws governing arrivals, servicing times, and the order in which arriving units are taken into service are known, then the nature of this waiting situation can be studied and analyzed mathematically. In this chapter we present some of the more elementary theory of waiting lines and some simple applications.

Arriving units may form one line and be serviced through only one station, as in a doctor's office; they may form one line and be serviced through several stations, as in a barber shop; or they may form several lines and be served through as many stations, as at the checkout counters of a supermarket. In this chapter we assume only one kind of queue discipline: first-in, first-out; with a unit going into service at the moment a station becomes empty.

A general assumption running through the chapter is that the waiting-line process will eventually become "stable," in the sense that the probability that n units are waiting at any instant remains the same as time passes. We shall not treat the transient case (a waiting line whose corresponding probabilities have not yet settled down to their stable values) or the explosive case (a waiting line that increases indefinitely with time).

The various properties of a waiting line, such as the number in line at any instant or the waiting time experienced by a particular arrival, are random variables in the sense of Chapter Two. The reason that these variables are random, rather than functionally dependent on time, is that arrivals are, in general, random events in time, and service times are random variables as well. Thus we shall be concerned with estimating only the *average* length of the line at any instant, the *average* idle time of the service facility in a 24-hour period, and so on.

When confronted with a problem involving waiting lines and the costs arising from them, the decision maker would use his knowledge of the average characteristics of the queue in attempting to reduce costs, maximize output, or whatever. Some of the changes he might recommend are: changing the number of servicing stations, changing the average service time in one or more stations, splitting a single queue or amalgamating several queues, and so on. Such changes would be evaluated by first considering their effect on the average characteristics of the waiting line, and then translating these changes in average characteristics into changes in the chosen measure of effectiveness.

POISSON ARRIVALS AND EXPONENTIAL SERVICE TIMES

In this section, we discuss a class of waiting-line situations that lend themselves to a relatively simple analytic treatment. Although the assumptions are fairly restrictive, the results apply to some situations met with in practice. In any case, the mode of approach described here should prove useful as an indication of an attack on more complicated queueing problems.

Arrivals and Services Considered Separately

In general, arrivals do not occur at regular intervals in time, but tend to be clustered or scattered in some fashion. The "Poisson assumption" specifies the behavior of arrivals, by postulating the existence of a constant λ, which is independent of time, queue length, or any other random property of the queue, such that

(6.1) $P\{\text{an arrival occurs between time } t \text{ and time } t+\Delta t\} = \lambda \, \Delta t$

if the interval Δt is sufficiently small. A waiting line for which arrivals occur in accordance with (6.1) is called a queue with *Poisson arrivals*. This terminology may seem surprising, but is justified by the following result.* Let n be a discrete random variable representing

---

* For a proof, see William Feller, *Probability Theory and Its Applications*, 2nd ed., p. 400 et seq., John Wiley & Sons, New York, 1957.

the number of arrivals in some time interval of fixed length T. Then, if equation (6.1) is satisfied, n obeys a Poisson distribution with parameter λT:

(6.2) $\qquad f_T(n) = P\{n \text{ arrivals in time } T\} = \dfrac{(\lambda T)^n e^{-\lambda T}}{n!}$

A further consequence is that if T is a random variable representing the time between consecutive arrivals, then T obeys an exponential distribution with parameter λ:

(6.3) $\qquad g(T) = \text{density function for } T = \lambda e^{-\lambda T}$

Actually, any or all of the relations (6.1), (6.2), and (6.3) may be taken as characterizing Poisson-type arrivals, since it is possible to prove any one of the relations starting with any other.

The *mean arrival rate* in a waiting-line situation is defined, as might be anticipated, as the expected number of arrivals occurring in a time interval of length unity. If arrivals are Poisson, we see from equation (6.2) that the expected number of arrivals in a time interval of length T is λT. Setting $T = 1$, it follows that the mean arrival rate for Poisson arrivals is just λ. The mean arrival rate λ is a dimensional number, whose units are arrivals per time unit.

The expected time between consecutive arrivals is just the mean of the random variable T whose density function is given by (6.3). This mean time between arrivals is easily computed to be $1/\lambda$. (Note: the reciprocal relation between the mean arrival rate and the mean time between arrivals is one of the implications of the Poisson assumption for arrivals, and may not hold true for other arrival distributions.)

Discussion of the properties of the servicing facility is complicated somewhat by the fact that servicing can take place only when there is a unit in the system requiring service. This explains the conditioning event in the following assumption. The statement (6.4) is analogous to (6.1) and is assumed to hold for each servicing station:

(6.4) $\quad P\{$a serviced unit is turned out in the interval t

$\qquad$ to $t+\Delta t$ given that a unit is being serviced at time $t\} = \mu \Delta t$

where μ is some constant. Here it is assumed that the constant of proportionality μ is independent of time, of queue length, and of any other random characteristic of the waiting-line system. It can be shown that, if the output of serviced units obeys (6.4), then servicing time is subject to the exponential distribution. More precisely, if s is a random variable representing the time it takes the station to complete service on a unit, then

$$(6.5) \qquad g(s) = \text{density function of } s = \mu e^{-\mu s}$$

The *mean servicing rate* for a particular station is defined as the conditional expectation of the number of services completed in one time unit, given that servicing is going on throughout the entire time unit. If servicing times are exponential, it turns out that the mean servicing rate is μ, which thus has dimensions of services per time unit. Roughly, μ may be regarded as the quotient of the output of the servicing station over some long time interval, divided by the portion of the time interval that the servicing station is actually in operation. The *mean servicing time* has the obvious interpretation as the mean of the random variable s mentioned above; for exponential service times, we find from (6.5) that the mean service time is $1/\mu$.

To complete the analogy between Poisson arrivals and exponential service times, we note that, if n is the number of *potential* services in time T, i.e., the number of units the servicing station could turn out in time T if there were no enforced idle time, then n obeys a Poisson distribution with parameter μT:

$$(6.6) \qquad \phi_T(n) = P\{n \text{ services in time } T \text{ given that servicing is going on throughout } T\}$$

$$= \frac{(\mu T)^n e^{-\mu T}}{n!}$$

As with Poisson arrivals, the relations (6.4), (6.5), and (6.6) are all equivalent.

The Basic Equations Governing the Queue

In this subsection, we show how the assumptions concerning arrivals, service times, queue discipline, and stability in time may be combined to furnish information concerning the total behavior of the waiting-line system. This information will take the form of a set of recursion relations which lead directly to the probability distribution for the random variable n, where n is the number of units in the system at any specified instant after stability has been achieved.

The recursion relations stated below apply to the general case of k servicing stations, each with mean service rate μ. These k stations are fed from one queue, with mean arrival rate λ. Though the proof for general k is not given here, the proof offered later for two servicing stations will illustrate the main ideas.

Let

n = number in system (number in queue plus number being serviced)

P_n = probability that there are n units in the system at time t (or at any other time)

k = number of servicing stations

The P_i may be calculated successively in terms of P_0 by

$$P_1 = \frac{\lambda}{\mu} P_0$$

(6.7) $\quad P_n = \dfrac{\lambda + (n-1)\mu}{n\mu} P_{n-1} - \dfrac{\lambda}{n\mu} P_{n-2} \qquad n = 2, 3, \cdots, k$

$$P_n = \frac{\lambda + k\mu}{k\mu} P_{n-1} - \frac{\lambda}{k\mu} P_{n-2} \qquad n \geq k+1$$

The evaluation of P_0 itself, once the P_n have all been expressed in terms of P_0, is accomplished by use of the relation

(6.8) $$\sum_{n=0}^{\infty} P_n = 1$$

We derive the governing equations for the special case $k = 2$, for which equations (6.7) specialize to

$$P_1 = \frac{\lambda}{\mu} P_0$$

(6.9) $\qquad P_2 = \dfrac{\lambda + \mu}{2\mu} P_1 - \dfrac{\lambda}{2\mu} P_0$

$$P_n = \frac{\lambda + 2\mu}{2\mu} P_{n-1} - \frac{\lambda}{2\mu} P_{n-2} \qquad n \geq 3$$

A diagram of the waiting-line system is presented as Figure 6.1. At the instant pictured, there are 3 units in the queue and 5 units in

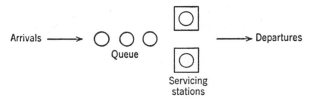

Figure 6.1.   A queue with two servicing stations.

the system. We assume, as usual, that queue discipline is such that an arrival moves immediately into a servicing station if there is a station vacant.

In this situation we note that the probability of an arrival in a small time interval of length Δt is $\lambda \Delta t$. The probability of a serviced unit being turned out in the interval $(t,\ t+\Delta t)$ is:

0   if there are no units in the system at t.

$\mu \Delta t$ if there is one unit in the system at t.

$2\mu \Delta t$ if there are two or more units in the system at t.

The probabilities of more than one arrival in the interval Δt, of more than one service, or of an arrival and a service both occurring in this interval are all taken to be zero, since they are proportional to the second-order small quantity $(\Delta t)^2$.

The following two events I_0 and II_0 are equivalent, since event II_0 is simply a listing of all the ways event I_0 can occur:

Event I_0:   {0 units in system at time $t+\Delta t$}.

Event II_0:   {0 units at time t, no arrivals in Δt}
                + {1 unit at time t, 1 service in Δt}.

Since the events are equivalent, the probability of occurrence of both events must be the same. Thus

$$P\{\text{event } I_0\} = P_0 = P\{\text{event } II_0\} = P_0(1 - \lambda\ \Delta t) + P_1\mu\ \Delta t$$

Then

$$P_0 = P_0(1 - \lambda\ \Delta t) + P_1\mu\ \Delta t$$

which reduces to

$$P_1 = \frac{\lambda}{\mu} P_0$$

This proves the first equation of (6.9).

To obtain the second equation of (6.9), we apply the same procedure to the events I_1 and II_1:

Event I_1:   {1 unit in system at time $t+\Delta t$}.

Event II_1:   {1 unit at t, no arrivals or services in Δt}
                + {0 units at t, 1 arrival in Δt}
                + {2 units at t, 1 service in Δt}.

This leads to

$$P_1 = P_1\{1 - (\lambda + \mu)\ \Delta t\} + P_0\lambda\ \Delta t + P_2(2\mu)\ \Delta t$$

and hence

$$P_2 = \frac{\lambda + \mu}{2\mu} P_1 - \frac{\lambda}{2\mu} P_0$$

which is the second equation of (6.9).

For the events I_r and II_r with $r \geq 2$, the over-all service rate is seen to be 2μ for all the subevents of II_r:

Event I_r: {r units in system at time $t + \Delta t$}.
Event II_r: {r units at t, no arrivals or services in Δt}
+ {$r-1$ units at t, 1 arrival in Δt}
+ {$r+1$ units at t, 1 service in Δt}.

Then

$$P_r = P_r\{1 - (\lambda + 2\mu) \Delta t\} + P_{r-1}\lambda \Delta t + P_{r+1}(2\mu) \Delta t$$

and

$$P_{r+1} = \frac{\lambda + 2\mu}{2\mu} P_r - \frac{\lambda}{2\mu} P_{r-1} \qquad r \geq 2$$

The substitution $n = r + 1$ yields the final equation of (6.9).

Once the P_n are determined, the various characteristics of the waiting-line system such as average queue length, idle time of the service facility, etc., are readily computed by the probability methods of Chapter Two. The following subsections are devoted to examples illustrating the way the technique works out in practice.

Queues: One Servicing Station

For the case of one servicing station, Poisson arrivals with mean arrival rate λ, and exponential service times with mean service rate μ, the governing equations (6.7) specialize to

$$P_1 = \frac{\lambda}{\mu} P_0$$

(6.10)

$$P_n = \frac{\lambda + \mu}{\mu} P_{n-1} - \frac{\lambda}{\mu} P_{n-2} \qquad n \geq 2$$

An easy induction shows that

$$P_n = \left(\frac{\lambda}{\mu}\right)^n P_0 \qquad n \geq 0$$

and the use of the condition

$$\sum_{n=0}^{\infty} P_n = 1$$

then yields

(6.11) $$P_n = \left(1 - \frac{\lambda}{\mu}\right)\left(\frac{\lambda}{\mu}\right)^n \qquad n \geq 0$$

Equation (6.11) is valid only when the mean service rate μ exceeds the mean arrival rate λ.

For the applications, we need the distribution of such random variables as the waiting time of an arrival before being taken into service (we shall call this random variable w) and the total time of an arrival in the system (denoted by v; $v = w$ plus service time).

Inasmuch as there is a positive probability $1 - (\lambda/\mu) = P_0$ that an arrival will not have to wait at all before going into service, the distribution for w is part discrete (at $w = 0$) and part continuous (for $w > 0$). If $\psi(w)\,dw$ is the probability of the event $\{w < \text{waiting time} < w + dw\}$, the resulting distribution for w is

$$P\{w=0\} = 1 - \frac{\lambda}{\mu}$$

(6.12)

$$\psi(w)\,dw = \left(1 - \frac{\lambda}{\mu}\right)\lambda e^{(\lambda-\mu)w}\,dw \qquad w > 0$$

Note that $\displaystyle\int_0^\infty \psi(w)\,dw$ has the value λ/μ and not unity, inasmuch as the event $\{w > 0\}$ is not a certain event.

The proof of (6.12) relies on the fact that the event {waiting time of an arrival is between w and $w+dw$} is the composition, for n ranging from 1 to ∞, of the events $\{n$ in system just before the arrival, $n - 1$ services in the time interval w, 1 service in time $dw\}$. The reader can fill in the details of the proof, using equations (6.4), (6.6), and (6.11).

If we are interested in the conditional density function for waiting time, given that a person has to wait, we divide $\psi(w)$ by $P\{w > 0\}$, and obtain

(6.13) $$\psi(w\,|\,w > 0) = (\mu - \lambda)e^{(\lambda-\mu)w} *$$

---

* The interpretation of the conditional density function $\psi(w\,|\,w > 0)$ is as follows. By definition, $\psi(w\,|\,w > 0)\,dw$ is the conditional probability of the event "waiting time is between w and $w+dw$," given the event "waiting time is greater than zero." The conditional mean $E(w\,|\,w > 0)$ is defined as the mean of the random variable w with density function $\psi(w\,|\,w > 0)$. The definitions of conditional distribution and conditional mean for a discrete random variable are analogous.

(Here

$$\int_0^\infty \psi(w|w > 0)\, dw = 1$$

since $P\{w > 0 | w > 0\} = 1$.)

The density function $\theta(v)$ for the total time an arrival spends in the system (waiting time plus service time) may be calculated in a similar fashion, and turns out to be identical with (6.13), viz.:

(6.14) $$\theta(v) = (\mu - \lambda)e^{(\lambda-\mu)v}$$

From (6.11), (6.12), (6.13), and (6.14) we may readily compute the expectations of the various random variables. The results are listed below.

(6.15) $$E(m) = \frac{\lambda^2}{\mu(\mu - \lambda)}$$ average queue length

(6.16) $$E(m|m > 0) = \frac{\mu}{\mu - \lambda}$$ average length of non-empty queues

(6.17) $$E(n) = \frac{\lambda}{\mu - \lambda}$$ average number of units in system

(6.18) $$E(w) = \frac{\lambda}{\mu(\mu - \lambda)}$$ average waiting time of an arrival

(6.19) $$E(w|w > 0) = \frac{1}{\mu - \lambda}$$ average waiting time of an arrival who waits

(6.20) $$E(v) = \frac{1}{\mu - \lambda}$$ average time an arrival spends in the system

Example 1

Arrivals at a telephone booth are considered to be Poisson, with an average time of 10 minutes between one arrival and the next. The length of a phone call is assumed to be distributed exponentially, with mean 3 minutes.

(a) What is the probability that a person arriving at the booth will have to wait?

(b) What is the average length of the queues that form from time to time?

(c) The telephone company will install a second booth when convinced that an arrival would expect to have to wait at least three minutes for the phone. By how much must the flow of arrivals be increased in order to justify a second booth?

SOLUTION

Here $\qquad\lambda = 0.1$ arrival per minute

$$\mu = 0.33 \text{ service per minute}$$

(a) $\qquad P\{\text{an arrival has to wait}\} = 1 - P_0$

$$= \lambda/\mu, \qquad \text{by (6.11)}$$

$$= 0.1/0.33 = 0.3$$

(b) $\qquad E(m \mid m > 0) = \dfrac{\mu}{\mu - \lambda} \qquad \text{by (6.16)}$

$$= \dfrac{0.33}{0.23} = 1.43 \text{ persons}$$

(c) $\qquad E(w) = \dfrac{\lambda}{\mu(\mu - \lambda)} \qquad \text{by (6.18)}$

$$= \dfrac{\lambda}{0.33(0.33 - \lambda)} \qquad \text{if we fix } \mu \text{ at } 0.33$$

We seek the new value λ' for which $E(w) = 3$ minutes. Solving the equation

$$3 = \dfrac{\lambda'}{0.33(0.33 - \lambda')}$$

we obtain an answer of $\lambda' = 0.16$ arrival per minute. So we must increase the flow of arrivals from 6 per hour, the present figure, to 10 per hour.

Example 2

As in Example 1, we have a telephone booth with Poisson arrivals spaced 10 minutes apart on the average, and exponential call lengths averaging 3 minutes.

(a) What is the probability that an arrival will have to wait more than 10 minutes before the phone is free?

(b) What is the probability that it will take him more than 10 minutes altogether to wait for the phone and complete his call?

(c) Estimate the fraction of a day that the phone will be in use.

SOLUTION

(a) Again, we have $\lambda = 0.1$ arrival per minute

$\mu = 0.33$ service per minute

$$P\{\text{waiting time} \geq 10\} = \int_{10}^{\infty}\left(1 - \frac{\lambda}{\mu}\right)\lambda e^{(\lambda-\mu)w}dw$$

from equation (6.12),

$$= \frac{\lambda}{\mu}e^{(\lambda-\mu)w}\Big]_{\infty}^{10} = 0.3e^{-2.3} = 0.03$$

(b) $P\{\text{time in system} \geq 10\} = \int_{10}^{\infty}(\mu - \lambda)e^{(\lambda-\mu)v}\,dv$

from equation (6.14)

$$= e^{10(\lambda-\mu)} = e^{-2.3} = 0.10$$

(c) The expected fraction of a day that the phone will be in use is seen to be the same as the expected fraction of any other time interval that the phone will be in use. In particular, it is the same as the expected fraction of a small time interval Δt that the phone will be in use, which is the same as the probability that the booth is occupied at a random instant. Thus the answer is $P\{n > 0\} = 1 - P_0 = \lambda/\mu = 0.3$.

Example 3

A repairman is to be hired to repair machines which break down at an average rate of three per hour. Breakdowns are distributed in time in a manner that may be regarded as Poisson. Non-productive time on any one machine is considered to cost the company $5 per hour. The company has narrowed the choice down to two repairmen, one slow but cheap, the other fast but expensive. The slow cheap repairman asks $3 per hour; in return, he will service broken-down machines exponentially at an average rate of four per hour. The fast expensive repairman demands $5 an hour, and will repair machines exponentially at an average rate of six per hour. Which repairman should be hired?

SOLUTION

We shall calculate the total expected cost for an 8-hour day for each repairman, and shall choose that repairman for which the total expected cost is least.

First, consider the slow cheap repairman. His salary for the day represents a $24 cost to the company. To compute the cost of non-productive time, we note that broken-down machines may be regarded as forming a queue, and the single repairman (whichever is chosen) as a single servicing station. The expected non-productive time in an 8-hour day is

$$8 \frac{\lambda}{\mu - \lambda}$$

from (6.17)

$$= 8 \frac{3}{4 - 3} = 24 \text{ machine-hours}$$

Then the expected cost of non-productive time is \$120; and the total expected cost with the slow cheap repairman is \$144.

For the fast expensive repairman, salary cost is \$40. Non-productive time cost is estimated as

$$8 \cdot \frac{3}{6 - 3} \cdot \$5 = \$40$$

So the total expected cost with the fast expensive repairman is \$40 + \$40 = \$80.

We hire the fast expensive repairman.

Example 4

A shipping company has a single unloading berth with ships arriving in a Poisson fashion at an average rate of three per day. The unloading time distribution for a ship with n unloading crews is found to be exponential with average unloading time $1/2n$ days. The company has a large labor supply without regular working hours, and to avoid long waiting lines the company has a policy of using as many unloading crews on a ship as there are ships waiting in line or being unloaded. (a) Under these conditions what will be the average number of unloading crews working at any time? (b) What is the probability that more than 4 crews will be needed?

SOLUTION

Let n = number of ships in the system at any specified instant (waiting in line or being unloaded). Then the mean servicing rate, for a ship entering service at a time when there are n ships in the system, is $2n$ ships per day. Since the mean servicing rate is not constant in this problem, we cannot use the formulas for P_n, $E(w)$, etc., given in the text. Instead, we obtain the governing equations for the statistical steady state:

$$P_1 = \frac{\lambda}{\mu} P_0$$

$$P_n = \frac{\lambda + (n-1)\mu}{n\mu} P_{n-1} - \frac{\lambda}{n\mu} P_{n-2} \qquad n \geq 2$$

(Here $\lambda = 3$ ships per day; $\mu =$ mean service rate with one unloading crew $= 2$ ships per day.) By induction we find

$$P_n = \frac{1}{n!} \left(\frac{\lambda}{\mu}\right)^n e^{-\lambda/\mu} \qquad n \geq 0$$

Then the expected number of crews working at any specified instant is

$$E(n) = \sum_{n=0}^{\infty} nP_n = \frac{\lambda}{\mu} = 1.5 \text{ crews}$$

The probability that a ship entering service will require more than four crews is the same as the probability that there are at least five ships in the system at any specified instant, given by

$$\sum_{n=5}^{\infty} P_n = 1 - P_0 - P_1 - P_2 - P_3 - P_4 = 0.019$$

Queues: Several Servicing Stations

In this subsection, we give properties and examples for k servicing stations, each with mean service rate μ, fed by a queue built up of arrivals with mean arrival rate λ. The governing equations (6.7) yield immediately the following expressions for the P_n in terms of P_0:

(6.21)

$$P_n = \frac{1}{n!} \left(\frac{\lambda}{\mu}\right)^n P_0 \qquad n = 0, 1, 2, \cdots, k-1$$

$$P_n = \frac{1}{k!k^{n-k}} \left(\frac{\lambda}{\mu}\right)^n P_0 \qquad n \geq k$$

The sequence P_n is seen to be composed of two dissimilar parts (if $k > 1$); and the resulting expression for P_0 is not simple. For this reason, it will be convenient to state queue properties in terms of P_0 as well as λ, μ, and k. In specific numerical examples, where it is usually necessary to evaluate P_0, the following expression for P_0 may be used:

$$(6.22) \qquad P_0 = \cfrac{1}{\left[\displaystyle\sum_{n=0}^{k-1} \frac{1}{n!}\left(\frac{\lambda}{\mu}\right)^n\right] + \frac{1}{k!}\left(\frac{\lambda}{\mu}\right)^k \frac{k\mu}{k\mu - \lambda}}$$

which is valid if $k\mu > \lambda$. (If $k\mu \leq \lambda$, none of the results of this section are applicable, since in that case the queue builds up indefinitely, and stability in time is never achieved.)

We recall that, for the case $k = 1$, the probability that an arrival has to wait for service is λ/μ. For the general case of k servicing stations, the probability that an arrival has to wait is just the probability that at any specified instant there are at least k units in the system. From (6.21) we may compute this probability:

$$(6.23) \qquad P\{n \geqq k\} = \sum_{n=k}^{\infty} P_n = \frac{\mu(\lambda/\mu)^k}{(k-1)!(k\mu - \lambda)} P_0$$

The formulas for average queue length, average number of units in the system, average waiting time for service, and average time in the system are listed below without proof.*

$$(6.24) \quad E(m) = \frac{\lambda\mu(\lambda/\mu)^k}{(k-1)!(k\mu - \lambda)^2} P_0 \qquad\qquad \text{average queue length}$$

$$(6.25) \quad E(n) = \frac{\lambda\mu(\lambda/\mu)^k}{(k-1)!(k\mu - \lambda)^2} P_0 + \frac{\lambda}{\mu} \qquad \begin{array}{l}\text{average number of}\\ \text{units in system}\end{array}$$

$$(6.26) \quad E(w) = \frac{\mu(\lambda/\mu)^k}{(k-1)!(k\mu - \lambda)^2} P_0 \qquad\qquad \begin{array}{l}\text{average waiting time}\\ \text{of an arrival}\end{array}$$

$$(6.27) \quad E(v) = \frac{\mu(\lambda/\mu)^k}{(k-1)!(k\mu - \lambda)^2} P_0 + \frac{1}{\mu} \qquad \begin{array}{l}\text{average time an arrival}\\ \text{spends in the system}\end{array}$$

Example 5

An insurance company has three claims adjusters in its branch office. People with claims against the company are found to arrive in a Poisson

---

*The derivation of these formulas is more complicated than the analogous formulas for the case $k = 1$. For the mode of proof, see Philip M. Morse, *Queues, Inventories, and Maintenance*, John Wiley & Sons, New York, 1958.

fashion, at an average rate of 20 per 8-hour day. The amount of time that an adjuster spends with a claimant is found to have an exponential distribution, with mean service time 40 minutes. Claimants are processed in the order of their appearance.

(*a*) How many hours a week can an adjuster expect to spend with claimants?

(*b*) How much time, on the average, does a claimant spend in the branch office?

SOLUTION

(*a*) Here $\qquad \lambda = \dfrac{5}{2}$ arrivals per hour

$$\mu = \dfrac{3}{2} \text{ services per hour for each adjuster}$$

$$P_0 = \cfrac{1}{1 + \dfrac{5}{3} + \dfrac{1}{2}\left(\dfrac{5}{3}\right)^2 + \dfrac{1}{6}\left(\dfrac{5}{3}\right)^3 \dfrac{\frac{9}{2}}{\frac{4}{2}}}$$

$$= \dfrac{24}{139}$$

The expected number of idle adjusters, at any specified instant, is

$$3P_0 + 2P_1 + 1P_2 = 3\left(\dfrac{24}{139}\right) + 2\left(\dfrac{40}{139}\right)$$

$$+ 1\left(\dfrac{100}{3 \times 139}\right) = \dfrac{4}{3} \text{ adjusters}$$

Then the probability that any one adjuster will be idle at any specified time is 4/9; and the expected weekly time an adjuster spends with claimants is $(5/9)40 = 22.2$ hours. Note that the same answer would be obtained, in a simpler though less instructive fashion, if we divided the expected number of servicing minutes per week (4000) by the number of adjusters (3).

(*b*) The average time an arrival spends in the system is found from (6.27) to be 49.0 minutes.

Example 6

A steel company, which operates its own fleet of ships to import iron ore, is considering the construction of port facilities to support a new plant. Both the number of unloading berths and the type of installation in each berth must be decided—on the basis of minimizing total unloading costs.

A maximum of three berths can be built; and it is required that the same type of unloading installation be in each berth that is built. The choice of unloading installation lies among type A, type B, and type C, for which the following information is available:

Installation type	Fixed cost per day	Operating cost per day	Capacity: average tonnage unloaded per day of operation
A	$ 840	$ 840	3600 tons
B	1350	1350	5800 tons
C	1500	1600	6400 tons

Fixed costs include such items as the amortization of the original cost of the installation over its expected life, general maintenance, etc.; they apply to all days, whether the equipment is used or not. Operating costs are incurred only during the time intervals that the unloading equipment is actually in use.

Ships to be unloaded each carry 8000 tons of ore, and are considered to arrive in a Poisson fashion throughout the year with a mean arrival rate of five ships a week. Service times for a given type of installation are considered to be exponential, with mean service rate corresponding to the average capacity column in the table.

If time spent in the unloading system (waiting time plus unloading time) is considered to cost the company $2000 per ship per day, what type of unloading installation should be chosen, and how many berths should be constructed?

SOLUTION

There are nine possible policies, each involving a choice among installation types (A, B, or C) and number of berths (1, 2, or 3). The combination (A, 1) can be discarded immediately, since the mean arrival rate is $5/7 = 0.714$ ship per day while the mean service rate with the combination (A, 1) is $3600/8000 = 0.450$ ship per day. The other eight combinations are all feasible, because they all result in a mean service rate greater than the mean arrival rate and hence in a steady state with a finite expected queue.

The arrival rate λ for each of the eight policies remains constant at 0.714 ship per day. The service rate for a single berth will depend only on the type of unloading installation, viz.:

$$\mu_A = 0.450 \text{ ship per day}$$

$$\mu_B = 0.725 \text{ ship per day}$$

$$\mu_C = 0.800 \text{ ship per day}$$

We wish to compute the total expected cost per day for each policy. This will be the sum of three component costs:

1. the fixed cost of the installations.
2. the operating cost of the installations.
3. the cost of ship holding time.

The fixed cost (per day) for the various policies is computed from the second column of the above table:

Number of berths

		1	2	3
	A	—	1680	2520
Installation type	B	1350	2700	4050
	C	1500	3000	4500

(Fixed cost per day)

The operating cost per day for the various policies may be obtained by first computing the fraction of the time a berth must stay in operation in order to preserve a steady-state balance on the average between arrivals and services. Thus, for the policy $(A, 2)$, we have a system mean service rate of 0.900 ship per day; then the fraction of time that an individual berth will be in operation (called the "system utilization factor") is $\lambda/0.900 = 0.714/0.900 = 0.793$. Similar results for all the feasible policies are listed below.

	1	2	3
A	—	0.793	0.529
B	0.985	0.493	0.328
C	0.892	0.448	0.297

(System utilization factor)

The operating cost for the various policies is then given by:

(Number of berths) × (system utilization factor)

× (operating cost per day for one berth)

So we obtain

	1	2	3	
A	—	1332	1332	
B	1330	1330	1330	(Operating cost per day)
C	1427	1427	1427	

In order to obtain $E(w)$, the average amount of time a ship spends in the unloading system, we use equation (6.27) but must first compute the eight values of P_0 associated with the various policies. Results for P_0, obtained from equation (6.22), are:

	1	2	3	
A	—	0.115	0.190	
B	0.015	0.340	0.369	(Values of P_0)
C	0.108	0.383	0.406	

From these, we compute the various values of $E(w)$:

	1	2	3	
A	—	5.96	2.48	
B	90.90	1.82	1.43	(Values of $E(w)$, days)
C	11.60	1.56	1.29	

Multiplying by λ (the expected number of ships per day) and then by $2000 (ship holding cost for one day), we get

	1	2	3	
A	—	8511	3541	
B	129,805	2599	2042	(Ship holding cost per day)
C	16,565	2228	1842	

Adding the corresponding fixed costs per day, operating costs per day, and ship holding costs per day, we obtain the following total expected costs per day for the various policies:

	1	2	3	
A	—	11,523	7393	
B	132,485	6,629	7422	(Total unloading cost per day, $)
C	19,492	6,655	7769	

Conclusion: Build two berths, and equip them with installation type B.

POISSON ARRIVALS AND ERLANG SERVICE TIMES

In this section, we retain the assumption of Poisson arrivals, but broaden the family of service time distributions to a new family, which will include as special cases both the exponential distribution and the situation where service time is constant. Because of the complexity of the analysis, the discussion of this section will be confined to the case of a single servicing station.

The Erlang Family of Service Time Distributions

The exponential assumption for service times, as specified by (6.5), gives only a one-parameter family (the parameter is μ) of possible service time distributions. This assumption is found to be unduly restrictive, partly because the exponential distribution has the property that larger service times are inherently less probable than smaller service times. A two-parameter generalization of the exponential family, called the *Erlang * family* of service time distributions, is highly useful in waiting-line applications. The Erlang family $g(t; \mu, k)$ is defined by

$$g(t; \mu, 1) = C_1 e^{-\mu t}$$

$$g(t; \mu, 2) = C_2 t e^{-2\mu t}$$

(6.28)
$$g(t; \mu, 3) = C_3 t^2 e^{-3\mu t}$$

and generally

$$g(t; \mu, k) = C_k t^{k-1} e^{-k\mu t}$$

Since each member of the family is a probability density function on the range $0 \leq t < \infty$, the constants C_k are assigned so that the integral

* Named for A. K. Erlang, who did pioneer work in the field of stochastic processes in the early part of the century.

of the corresponding function over this range is unity. Values of the C_k are:

$$C_1 = \mu$$

$$C_2 = 4\mu^2$$

(6.29)
$$C_3 = \frac{27}{2}\mu^3$$

and generally

$$C_k = \frac{(\mu k)^k}{(k-1)!}$$

The Erlang family has many interesting properties. The members all share the common mean $1/\mu$. The mode is at $t = 0$ for $k = 1$; it is at $t = 1/2\mu$ for $k = 2$; for general k, the mode is located at

$$t = \frac{k-1}{\mu k}$$

The variance for the kth member of the family is $1/k\mu^2$. We see that the one-parameter family obtained by setting $k = 1$ is just the exponential family; as k increases, the mode moves to the right toward $1/\mu$, and the variance decreases toward zero. For $k = \infty$, the mode is at $1/\mu$, and the variance is zero; so we may interpret $g(t; \mu, \infty)$ as the

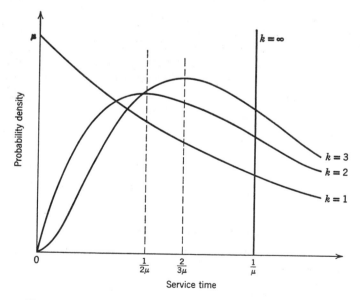

Figure 6.2.   The Erlang family of service time distributions.

family of situations for which the service time is *constant* and has the value $1/\mu$.

Figure 6.2 gives a suggestion of the way the density functions vary as k increases.

The Erlang family has a close tie with the exponential distribution, even beyond the fact that the first Erlang distribution is exponential. If we have r random variables $x_1, x_2, \cdots, x_r$, which are independent and have a common exponential distribution with mean $1/r\mu$, then the random variable $x_1 + x_2 + \cdots + x_r$ follows the rth Erlang distribution with parameter μ. Thus a servicing station in which a unit goes through r independent service phases, each exponential with mean time $1/r\mu$, will have service times obeying the rth Erlang distribution with parameter μ.

Even when this physical realization of the Erlang distribution is not present, some member of the family may give an adequate fit to the observed distribution of service times.

Queues: One Servicing Station

The derivation of queue properties for the case of Erlang services is based on the use of state probabilities, where an individual state is defined as the number in the system together with the current servicing phase of the unit presently in service, if any. The results, given here without proof, are for the case of Poisson arrivals with mean arrival rate λ, and service times following the rth Erlang distribution with mean service rate μ. The reader can verify that these results specialize to the results for the exponential case, when $r = 1$.

$$(6.30) \quad E(m) = \frac{r+1}{2r} \cdot \frac{\lambda^2}{\mu(\mu - \lambda)} \qquad \text{average queue length}$$

$$(6.31) \quad E(n) = \frac{r+1}{2r} \cdot \frac{\lambda^2}{\mu(\mu - \lambda)} + \frac{\lambda}{\mu} \qquad \begin{array}{l}\text{average number of units in} \\ \text{system}\end{array}$$

$$(6.32) \quad E(w) = \frac{r+1}{2r} \cdot \frac{\lambda}{\mu(\mu - \lambda)} \qquad \text{average waiting time}$$

$$(6.33) \quad E(v) = \frac{r+1}{2r} \cdot \frac{\lambda}{\mu(\mu - \lambda)} + \frac{1}{\mu} \qquad \text{average time in system}$$

Example 7

A barber with a one-man shop takes exactly 25 minutes to complete one haircut. If customers arrive in a Poisson fashion at an average rate of one every 40 minutes, how long on the average must a customer wait for service?

SOLUTION

For the case of constant service time, $r = \infty$, and equation (6.32) reduces to

$$E(w) = \frac{\lambda}{2\mu(\mu - \lambda)}$$

Here $\lambda = 0.025$ customer per minute, and $\mu = 0.04$ customer per minute.

$$E(w) = \frac{0.025}{(0.08)(0.015)} = 20.8 \text{ minutes}$$

Example 8

Repairing a certain type of machine which breaks down in a given factory consists of five basic steps that must be performed sequentially. The time taken to perform each of the five steps is found to have an exponential distribution with mean 5 minutes and is independent of the other steps. If these machines break down in a Poisson fashion at an average rate of two per hour, and if there is only one repairman, what is the average idle time for each machine that has broken down?

SOLUTION

According to the results stated in the early part of this section, service times will follow an Erlang distribution with $r = 5$ and $\mu = 0.04$ service per minute. The expected time out of operation for a machine that has broken down is given by equation (6.33) with $\lambda = 0.033$ arrival per minute. Thus

$$E(v) = \frac{6}{10} \cdot \frac{0.033}{(0.04)(0.007)} + 25$$

$$= 96 \text{ minutes}$$

MONTE CARLO SOLUTIONS

The Monte Carlo methods discussed in Chapter Three are extremely useful in waiting-line problems that are difficult or impossible to

analyze mathematically. Simulated sampling methods are appropriate, for example, when the simple first-in first-out assumption of this
chapter is replaced by a different type of queue discipline. In many
cases, the observed distributions of service times and time between
arrivals cannot be fitted by mathematical distributions, and the Monte
Carlo approach is the only hope for any sort of answer   Multistage
queueing, in which the departures from one queue form the arrivals
for the next, is another difficult area that can be handled comparatively
simply by Monte Carlo.

There are several advantages of the Monte Carlo approach over the
obvious sampling procedure of just looking at the actual process and
forming a history of arrivals, services, waiting times, queue lengths,
etc. For one thing, simulated sampling, especially when done on a
digital computer, can develop months or years of "data" in a matter
of a few minutes. Another advantage is that manipulation can be
made of those factors that are subject to control. For example, using
Monte Carlo methods, we can readily assess the effect of adding one
or more service facilities without actually having to go to the trouble
and expense of installing them. Changes in queue discipline can be
tried out experimentally on paper, without any disruption whatever
of the actual process itself, and so on.

The following examples are merely illustrative of the application
of Monte Carlo methods to queueing. They should not be taken as
models to follow in practice, both because the situations described are
perhaps oversimplified, and because far too few arrivals and services
are investigated.

Example 9

Buses are scheduled to pass a certain corner every 15 minutes, but
actually the arrival of a bus varies normally about its scheduled arrival
time, with a standard deviation of 3 minutes. People wishing to board
the bus arrive in a Poisson fashion with mean arrival rate of 4 persons
per hour, and the number of empty seats on the bus has a Poisson
distribution with mean 3/2. If no standees are permitted, find the
average waiting time of an arrival.

SOLUTION

The period investigated was taken to be approximately 8 hours.
The columns in Table 1 (I–VI) are labeled in the order in which they
are obtained. Columns I and II refer to bus arrival times and occupancy, and were obtained by Monte Carlo from the given distributions.
Column III refers to the time interval between the arrival of one person

TABLE 1. MONTE CARLO SOLUTION TO EXAMPLE 9

I Buses, number of empty seats, Monte Carlo	II Buses, time of arrival, Monte Carlo	V Assign- ment of arrivals to buses	IV People, time of arrival, from III	III People, time between arrivals, Monte Carlo	VI People, waiting time, from II, IV, V
3	17		8	8	9
2	28		13	5	4
1	46		18	4	10
1	58		22	5	6
1	75		49	27	9
2	96		58	9	17
2	111		71	13	25
0	122		91	20	5
1	130		133	42	23
0	148		139	6	17
2	156		154	15	31
3	185		189	35	3
3	192		207	18	2
1	209		216	9	10
2	226		223	7	3
1	241		247	24	5
3	252		341	94	7
2	267		350	9	9
4	286		352	2	20
2	304		369	17	3
2	313		401	32	3
0	332		402	1	—
3	348		403	1	—
1	359		416	13	—
3	372		425	9	—
1	388				
1	404				

and the next at the bus stop and was obtained by Monte Carlo from the exponential distribution e^{-4t}. All entries are in minutes, as measured from the starting time of the simulated sampling procedure.

Once the arrival times of people and buses are set down, the assignment of people to buses becomes automatic. The obvious principle is that a person is assigned to a bus if he is waiting when the bus comes and there is a seat available for him. Once a person is assigned to a bus, his waiting time (col. VI) is obtained by subtracting his arrival time from the arrival time of his bus.

Waiting times for 21 arrivals were obtained, totaling 221 minutes. Thus our estimate of the mean waiting time of an arrival is 10.5 minutes.

Example 10

This example involves what is known as a three-stage queueing process. Each arriving unit proceeds in its turn through three servicing stations, in a prescribed order. Arrivals are Poisson, and occur every 20 minutes on the average. Service times in the three stages are distributed in the following fashion:

Stage 1: Normal, mean 10 minutes, S.D. 5 minutes.
Stage 2: Exponential, with $\mu = 1/15$ service per minute.
Stage 3: Service time constant, at 15 minutes.

Using Monte Carlo methods, find the expected time in the system and the expected time spent waiting, for a typical arrival.

SOLUTION

We investigate the history of 36 arrivals, over a time interval that turns out to be of the order of 15 hours. To obtain representative time intervals between arrivals, we work with the cumulative distribution $e^{-0.05T}$, and obtain

$$T = 20 \ln (1/y)$$

where y is a random number between 0 and 1. To obtain representative service times for the first stage, we use tables of random normal numbers as explained in Chapter Three. For the second service stage, we work with the cumulative distribution $e^{-(1/15)T}$. The results obtained for the 36 units considered are given in Table 2.

These numbers are translated into the actual diary of an arrival, in Table 3, by the usual considerations. A unit proceeds immediately into a service stage if it is unoccupied; otherwise, it waits until the servicing station is free. All times are in minutes, measured from the arrival time of the item immediately preceding arrival 1.

TABLE 2. MONTE CARLO SOLUTION TO EXAMPLE 10

Arrival	Arrival time measured from previous arrival	Service time, first service stage	Service time, second service stage
1	25	11	9
2	7	13	4
3	10	6	12
4	31	8	26
5	21	5	13
6	12	11	7
7	36	9	18
8	32	15	50
9	7	18	2
10	1	6	5
11	32	9	24
12	18	3	15
13	12	1	3
14	11	6	3
15	68	10	5
16	27	6	8
17	21	6	1
18	13	15	2
19	2	11	31
20	7	16	3
21	41	7	6
22	7	18	5
23	37	15	8
24	26	12	10
25	12	2	23
26	2	8	3
27	60	14	33
28	2	11	6
29	60	7	3
30	2	12	45
31	27	6	1
32	37	3	9
33	22	14	22
34	27	10	79
35	10	13	42
36	20	11	35

TABLE 3

Arrival	Arrival time	Time into first stage	Time out of first stage	Time into second stage	Time out of second stage	Time into third stage	Time out of third stage	Time in system
1	25	25	36	36	45	45	60	35
2	32	36	49	49	53	60	75	43
3	42	49	55	55	67	75	90	48
4	73	73	81	81	107	107	122	49
5	94	94	99	107	120	122	137	43
6	106	106	117	120	127	137	152	46
7	142	142	151	151	169	169	184	42
8	178	178	193	193	243	243	258	70
9	185	193	211	243	245	258	273	88
10	186	211	217	245	250	273	288	102
11	218	218	227	250	274	288	303	85
12	236	236	239	274	289	303	318	82
13	248	248	249	289	292	318	333	85
14	259	259	265	292	295	333	348	89
15	327	327	337	337	342	348	363	36
16	354	354	360	360	368	368	383	29
17	375	375	381	381	382	383	398	23
18	388	388	403	403	405	405	420	32
19	390	403	414	414	445	445	460	70
20	397	414	430	445	448	460	475	78
21	404	430	437	448	454	475	490	86
22	445	445	463	463	468	490	505	60
23	452	463	478	478	486	505	520	68
24	478	478	490	490	500	520	535	57
25	490	490	492	500	523	535	550	60
26	492	492	500	523	526	550	565	73
27	552	552	566	566	599	599	614	62
28	554	566	577	599	605	614	629	75
29	614	614	621	621	624	629	644	30
30	616	621	633	633	678	678	693	77
31	643	643	649	678	679	693	708	65
32	681	681	684	684	693	708	723	42
33	703	703	717	717	739	739	754	51
34	730	730	740	740	819	819	834	104
35	740	740	753	819	861	861	876	136
36	760	760	771	861	896	896	911	151
								2372

Average time in system $= 2372/36 = 65.9$ minutes

Average waiting time $= 65.9 - 10 - 15 - 15 = 25.9$ minutes

PROBLEMS FOR SOLUTION

Set VIII

1. A TV repairman finds that the time spent on his jobs has an exponential distribution with mean 30 minutes. If he repairs sets in the order in which they come in, and if the arrival of sets is approximately Poisson with an average rate of 10 per 8-hour day, what is the repairman's expected idle time each day? How many jobs are ahead of the average set just brought in?

[*Ans.* 3 hours; $1\frac{2}{3}$ jobs]

2. At what average rate must a clerk at a supermarket work in order to insure a probability of 0.90 that the customer will not have to wait longer than 12 minutes? It is assumed that there is only one counter, to which customers arrive in a Poisson fashion at an average rate of 15 per hour. The length of service by the clerk has an exponential distribution.

[*Ans.* 2.48 minutes per service]

3. A supermarket has two girls ringing up sales at the counters. If the service time for each customer is exponential with mean 4 minutes, and if people arrive in a Poisson fashion at the counter at the rate of 10 an hour:

(*a*) What is the probability of having to wait for service? [*Ans.* 0.167]
(*b*) What is the expected percentage of idle time for each girl? [*Ans.* 67%]

4. A telephone exchange has two long-distance operators. The telephone company finds that, during the peak load, long-distance calls arrive in a Poisson fashion at an average rate of 15 per hour. The length of service on these calls is approximately exponentially distributed with mean length 5 minutes. What is the probability that a subscriber will have to wait for his long-distance call during the peak hours of the day? If the subscribers will wait and are serviced in turn, what is the expected waiting time? [*Ans.* 0.48, 3.2 minutes]

5. A bank has two tellers working on savings accounts. The first teller handles withdrawals only. The second teller handles deposits only. It has been found that the service time distributions for both deposits and withdrawals are exponential with mean service time 3 minutes per customer. Depositors are found to arrive in a Poisson fashion throughout the day with mean arrival rate 16 per hour. Withdrawers also arrive in a Poisson fashion with mean arrival rate 14 per hour. What would be the effect on the average waiting time for depositors and withdrawers if each teller could handle both withdrawals and deposits? What would be the effect if this could only be accomplished by increasing the mean service time to 3.5 minutes?

[*Ans.* Initially 12 minutes and 7 minutes. Combined waiting time 3.86 minutes. Combined waiting time with increased service time 11.4 minutes.]

6. At a certain airport it takes exactly 5 minutes to land an airplane, once it is given the signal to land. Although incoming planes have scheduled arrival times, the wide variability in arrival times produces an effect which makes

the incoming planes appear to arrive in a Poisson fashion at an average rate of six per hour. This produces occasional stack-ups at the airport which can be dangerous and costly. Under these circumstances, how much time will a pilot expect to spend circling the field waiting to land? [*Ans.* $2\frac{1}{2}$ minutes]

7. Problems arrive at a computing center in a Poisson fashion at an average rate of five per day. The rules of the computing center are that any man waiting to get his problem solved must aid the man whose problem is being solved. If the time to solve a problem with one man has an exponential distribution with a mean time of $1/3$ day, and if the average solving time is inversely proportional to the number of people working on the problem, approximate the expected time in the center for a person entering the line. [*Ans.* 8 hours]

8. A warehouse in a small state receives orders for a certain item and sends them by truck as soon as possible to the customer. The orders arrive in a Poisson fashion at a mean rate of 0.9 per day. Only one item at a time can be shipped by truck from the warehouse, which is located in the central part of the state. Because the customers are located in various places in the state, the distribution of service time in days has a distribution with probability density $4te^{-2t}$. What is the expected delay between the arrival of an order and the arrival of the item to the customer? Service time is defined here as the time the truck takes to load, get to the customer, unload, and return to the warehouse. Loading and unloading times are small compared with travel time. [*Ans.* $7\frac{1}{4}$ days]

9. A hospital clinic has a doctor examining every patient brought in for a general checkup. The doctor averages 4 minutes on each phase of the checkup although the distribution of time spent on each phase is approximately exponential. If each patient goes through four phases in the checkup and if the arrivals of the patients to the doctor's office are approximately Poisson at an average rate of three per hour, what is the average time spent by a patient waiting in the doctor's office? What is the average time spent in the examination? What is the most probable time spent in the examination?
[*Ans.* 40 minutes, 16 minutes, 12 minutes]

10. Attendants at a gas station are paid at the rate of $15 each per 8-hour day. Cars arrive for service in a Poisson fashion at an average rate of one car every 3 minutes. Each car is serviced by a single attendant, and the resultant profit per car serviced is estimated to average $1.00. The service time per car is exponentially distributed with mean 8 minutes. When the number of cars waiting for service exceeds two, arrivals become discouraged and drive on (lost business). Use Monte Carlo methods to estimate the optimum number of attendants.

11. Before parts are assembled into a vacuum tube, they must be cleaned in a degreaser. Batches of parts are brought in randomly (Poisson) at an average rate of λ batches per hour, and are cleaned at an average rate of μ batches per hour. The cost of waiting is C_1 dollars per batch per hour; and the cost of owning and operating a degreaser that works at an average rate μ is μC_2 dollars per hour. How large should μ be?
[*Ans.* For least expected hourly cost, $\mu = \lambda + \sqrt{C_1\lambda/C_2}$]

12. Devise a time line (or set of time lines) which will represent visually the history of the first 10 arrivals in the three-stage queueing problem of Example 10 in the text.

13. Prove the result given in equation (6.2), which states in effect that, if arrivals occur at random in time, then the number of arrivals occurring in a fixed time interval follows a Poisson distribution. [*Hint:* Divide the interval T into N subintervals of length Δt. The probability of n arrivals is seen to follow a binomial distribution with parameter $\lambda \, \Delta t$. What happens to this binomial distribution as N tends to infinity?]

14. Following the hint given in the text, derive equation (6.12), which gives the unconditional distribution of waiting time for a Poisson situation with one servicing station.

15. Prove that, for the Erlang distribution with parameters μ and k, the mode is at $(1 - 1/k)(1/\mu)$, the mean is $1/\mu$, and the variance is $1/k\mu^2$.

REFERENCES

Brockmeyer, E., H. L. Holstrom, and A. Jensen, *The Life and Works of A. K. Erlang* (in English), Copenhagen Telephone Co., Copenhagen, 1948.

Feller, William, *An Introduction to Probability Theory and Its Applications*, 2nd ed., Chapter 17, John Wiley & Sons, New York, 1957.

Fry, Thornton C., *Probability and Its Engineering Uses*, Chapter 10, D. Van Nostrand Co., New York, 1928.

Morse, Philip M., *Queues, Inventories, and Maintenance*, John Wiley & Sons, New York, 1958.

Saaty, Thomas L., "Résumé of Useful Formulas in Queueing Theory," *Operations Research*, Vol. 5, no. 2 (Apr. 1957).

Competitive
strategies

Competitive situations are characterized by the fact that two or more individuals are making decisions in situations that involve conflicting interests and in which the outcome is controlled by the decisions of all the parties involved. Many conflict situations of this type are found in economic, social, political, or military problems.

Many of these situations will involve elements of chance, as for example the weather during a military attack, or the cards dealt in a poker hand. However, in all these competitive situations, one may assume that each opponent is going to act in some rational manner and will attempt to resolve the conflict of interests in his favor.

The approach to competitive problems developed by von Neumann utilizes the minimax principle which has as its fundamental idea the minimization of maximum loss. Von Neumann's ideas have led to the development of a branch of mathematics known as game theory which is useful in handling many competitive situations. However, not all the competitive situations that may arise can be analyzed with the mathematics of game theory.

In this chapter we shall examine a number of competitive problems, and attempt to develop methods for optimizing the strategy of a competitor.

COMPETITIVE GAMES

We shall call a competitive situation a *competitive game* if it has the following four properties:

(*a*) There are a finite number of *competitors.*

(*b*) Each of the N competitors has available to him a finite list of possible *courses of action;* this list need not be the same for each competitor.

(*c*) A *play* of the game results when each of the competitors chooses a single course of action from the list of courses available to him. The choices are assumed to be made simultaneously, so that no competitor knows his opponents' choices until he is already committed to his own.

(*d*) The *outcome* of a play consists of the particular set of courses of action undertaken by the competitors. Each outcome determines a set of payments (positive, negative, or zero), one to each competitor.

In a game where there are N competitors, and competitor i has n_i courses of action available to him, there are $n_1 n_2 \cdots n_N$ possible outcomes to a play of the game. A particular outcome θ results in a payment $R(i, \theta)$ to competitor i. If for every possible outcome θ, we have

$$\sum_i R(i, \theta) = 0$$

then the game is called a *zero-sum* game. That is, a game is a zero-sum game if the sum of payments to all competitors after a play of the game is restricted to be zero.

The *strategy* of competitor i is the decision rule he uses for making the choice from his list of courses of action. This decision rule should not require definite information about the opponents' choice, inasmuch as all choices are understood to be made simultaneously and divulged at the same instant. Here we restrict our attention to two types of strategy. A *pure* strategy is a decision, in advance of all plays, always to choose a particular course of action i_0. A *mixed* strategy is a decision, in advance of all plays, to choose a course of action for each play in accordance with some particular probability distribution. For example, a person with two possible courses of action might flip a coin before each play to decide which course he should take. The advantage of a mixed strategy over a pure strategy, after the pattern of play has become evident, is that the opponents are kept guessing as to what a player's actual course of action will be.

A pure strategy may be identified by a number representing the course of action chosen. A mixed strategy, for a player with m possible courses of action, is denoted by the set X of m non-negative numbers whose sum is unity, representing the probabilities with which each course of action is chosen If x_i is the probability of choosing course i, we have

$$X = (x_1, x_2, \cdots, x_m)$$

where

$$x_i \geq 0 \qquad (i = 1, 2, \cdots, m)$$

and

$$\sum_{i=1}^{m} x_i = 1$$

It will be realized that a pure strategy is a special case of a mixed strategy, where all but one of the x_i are zero, and the exception has the value one. A competitor may choose from only m pure strategies, but he has an infinite number of mixed strategies to choose from.

Before we can attempt to find an optimal strategy for a competitor, we must have a criterion of optimality. Throughout this section, we shall use what is known as the *maximin* criterion. The exact meaning of this criterion will become more clear as we proceed. Roughly, it may be visualized as follows. A player lists each of his potential (mixed or pure) strategies together with the worst outcome, from his point of view, that can result from combinations of his competitors' potential strategies. He chooses the strategy that corresponds to the best of these worst possible outcomes.

We shall say that a game has a *solution* if the set of optimal strategies for the various players has the following property. If the players adopt these strategies initially, and after repeated plays gain knowledge of the others' chosen strategies, they will still see fit to maintain their initial strategies as giving them the maximum expected gain. The *value* of a solvable game to a player is his expected gain in one play of the game with all players using their stable optimal strategies.

In this chapter, we shall confine our attention to two-person zero-sum games. For a discussion of n-person games, the reader is referred to one of the several textbooks on the subject of game theory.

Two-Person Zero-Sum Games

A game with only two competitors A and B is most conveniently described by means of a pair of matrices. Row designations for each matrix are the courses of action available to A; column designations are the courses available to B; cell entries are the corresponding payments to A for the one matrix and to B for the other matrix.

With a zero-sum two-person game, the cell entry in B's payoff matrix will be the negative of the corresponding cell entry in A's payoff matrix; and the matrices will appear as follows:

		B						B		
	1	2	$\cdots$	n		1	2	$\cdots$	n
1	a_{11}	a_{12}	$\cdots$	a_{1n}	1	$-a_{11}$	$-a_{12}$	$\cdots$	$-a_{1n}$
2	a_{21}	a_{22}	$\cdots$	a_{2n}	2	$-a_{21}$	$-a_{22}$	$\cdots$	$-a_{2n}$
m	a_{m1}	a_{m2}	$\cdots$	a_{mn}	m	$-a_{m1}$	$-a_{m2}$	$\cdots$	$-a_{mn}$

A's payoff matrix $\qquad\qquad$ B's payoff matrix

For brevity, we shall usually omit B's payoff matrix, with the understanding that it is just the negative of the payoff matrix displayed for A.

We shall see later that all two-person zero-sum games are solvable; i.e., that stable optimal strategies exist in the sense above. The simplest type of game to solve is one where the stable optimal strategies are pure strategies. This is the case if and only if the payoff matrix contains a *saddle point*; a saddle point is an element of a matrix that is both the lowest element in its row and the highest element in its column. Equivalently, a saddle point can be defined as an element of a matrix that is at once the largest of the row minima and the smallest of the column maxima.

The solution in such cases is for player A to use his pure strategy corresponding to the row through the saddle point, and for B to use his pure strategy corresponding to the column through the saddle point. The value of the game to A is the element at the saddle point, and the value to B is its negative. We shall not prove these statements here; however, the proof follows the discussion of Example 2 where optimal mixed strategies for a two-person game are obtained. Since it is so easy to discover whether or not a given matrix contains a saddle point, the first step in the solution of any two-person zero-sum game is to examine the matrix to see whether a saddle point exists.

Example 1

The payoff matrix of a game is given below. Find the best strategy for each player, and the value of a play of the game to A and B.

$$B$$

	I	II	III	IV	V
I	9	3	1	8	0
II	6	5	4	6	7
III	2	4	3	3	8
IV	5	6	2	2	1

A

SOLUTION

If we circle the row minima and put squares around the column maxima, we obtain

$$B$$

	I	II	III	IV	V
I	[9]	3	1	[8]	(0)
II	6	5	(4)	6	7
III	(2)	4	3	3	[8]
IV	5	[6]	2	2	(1)

A

We see that the matrix has a saddle point of 4, in the second row and third column. According to the rule, the optimal strategies are pure strategies, viz.:

    Player A: Strategy II.
    Player B: Strategy III.

The value of the game is 4 to A, -4 to B. Note that these strategies are truly stable in the minimax sense. When B becomes aware that A is always playing II, he will maintain strategy III because it cuts his loss to the lowest possible value. Similarly, A will continue with II even after discovering that B is sticking to III, since strategy II gives him the greatest possible gain.

If there is no saddle point, the best strategies are mixed strategies, and the solution of the game consists of evaluating the probabilities with which each pure strategy should be used. If mixed strategies are used, we cannot guarantee a minimum gain at any particular play. Instead we endeavor to insure that the minimum possible value of the average or expected gain shall be as large as possible.

In Example 2 we will see how the above rule fails when there is no saddle point, and why in these circumstances a mixed strategy is inevitable.

Example 2

The payoff matrix for A in a two-person zero-sum game is given below. Determine the value of the game and the optimum strategies for both players.

$$
\begin{array}{c c}
 & \begin{array}{ccc} & B & \\ \text{I} & \text{II} & \text{III} \end{array} \\
A \begin{array}{c} \text{I} \\ \text{II} \\ \text{III} \end{array} & \left[\begin{array}{ccc} -1 & 2 & 1 \\ 1 & -2 & 2 \\ 3 & 4 & -3 \end{array}\right]
\end{array}
$$

SOLUTION

If A is looking for a pure strategy he examines the rows and discovers the row minima to be

Row	I	II	III
Minimum	-1	-2	-3

He therefore decides to use I, insuring himself of a gain of at least -1. By similar reasoning B decides to use his third strategy, thus insuring that he cannot lose more than 2.

Now suppose A and B start playing with these pure strategies. As soon as A discovers that B always plays III, he realizes that he (A) can increase his gains from 1 to 2 by playing II. When B realizes A is playing II, he will change his strategy to II so that he (B) can gain 2 at each play. When A sees this, he will change to III, and so on. The strategies will never become fixed, because, whenever one player discovers the current pure strategy of his opponent, he finds that a change in his own pure strategy will increase his gains. In contrast, when a saddle point exists, if one player changes from his pure strategy through the saddle point while the other player maintains his strategy, the player who changes will never increase his gains. Of course even with a saddle point, if either player is foolish, and consistently chooses the wrong strategy, the other player can use this to his advantage. However, we are assuming that the players behave rationally and that both use the strategy that is optimal from their own viewpoint.

Returning to our problem with no saddle point, it is clear that neither A nor B will use a single pure strategy. It is also clear that, if one player ever realizes that the other player is using a fixed sequence of pure strategies, he will be able to anticipate the next play of his opponent and take advantage of the situation. A good way to avoid a fixed sequence is to make the strategy for each play a random variable: i.e., to use a mixed strategy.

Let $X = (x_1, x_2, x_3)$ and $Y = (y_1, y_2, y_3)$ denote the optimum mixed strategies for A and B, respectively. Then the probability that A plays i is x_i, and the probability that B plays j is y_j. The gain to A at each play is now a random variable α, and the expected value of a play to A is

$$E(\alpha; X, Y) = \sum_{ij} a_{ij}x_iy_j$$

where a_{ij} is the gain to A when A plays i and B plays j.

A wishes to choose X so that, regardless of the nature of Y, his expectation at each play exceeds some amount v_1; v_1 is to be as large as possible.

Similarly the expected gain for B is

$$E(-\alpha; X, Y) = \sum_{ij} (-a_{ij})x_iy_j$$

and B will play so that the expected value of his gain exceeds some number v_2; v_2 is to be as large as possible.

Using X_o and Y_o to denote the optimum strategies for A and B respectively, we require X_o, Y_o, v_1, v_2 to satisfy the conditions

$$E(\alpha; X_o, Y) \geq v_1 \quad \text{for all } Y$$

and

$$E(-\alpha; X, Y_o) \geq v_2 \quad \text{for all } X$$

There is a remarkable theorem due to von Neumann which states that in any zero-sum two-person game the quantities v_1, v_2 introduced above are the negatives of each other. We will write v for v_1 and $-v$ for v_2.

Then we have

(7.1) $$E(\alpha; X_o, Y) \geq v \quad \text{for all } Y$$

(7.2) $$E(\alpha; X, Y_o) \leq v \quad \text{for all } X$$

Hence

$$E(\alpha; X_o, Y_o) = v$$

This means that, if both players use their optimal minimax strategies, their achieved expected gains coincide with their minimax expected gains.

Substituting the numerical values of a_{ij} in (7.1) yields

$$y_1(-x_1 + x_2 + 3x_3) + y_2(2x_1 - 2x_2 + 4x_3) + y_3(x_1 + 2x_2 - 3x_3) \geq v$$

Since this is to be true of all y_j, it is true when any two of the y_j are zero and the third is one. The three implied inequalities are:

$$-x_1 + x_2 + 3x_3 \geq v$$

(7.3)
$$2x_1 - 2x_2 + 4x_3 \geq v$$

$$x_1 + 2x_2 - 3x_3 \geq v$$

Similarly, from (7.2) we obtain

$$-y_1 + 2y_2 + y_3 \leq v$$

(7.4)
$$y_1 - 2y_2 + 2y_3 \leq v$$

$$3y_1 + 4y_2 - 3y_3 \leq v$$

In addition we have

$$x_1 + x_2 + x_3 = 1$$

(7.5)

$$y_1 + y_2 + y_3 = 1$$

and

$$x_i \geq 0 \qquad i = 1, 2, 3$$

(7.6)

$$y_i \geq 0 \qquad i = 1, 2, 3$$

The equations and inequations (7.3) through (7.6) serve to determine all seven of the unknowns x_i, y_j, and v.

We note first that altogether we have 14 relationships among 7 variables. It is clear that not all the x_i and y_j can be zero, but it is possible for equality signs to hold in all the relationships of (7.3) and (7.4). We first assume that this is so, and attempt to solve the following set of eight equations in the seven unknowns:

$$-x_1 + x_2 + 3x_3 = v$$

$$2x_1 - 2x_2 + 4x_3 = v$$

$$x_1 + 2x_2 - 3x_3 = v$$

$$-y_1 + 2y_2 + y_3 = v$$

(7.7)
$$y_1 - 2y_2 + 2y_3 = v$$

$$3y_1 + 4y_2 - 3y_3 = v$$

$$x_1 + x_2 + x_3 = 1$$

$$y_1 + y_2 + y_3 = 1$$

If these equations are found to be consistent, and have positive solutions for the x_i and y_j, we have a set of values satisfying all the relationships (7.3) through (7.6). If not, we have to replace one or more of the equality signs in (7.7) by strict inequalities until we find a suitable set of non-negative solutions.

In this particular problem it is easy to verify that the eight equations are consistent and have the solution

x_1	x_2	x_3	y_1	y_2	y_3	v
17/46	20/46	9/46	14/46	12/46	20/46	30/46

Consequently we have a solution to the game. Note that A now has an expected gain per play of 30/46, whereas, if he were to stay with his best pure strategy, he could only be sure of not losing more than 1. B now has an expected loss of $-30/46$, whereas with a pure strategy he cannot be sure he will lose less than 2.

Example 3

Show that, for any zero-sum two-person game where the optimal strategies are not pure strategies (i.e. there is no saddle point), and for which A's payoff matrix is

$$\begin{bmatrix} a_{11} & a_{12} \\ a_{21} & a_{22} \end{bmatrix}$$

the optimal strategies (x_1, x_2) and (y_1, y_2) are determined by

$$(7.8) \qquad \frac{x_1}{x_2} = \frac{a_{22} - a_{21}}{a_{11} - a_{12}}, \qquad \frac{y_1}{y_2} = \frac{a_{22} - a_{12}}{a_{11} - a_{21}}$$

and the value v of the game to A is

$$(7.9) \qquad v = \frac{a_{11}a_{22} - a_{12}a_{21}}{a_{11} + a_{22} - (a_{12} + a_{21})}$$

SOLUTION

Since there is no saddle point, the largest and second largest elements of the matrix must constitute one of the diagonals. This means that there are only 8 possibilities (instead of 24) for the ordering of the entries a_{11}, a_{12}, a_{21}, a_{22}. They are:

$$a_{11} \geq a_{22} \geq a_{12} \geq a_{21}$$

$$a_{11} \geq a_{22} \geq a_{21} \geq a_{12}$$

$$a_{22} \geq a_{11} \geq a_{12} \geq a_{21}$$

(7.10)
$$a_{22} \geq a_{11} \geq a_{21} \geq a_{12}$$

$$a_{12} \geq a_{21} \geq a_{11} \geq a_{22}$$

$$a_{12} \geq a_{21} \geq a_{22} \geq a_{11}$$

$$a_{21} \geq a_{12} \geq a_{11} \geq a_{22}$$

$$a_{21} \geq a_{12} \geq a_{22} \geq a_{11}$$

The six relations for determining optimal strategies are, regardless of the ordering,

$$x_1 + x_2 = 1$$

$$y_1 + y_2 = 1$$

$$a_{11}x_1 + a_{21}x_2 \geq v$$

$$a_{12}x_1 + a_{22}x_2 \geq v$$

$$a_{11}y_1 + a_{12}y_2 \leq v$$

$$a_{21}y_1 + a_{22}y_2 \leq v$$

The third and fourth restrictions, regarded as equalities, together yield

$$\frac{x_1}{x_2} = \frac{a_{22} - a_{21}}{a_{11} - a_{12}}$$

The right-hand side is positive for each of the eight orderings in (7.10). Hence we may proceed to evaluate x_1 and x_2 separately, using the first of the six relations, and obtain

$$x_1 = \frac{a_{22} - a_{21}}{a_{11} + a_{22} - (a_{12} + a_{21})}$$

$$x_2 = \frac{a_{11} - a_{12}}{a_{11} + a_{22} - (a_{12} + a_{21})}$$

We compute the value of the game to A by substituting these quantities in either the third or fourth relation regarded as an equality. The result is

$$v = \frac{a_{11}a_{22} - a_{12}a_{21}}{a_{11} + a_{22} - (a_{12} + a_{21})}$$

By using the fifth and sixth inequalities, we obtain

$$\frac{y_1}{y_2} = \frac{a_{22} - a_{12}}{a_{11} - a_{21}}$$

which again is positive for each of the eight orderings (7.10).

It should be pointed out that, if the matrix has a saddle point, equations (7.8) and (7.9) may give an incorrect solution.

Example 4

In a game of matching coins with two players, suppose A wins one unit of value when there are two heads, wins nothing when there are two tails, and loses $\frac{1}{2}$ unit of value when there are one head and one tail. Determine the payoff matrix, the best strategies for each player, and the value of the game to A.

SOLUTION

The payoff matrix (for A) is seen to be:

$$
\begin{array}{cc}
 & B \\
 & \begin{array}{cc} H & T \end{array} \\
A \;\; \begin{array}{c} H \\ T \end{array} & \left|\begin{array}{cc} +1 & -\frac{1}{2} \\ -\frac{1}{2} & 0 \end{array}\right.
\end{array}
$$

Since there is no saddle point, we know that the optimal strategies will be mixed strategies. The solution is obtained most easily by use of the formulas given in Example 3. We have

$$\frac{x_1}{x_2} = \frac{1}{3}$$

So
$$x_1 = \frac{1}{4}, \qquad x_2 = \frac{3}{4}$$

$$\frac{y_1}{y_2} = \frac{1}{3}, \qquad y_1 = \frac{1}{4}, \qquad y_2 = \frac{3}{4}$$

$$v = \frac{0 - \frac{1}{4}}{1 + 1} = -\frac{1}{8}$$

Thus each player should show heads 1/4 of the time and tails 3/4 of the time. The game is unfair to A, as he will lose on average 1/8 unit each time the game is played.

Example 5

In a campaign for mayor, the Whigs and Populists are each planning to nominate a candidate in closed session, with the results to be announced simultaneously. Gamblers are expected to offer the following odds for the possible combinations of candidates:

Whigs	Odds	Populists
Eise	2:1	Fogg
Eise	3:1	Kale
Eise	1:2	Smith
Nix	3:7	Fogg
Nix	3:2	Kale
Nix	1:3	Smith
Humph	3:1	Fogg
Humph	1:4	Kale
Humph	2:1	Smith

The political bosses wish to select candidates in accordance with standard minimax criteria. What are optimal strategies for the two parties?

SOLUTION

If the payoff for a party were taken as its probability of winning, the two payoff matrices in this "game" would be as follows:

		Populists F	K	S				Populists F	K	S
	E	0.667	0.750	0.333			E	0.333	0.250	0.667
Whigs	N	0.300	0.600	0.250		Whigs	N	0.700	0.400	0.750
	H	0.750	0.200	0.667			H	0.250	0.800	0.333

Whigs payoff matrix — Populists payoff matrix

With these payoff matrices, the game is not zero-sum. The game can be converted to zero-sum by taking the payoffs to be the *differences* between the corresponding win probabilities. This change may be justified, to some extent, by noting that the original payoffs and the new payoffs increase and decrease together. The payoff matrix for the

Whigs becomes

Populists

		F	K	S
	E	0.333	0.500	−0.333
Whigs	N	−0.400	+0.200	−0.500
	H	0.500	−0.600	0.333

The payoff matrix for the Populists is, of course, just the negative of that for the Whigs.

To solve this game, we first check whether the optimal strategies are pure strategies. The largest row minimum is −0.333, and the smallest column maximum is +0.333. Hence the optimal strategies will be mixed strategies.

The next step is to try to reduce the dimensionality of the game by the elimination of *recessive* pure strategies. A pair of pure strategies i and j are said to be in a dominant–recessive relationship if pure strategy i has a payoff greater than or equal to pure strategy j for each possible course of action of the opponent. If a pure strategy is recessive, it can be shown that its choice probability in the optimal mixed strategy is zero. Hence the rows (columns) corresponding to the various recessive pure strategies can be eliminated from the payoff matrix, in computing optimal strategies.

For the Whigs, we find that Eise dominates Nix; and, for the Populists, Smith dominates Fogg. Nix is nixed, Fogg is lifted, and the Whigs' payoff matrix becomes 2 by 2, viz.:

Populists

		K	S
Whigs	E	0.500	−0.333
	H	−0.600	0.333

By the simple formulas of Example 3, we find that

$$\frac{x_1}{x_2} = \frac{0.933}{0.833}, \qquad x_1 = 0.528, \qquad x_2 = 0.472$$

$$\frac{y_1}{y_2} = \frac{0.666}{1.100}, \qquad y_1 = 0.378, \qquad y_2 = 0.624$$

Both Whigs and Populists should use a random process in selecting their candidate. The process used by the Whigs should have a 0.528 chance of selecting Eise and a 0.472 chance of selecting Humph. The Populists should be 0.378 sure of picking Kale, and 0.624 sure of backing Smith.

The value of the game to the Whigs is -0.019; so it seems that the Populists have a slight edge. This supposition is strengthened by the fact that, when the optimal mixed strategies are used, the Populists' probability of winning the election is 0.510.

Example 6

In the following 3-by-3 game we wish to find optimal strategies and the value of the game

$$
\begin{array}{c}
 & & B \\
 & & 1 \quad\; 2 \quad\; 3 \\
\begin{array}{c} \\ 1 \\ A\;\; 2 \\ 3 \end{array} &
\left[\begin{array}{rrr}
3 & -2 & 4 \\
-1 & 4 & 2 \\
2 & 2 & 6
\end{array}\right]
\end{array}
$$

SOLUTION

As in Example 2, we arrive at the following relationships:

$$3x_1 - x_2 + 2x_3 \geq v$$

$$-2x_1 + 4x_2 + 2x_3 \geq v$$

$$4x_1 + 2x_2 + 6x_3 \geq v$$

$$3y_1 - 2y_2 + 4y_3 \leq v$$

(7.12)
$$-y_1 + 4y_2 + 2y_3 \leq v$$

$$2y_1 + 2y_2 + 6y_3 \leq v$$

$$x_1 + x_2 + x_3 = 1$$

$$y_1 + y_2 + y_3 = 1$$

$$x_i \geq 0 \qquad i = 1, 2, 3$$

$$y_i \geq 0 \qquad i = 1, 2, 3$$

We attempt to find a solution by taking any four of the first six relations as equalities, together with the seventh and eighth, and solving these six equations for the x_i and y_j in terms of v. If these equations are consistent and if a value of v can be found that results in positive values for the x_i and y_j, and if these latter values also satisfy the two remaining unused relations, then we have a solution to the game.*

For example, if we took the first four relations as equalities, we would obtain the system

(7.13)
$$3x_1 - x_2 + 2x_3 = v$$
$$-2x_1 + 4x_2 + 2x_3 = v$$
$$4x_1 + 2x_2 + 6x_3 = v$$
$$3y_1 - 2y_2 + 4y_3 = v$$
$$x_1 + x_2 + x_3 = 1$$
$$y_1 + y_2 + y_3 = 1$$

The first three equations imply $x_1 = x_2 = -x_3$, $v = 0$; since all x_i are non-negative, we have $x_1 = x_2 = x_3 = 0$. However, these values do not satisfy the fifth equation; and so this trial set of six equations cannot furnish a solution to the game. We then try another set of equations, and hope for a legitimate solution. Continuing in this way, we will eventually try the set of equations

(7.14)
$$3x_1 - x_2 + 2x_3 = v$$
$$-2x_1 + 4x_2 + 2x_3 = v$$
$$-y_1 + 4y_2 + 2y_3 = v$$
$$2y_1 + 2y_2 + 6y_3 = v$$
$$x_1 + x_2 + x_3 = 1$$
$$y_1 + y_2 + y_3 = 1$$

We find that these six equations in seven unknowns are consistent, and have the solution $X = (0, 0, 1)$; $Y = (\frac{2}{5}, \frac{3}{5}, 0)$; $v = 2$. This proposed solution is seen, by substitution, to satisfy all the requirements (7.12), and hence is an actual solution to the game. (There are other solutions as well; see problem 3 in the list at the end of this chapter.)

---

* The careful reader may have noted that the dimension of this particular game could have been reduced by the elimination of B's strategy 3, which is dominated by strategy 1. The game is worked out as a 3-by-3 game in order to illustrate the algebraic techniques involved in the general case.

Before proceeding to a quick method for approximating the solution of a game, we summarize the analytical procedure:

1. Look for a saddle point.
2. Look for dominance, and eliminate recessive strategies.
3. If the elimination of recessive strategies yields a 2-by-2 matrix, use the formula of Example 3. If it yields a 2-by-m or an m-by-2 matrix, a graphical modification of the algebraic method as explained in problem 2 of Set IX is probably quickest. If it yields a matrix whose small dimension exceeds 2, solve by the algebraic method.

Approximate Solution of Two-Person Zero-Sum Games

Games with large matrices are extremely tedious to solve by standard methods. An approximate method exists which may be used to find the value of the game to any desired accuracy. Optimal strategies can also be approximated. The basic idea in solving the game in this manner is that each player acts under the assumption that the past is the best guide to the future and will play in such a manner as to maximize his expectation. The method, which will work for any size matrix, is best illustrated by an example.

Example 7

The matrix of a certain two-person zero-sum 3-by-3 game is given below. Show how to obtain an approximate solution by iteration.

$$
\begin{array}{cc|ccc}
 & & & B & \\
 & & 1 & 2 & 3 \\
\hline
 & 1 & 1 & 0 & 2 \\
A & 2 & 3 & 0 & 0 \\
 & 3 & 0 & 2 & 1 \\
\end{array}
$$

SOLUTION

Player A arbitrarily selects any row and places it under the matrix. Here we shall arbitrarily select row 1. Player B examines this row and chooses a column corresponding to the *smallest* number in the row. This is column 2. Column 2 is then placed to the right of the matrix. Player A examines this column and chooses a row corresponding to the *largest* number in this column. This is row 3. Row 3 is then added to the row last chosen and the sum of the two rows is placed beneath the row last chosen. Player B chooses a column corresponding to the *smallest* number in the new row and adds this column to the column last chosen. In case of a tie that row or column must be chosen by some consistent mechanism. A coin flip will do, but in this example we shall arbitrarily say that in case of a tie the player will select the row or column different from his last choice. This procedure may be continued in the same manner. Ten iterations are shown below with the smallest numbers in each succeeding row and largest numbers in each succeeding column circled. The approximate strategies after 10

$$
\begin{array}{c}
& & & B \\
& & 1 \quad 2 \quad 3 \\
\end{array}
$$

		1	2	3											
	1	1	0	2	0	1	1	3	4	⑥*	6	7	7	9	$\frac{1}{10}$
A	2	3	0	0	0	③	3	3	⑥	6	6	⑨	9	9	$\frac{3}{10}$
	3	0	2	1	②	2	④	⑤	5	6	⑧	8	⑩	⑪	$\frac{6}{10}$

1	⓪	2
①	2	3
4	②	3
4	4	④*
④	6	5
7	6	⑤
8	⑥	7
⑧*	8	8
11	⑧*	8
11	10	⑨

$$\frac{3}{10} \quad \frac{4}{10} \quad \frac{3}{10}$$

* Choice made by tie-breaking rules given above.

iterations are found by dividing the number of circled numbers in each row or column by the total number of circled numbers. Thus A's approximate strategy is $(\frac{1}{10}, \frac{3}{10}, \frac{6}{10})$ and B's approximate strategy is $(\frac{3}{10}, \frac{4}{10}, \frac{3}{10})$.

Upper and lower bounds for the value of the game can be determined by dividing the highest number in the last column, 11, by the total number of iterations, 10, and by dividing the lowest number in the last row by the number of iterations, 10. Thus

$$\frac{9}{10} \leq v \leq \frac{11}{10}$$

Sometimes narrower bounds can be determined by examining the restrictions given by all the rows and columns. For example, the third last row indicates that a lower bound for $v = \frac{8}{8}$. This is a greater lower bound than $\frac{9}{10}$. And the sixth column indicates a lower upper bound, $\frac{6}{6}$. Thus

$$\frac{8}{8} \leq v \leq \frac{6}{6}$$

In this case we have determined the value of the game exactly as $v = 1$. In general, we do not get exact convergence in this manner but only a continual narrowing of the upper and lower bounds.

The exact solution of this game is $v = 1$ with optimal strategy for player A, $(\frac{1}{4}, \frac{1}{4}, \frac{1}{2})$ and optimal strategy for player B, $(\frac{1}{3}, \frac{1}{3}, \frac{1}{3})$. The approximate solutions are not too far off, and would get better with more iterations. If there is more than one solution, the approximate strategy may not converge on any given solution. However, at any point the approximate strategy will approximate one of the several solutions of the game.

The iterative method is very powerful for handling large games. It is the kind of method that is easily adaptable to machine computations.

OTHER COMPETITIVE SITUATIONS

In this section we consider some competitive situations which are not competitive games in the strict sense of the previous section, but which are amenable to simple analysis. The first two examples show how to determine optimal bidding strategies in two common types of bidding situations. The third example deals with a poker hand; and the last two discuss a very idealized competitive marketing situation.

The reader will note that the criterion used in this section is maximum gain rather than minimax (or, more correctly, maximin) gain. This was selected not because one criterion is considered superior to the other but because the application of minimax methods to problems where the choice variable is continuous usually involves techniques more advanced than those given in this book.

Example 8

A manufacturer engaged in bidding for contracts makes it a practice to record, in addition to his own submitted bid, his cost estimate K and the lowest opponent bid B on each job. He finds that the random variable x, where

$$x = \frac{B - K}{K}$$

follows a normal distribution $f(x)$ with mean 0.15 and standard deviation 0.05.

If the manufacturer is interested in maximizing his expected profit on each job, and if it is assumed that his competitors' bidding habits will not change, what should the manufacturer's bidding strategy be?

SOLUTION

Let A be the manufacturer's bid, and B be the lowest opponent's bid. Then his profit P will be

$$A - K \quad \text{if} \quad A < B$$

$$0 \quad \text{if} \quad A > B$$

Let $E(P; A)$ denote the expected profit with bid A. Then

$$E(P; A) = (A - K) P\{B > A\}$$

We replace the decision variable A by the equivalent variable z, where

$$z = \frac{A - K}{K}$$

Then

$$E(P; A) = KzP\{x > z\}$$

$$= Kz \int_z^\infty f(x)\, dx$$

where x is the random variable in the statement of the problem, and $f(x)$ is its density function.

The quantity

$$z \int_z^\infty f(x)\, dx$$

is maximized by the solution z of the equation

(7.15)
$$\int_z^\infty f(x)\, dx - z f(z) = 0$$

Graphically, $E(P; z)$ is a maximum when the two cross-hatched areas in Figure 7.1 are equal.

Numerically, z may be found by using tables of ordinates and areas of the normal distribution. It turns out that $z = 0.117$ is a solution to the preceding equation. Thus the manufacturer's optimum bidding strategy is to add 11.7% to his own cost estimate in submitting a bid.

A critical assumption in the statement of the problem is that the competitors' bidding habits will not change. It will be realized that any of the earlier examples of this chapter could have been "solved" by making a similar assumption about an opponent's strategy. However, when there is only one opponent, it seems more plausible to assume that he will behave rationally, i.e. that he will use to his advantage the knowledge that accrues to him concerning our strategy. In a bidding situation, the competition is from an amorphous collection

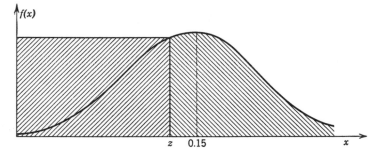

Figure 7.1. Graphical solution of equation (7.15).

of opponents, and it is more reasonable to suppose (at least in the short run) that their actions viewed as a group will not change.

Example 9

Two objects of value $100 and $130 are to be auctioned at a public sale. Only two bidders are interested in these items. Bidder A has $100 available, and bidder B has $80 available. What should be their strategies if each bidder is interested in maximizing his own gain?

SOLUTION

Let us assume for simplicity that successive bids increase in steps of Δ. At any stage of the bidding, a player has the option of letting his opponent's bid stand, or of increasing it by Δ and leaving the next decision up to his opponent.

Suppose that bidder B has just bid x dollars for the first object. Let $\alpha(x, 0)$ be A's gain if he lets B's bid stand, and $\alpha(x, \Delta)$ be A's gain if he increases the bid to $x+\Delta$ and B lets him win. If A lets B take the first object for x, then A is sure to win the second object with a bid of

$$80 - x + \Delta$$

since B's total capital is $80. Thus

$$\alpha(x, 0) = 130 - [80 - x + \Delta] = 50 + x - \Delta$$

If A wins with a bid of $x+\Delta$, then B will win the second object (if $x \geq \$20$) with a bid of

$$130 - (x + \Delta) + \Delta = 130 - x$$

Thus

$$\alpha(x, \Delta) = 100 - (x + \Delta) = 100 - x - \Delta$$

We see that A should bid $x+\Delta$ provided $100 - x - \Delta \geq 50 + x - \Delta$: i.e. provided $x \leq 25$. If $x > 25$, A should let B win the first object for that amount.

Player B has a similar decision to make. If A has just bid x (and if $x \geq 20$) then B's gains $\beta(x, 0)$ and $\beta(x, \Delta)$ are given by

$$\beta(x, 0) = 130 - (100 - x + \Delta) = 30 + x - \Delta$$

$$\beta(x, \Delta) = 100 - (x + \Delta) = 100 - x - \Delta$$

So B should bid $x+\Delta$ on item 1 provided $x \leq 35$.

It is clear that B will take the less expensive object for about \$25, and A will take the more expensive object for about \$55. Both parties end up with the same net gain; and if the other item were offered first, the results would be exactly the same. The order of the items is immaterial in all such problems, regardless of the relative values of the two items and the relative resources of the competitors. The net gains will be equal when conditions are such that the optimal strategies lead to a division of the two items between the competitors; otherwise, of course, the net gain for one of the parties will be zero.

Example 10

A and B are playing a variety of poker in which all the cards dealt are face up. After four cards have been dealt to each person the hands are as follows:

A: ace of clubs, ace of diamonds, ace of hearts, deuce of hearts.
B: four of hearts, five of hearts, six of hearts, seven of hearts.

At this point there is \$1.00 in the pot and A bets \$1.00. One more card is to be dealt to each player. What should B do? At what size bet by A would B be wise to drop?

SOLUTION

The rationale of poker is to bet only if one's expectation of the final pot is greater than or equal to the amount one must put in to reach the final pot. In this problem, all the cards can be seen, and the expectations can be calculated exactly. In a general poker problem cards are hidden and expectations must be estimated. Potential improvements in the two hands by the fifth card are:

A: Four of a kind—1 chance. Full house—3 chances.
B: Straight flush—2 chances. Straight—6 chances.
Flush—5 chances.

The probability of B's winning is the probability of a straight flush, plus the probability of a flush or straight times the probability A does not improve:

$$\Pr\{B \text{ wins}\} = \tfrac{2}{44} + \tfrac{11}{44} \cdot \tfrac{39}{43} = 0.273$$

If B meets the raise and calls, he will put \$1.00 in the pot. There will be \$3.00 in the pot and his expectation will be

$$0.273 \times \$3.00 = \$0.82$$

This indicates that B's calling of A's bet would be a bad investment.

Suppose that A had raised the amount x. Then there would be $1+2x$ dollars in the pot if B called. He should call if

$$0.273 \, (1 + 2x) \geq x$$

$$0.60 \geq x$$

As long as A does not bet more than 60 cents, B should meet the raise and call. Otherwise B should drop out.

Example 11

Two competitors A and B dominate an industry, and have fixed amounts X and Y, respectively, available for advertising and sales promotion. The country has been divided into n sales districts, which are the same for both companies. In district i the industry sales potential is s_i, and this sales potential is actually achieved in each area regardless of the total amount of sales promotion and advertising devoted to that area. Assuming that the industry sales in each district are divided between the two competitors in proportion to the amount spent on advertising and promotion within the district, how should the competitors divide their promotion funds among the n districts?

SOLUTION

Let x_i = amount spent by A in ith area
y_i = amount spent by B in ith area

Then the total amount of A's sales will be

$$\sum_{i=1}^{n} \left(\frac{x_i}{x_i + y_i}\right) s_i$$

and the total amount of B's sales will be

$$\sum_{i=1}^{n} \left(\frac{y_i}{x_i + y_i}\right) s_i$$

Since the total sales $S(=\Sigma s_i)$ is a constant, A will maximize his total sales if and only if he maximizes the difference between his sales and B's sales. That is, A wishes to maximize the quantity D, where

(7.16)
$$D = \sum_{i=1}^{n} \left(\frac{x_i - y_i}{x_i + y_i}\right) s_i$$

This can be regarded as a zero-sum game. A chooses a set of positive x_i adding up to X; B chooses a set of positive y_i adding up to Y. A's payoff is $D(x_1 \cdots x_n, y_1 \cdots y_n)$, B's payoff is $-D(x_1 \cdots x_n, y_1 \cdots y_n)$. The simple methods of the previous section, however, do not suffice to solve this game, since the competitors each have a non-denumerably infinite number of courses of action.

Unfortunately, a motivated discussion of the solution of continuous games cannot be presented within the confines of an example. We shall, however, state the solution and prove that it comprises the optimal strategy for each competitor. The solution is

(7.17)
$$x_i = \frac{s_i}{S} X \qquad \text{for all } i$$

(7.18)
$$y_i = \frac{s_i}{S} Y \qquad \text{for all } i$$

and with these values for x_i and y_i

(7.19)
$$D = \frac{X - Y}{X + Y} S$$

To prove that this is a solution, suppose that A adopts the strategy (7.17), and that B deviates slightly from (7.18), viz.:

(7.20)
$$y_i = \frac{s_i}{S} Y + \Delta_i$$

where each Δ_i is small and $\Sigma \Delta_i = 0$. The payoff D' to A is now expressed by

(7.21)
$$D' = \sum_{i=1}^{n} \left[\frac{s_i(X - Y) - S\Delta_i}{s_i(X + Y) + S\Delta_i}\right] s_i$$

We note that each term in the sum has the form

$$k \frac{a - \epsilon}{b + \epsilon}$$

with ϵ small. By elementary expansions, we easily obtain the approximate result

$$k \frac{a - \epsilon}{b + \epsilon} = \frac{ka}{b} \left[1 - \frac{\epsilon}{a} - \frac{\epsilon}{b} + \left(\frac{1}{ab} + \frac{1}{b^2} \right) \epsilon^2 \right]$$

Applying this to (7.21), with $k = s_i$, $a = s_i(X - Y)$, $b = s_i(X + Y)$, $\epsilon = S\Delta_i$, the result is

$$D' = \sum_{i=1}^{n} \left\{ \frac{X - Y}{X + Y} \left[1 - \frac{S\Delta_i}{s_i(X - Y)} - \frac{S\Delta_i}{s_i(X + Y)} \right. \right.$$

$$\left. \left. + \frac{S^2\Delta_i^2}{s_i^2(X^2 - Y^2)} + \frac{S^2\Delta_i^2}{s_i^2(X + Y)^2} \right] \right\} s_i$$

$$= \frac{X - Y}{X + Y} \left\{ S - S \left[\frac{1}{X - Y} + \frac{1}{X + Y} \right] \Sigma\Delta_i \right.$$

$$\left. + S^2 \left[\frac{1}{X^2 - Y^2} + \frac{1}{(X + Y)^2} \right] \right\} \Sigma \frac{\Delta_i^2}{s_i}$$

Since $[(X - Y)/(X + Y)]S = D$, and $\Sigma\Delta_i = 0$, we may write D' as

$$D' = D + [S^2][X + Y]^{-2} \left[1 + \frac{X - Y}{X + Y} \right] \left[\Sigma \frac{\Delta_i^2}{s_i} \right]$$

Note that each term in brackets is intrinsically positive. This implies that $D' > D$; we conclude that the strategy (7.17) used by A is optimal. In a similar fashion, we can show that (7.18) is the optimal strategy for B.

Example 12

The situation is the same as in the previous example, with the exception that B's allocations to districts are arrived at by executive fiat, and are not the optimal allocations as indicated in the last example. If A knows B's intended allocations, how should A react to take advantage of the fact that B's allocations are non-optimal?

SOLUTION

The function to be maximized with respect to the x_i is

$$\sum_i \left(\frac{x_i - y_i}{x_i + y_i} \right) s_i \qquad y_1, \cdots, y_n \text{ parameters}$$

subject to the restriction $\sum_i x_i = X$. Here the Lagrangian multiplier technique can be used. Form the functional

$$F = \sum_i \left(\frac{x_i - y_i}{x_i + y_i} \right) s_i - \lambda \left(\sum_i x_i - X \right)$$

Differentiating F with respect to each of the x_i and λ, we find

$$\frac{2s_1 y_1}{(x_1 + y_1)^2} - \lambda = 0$$

$$\frac{2s_2 y_2}{(x_2 + y_2)^2} - \lambda = 0$$

$$\vdots$$

$$\frac{2s_n y_n}{(x_n + y_n)^2} - \lambda = 0$$

$$\sum_i x_i - X = 0$$

A solution for λ is obtained by solving each of the first n equations for the term $x_i + y_i$, and then adding. The result is

$$\lambda = \left(\frac{\sum_i \sqrt{2 s_i y_i}}{X + Y} \right)^2$$

Thus, since the y_i are parameters, we have

$$x_i = \frac{\sqrt{s_i y_i}}{\sum_i \sqrt{s_i y_i}} (X + Y) - y_i$$

To illustrate this result, let $s_1 = 50$, $s_2 = 100$, $s_3 = 70$, $X = Y = 30$. Suppose $y_1 = 8$, $y_2 = 15$, $y_3 = 7$. The analysis is shown in Table 1.

TABLE 1

s_i	y_i	$\sqrt{s_i y_i}$	x_i	Minimax value of x_i and y_i
50	8	20.0	6.8	6.8
100	15	38.8	13.8	13.6
70	7	22.2	9.4	9.6

Notice that the x_i's in the fourth column do not deviate very much from the minimax strategy as given by the previous example.

PROBLEMS FOR SOLUTION

Set IX

1. The following games have saddle-point solutions. Determine the optimal minimax strategies for each player.

(a)
$$\begin{vmatrix} 6 & 8 & 6 \\ 4 & 12 & 2 \end{vmatrix}$$

(b)
$$\begin{vmatrix} -5 & 2 & 0 & 7 \\ 5 & 6 & 4 & 8 \\ 4 & 0 & 2 & -3 \end{vmatrix}$$

2. Find the solution of the following game:

$$\begin{vmatrix} 1 & 3 & 11 \\ 8 & 5 & 2 \end{vmatrix}$$

[*Hint:* This problem may be worked by the algebraic methods of the text. However, the following graphical method, which is applicable to any m-by-2 or 2-by-m game, may give quicker results. The restrictions on the x_i may be rewritten as

R_1: $7x_1 + v \leq 8$.
R_2: $2x_1 + v \leq 5$.
R_3: $-9x_1 + v \leq 2$.

Plotting the relaxed inequalities on a graph with x_1 as abscissa and v as ordinate gives a diagram such as Figure 7.2. The pair (v, x_1) in the final solution of the game must be below all three lines, and yet have as great a v as possible. (Why?) Clearly this pair is the point of intersection of R_2 and R_3, which is $x_1 = 3/11$, $v = 49/11$. So the value of the game is $49/11$, and A's optimal strategy is $(3/11, 8/11)$. The final step is the calculation of B's optimal strategy, which is easily done algebraically once v is known.]

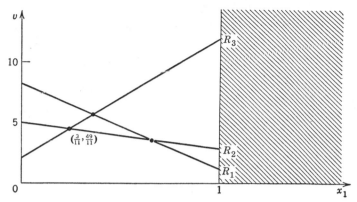

Figure 7.2. Graphical solution of a 2-by-m game.

3. Rework Example 6 of the text, taking advantage of the existing dominance relationship.

[*Hint:* After eliminating B's strategy 3, we have a 3-by-2 game. Apply the graphical method of the previous problem to obtain B's optimal strategy, remembering that the payoff matrix for B is the negative of that for A.]

[*Ans. A:* $(0, 0, 1)$; $B:$ $(a, 1-a, 0)$ where a is an arbitrary number between 2/5 and 4/5; $v = 2$.]

4. A and B play a game in which each has three coins: a penny, a nickel, and a dime. Each selects a coin without knowledge of the other's choice. If the sum of the coins is an odd amount, A wins B's coin; if the sum is even, B wins A's coin. Find the best strategy for each player and the value of the game. [*Ans. A:* $(1/2, 0, 1/2)$; $B:$ $(10/11, 0, 1/11)$; $v = 0$.]

5. Two items of value $80 and $100 are to be bid for simultaneously (with sealed bids) by A and B. Both bidders announce their intention of devoting a total of $110 to the two bids. If each uses a minimax criterion, what are the resulting bids?

[*Ans.* $65 for the more valuable item, $45 for the less valuable.]

[*Hint:* Let x be A's bid and y be B's bid for the more valuable item. If A wins with a bid of x, he does not win the second item, and his gain is $100-x$. If A does not win with a bid of x, he wins the second item with a resultant gain of $x-30$. For a given x, let $R(x)$ be the smaller of $100-x$ and $x-30$. Then $R(x)$ is maximized by a value of x equal to 65.]

6. If we build an m-by-n matrix by drawing each element at random from a continuous distribution, what is the probability that it has a saddle point?

[*Hint:* Since the distribution is continuous, the matrix can have at most one saddle point. This means that saddle points in various positions of the matrix are mutually exclusive events, and hence that the probabilities of these events are additive. Calculate the probability that the upper left-hand corner element is a saddle point, and multiply by mn.]

$$\left[Ans. \frac{m!\, n!}{(m + n - 1)!} \right]$$

REFERENCES

Churchman, C. W., R. L. Ackoff, and E. L. Arnoff, *Introduction to Operations Research*, John Wiley & Sons, New York, 1957.

Luce, R. D., and H. Raiffa, *Games and Decisions: Introduction and Critical Survey*, John Wiley & Sons, New York, 1957.

McKinsey, J. C. C., *Introduction to the Theory of Games*, McGraw-Hill Book Co., New York, 1952.

Thrall, R. M., C. H. Coombs, and R. L. Davis, eds., *Decision Processes*, John Wiley & Sons, New York, 1954.

Vajda, S., *The Theory of Games and Linear Programming*, John Wiley & Sons, 1956.

Williams, J. D., *The Compleat Strategyst*, McGraw-Hill Book Co., New York, 1954

EIGHT

Allocation

Problems of allocation arise whenever there are a number of activities to perform, but limitations on either the amount of resources or the way they can be spent prevent us from performing each separate activity in the most effective way conceivable. In such situations we wish to allot the available resources to the activities in a way that will optimize the total effectiveness.

The number of possible ways of allocating the resources to the activities can be finite or infinite. In problems with a finite number of choices we could, in theory, enumerate all possible choices. Unfortunately, in practical problems enumeration is far too lengthy; for example, there are 10! ways of allocating 10 contracts one apiece to 10 contractors. In the case of continuous choice (e.g., division of capital between possible investments), the restrictions on the choice variables are often of such a nature as to preclude the use of calculus.

It is only in recent years that mathematicians have realized that, for many practical purposes, solutions in principle (e.g. enumeration) are insufficient. Naturally enough, the first situations to be discussed were the comparatively simple ones where the effectiveness and the restrictions are stated in terms of linear functions of the allocations. The analysis of these situations is called *linear programming;* the techniques used can be divided into three main groups according to the methods used for solution.

Assignment Problems

This group comprises problems where we are given a matrix of effectiveness, showing what happens when we associate each of a number of "origins" with each of the *same* number of "destinations." Each origin is to be associated with one and only one destination, and we wish to make the associations in such a way as to minimize (maximize) the summed effectiveness. The previously cited example of awarding ten contracts to ten contractors is such a problem.

Transportation Problems

This class of problems is a generalization of the type described in the first group. The matrix of effectiveness is no longer necessarily square; it shows what happens to effectiveness when we associate each of a number of origins with each of a possibly different number of destinations. We are given the total movement from each origin, and the total movement to each destination, and we wish to determine how the associations should be made subject to the limitations on totals.

Simplex Problems

This group actually includes the first two groups, but the computations are so lengthy that the methods of groups 1 and 2 should be used whenever possible. The type of problem that can be solved by the simplex method is best illustrated by an example, and we will not give a formal mathematical statement of the problem, at this stage.

Suppose that a machine can make 400 items of product X per week and 300 of product Y. If production is changed from X to Y or vice versa during the week, a total of 600 items can be made. The profit from sales of X is \$2 per item and the profit from Y is \$5 per item. We wish to determine the amount x to be made of product X, and the amount y to be made of product Y, so that profit will be maximized.

The mathematical statement is that we wish to maximize the expression

$$2x + 5y$$

subject to the restrictions

$$0 \le x \le 400, \qquad 0 \le y \le 300, \qquad x + y \le 600$$

Generally, a simplex problem involves the maximization or minimization of a linear function of a set of non-negative variables, subject to a set of linear inequalities relating the variables.

It is not the purpose of this chapter to give detailed justification of the methods used in solving linear programming problems. We will outline some of the possible techniques and endeavor to make them sound plausible. It is well to bear in mind that, even with the techniques to be described, many practical problems involve so many variables that they are beyond the capacity of clerks with desk computers. It is probably not mere chance that linear programming methods have been developed at the same time that electronic computers have become available.

THE ASSIGNMENT PROBLEM

The assignment problem is a type of allocation problem in which n items are distributed among n boxes, one item to a box, in such a way that the return resulting from the distribution is optimized. For example, a department head may have five people available for assignment and five jobs to fill; which assignments will be best for the company? A trucking company has an empty truck in each of cities 1, 2, 3, 4, 5, 6 and needs an empty truck in each of cities 7, 8, 9, 10, 11, 12; how should the trucks be dispatched so as to minimize the total mileage?

The problem may be stated formally as follows. Given an n-by-n array of real numbers $[c_{ij}]$, where c_{ij} is the individual return associated with assigning the ith item to the jth box. Find, among all permutations $(i_1, i_2, \cdots, i_n)$ of the set of integers $(1, 2, \cdots, n)$, that permutation for which

$$c_{1i_1} + c_{2i_2} + \cdots + c_{ni_n}$$

takes its maximum (minimum) value.

There are $n!$ such permutations (i.e. $n!$ ways of assigning n items to n boxes). The method for choosing the optimal permutation or "assignment" is best explained with examples.

Example 1

A department head has four subordinates, and four tasks to be performed. The subordinates differ in efficiency, and the tasks differ in their intrinsic difficulty. His estimate of the times each man would take to perform each task is given in the effectiveness matrix below. How should the tasks be allocated, one to a man, so as to minimize the total man-hours?

		Man		
	I	II	III	IV
A	8	26	17	11
B	13	28	4	26
C	38	19	18	15
D	19	26	24	10

Task (label for rows A, B, C, D)

Solution

There are $4! = 24$ possible sets of associations that satisfy these conditions. The reader can write down all possible sets, together with the corresponding total man-hours.

A more systematic procedure is as follows:

We choose the smallest number in row A and subtract it from each element in the row. The result is:

$$
\begin{array}{cccc}
0 & 18 & 9 & 3 \\
13 & 28 & 4 & 26 \\
38 & 19 & 18 & 15 \\
19 & 26 & 24 & 10
\end{array}
$$

Now suppose that we have assigned one task to each man. Whatever assignment we have made, the total man-hours for the new matrix will be 8 less than for the old matrix. Thus an assignment that minimizes the total for one matrix also minimizes the total for the other.

This statement is generally true; the reader should verify the following theorem, which is the basis for our solution.

Theorem

If in an assignment problem we add a constant to every element of a row (or column) in the effectiveness matrix, then an assignment that minimizes the total effectiveness in one matrix also minimizes the total effectiveness in the other matrix.

We now proceed to subtract the minimum element in each row from all the elements in its row, yielding

$$
\begin{array}{cccc}
0 & 18 & 9 & 3 \\
9 & 24 & 0 & 22 \\
23 & 4 & 3 & 0 \\
9 & 16 & 14 & 0
\end{array}
$$

Next we subtract the minimum element in each column from all the elements in its column, obtaining

$$
\begin{array}{cccc}
0 & 14 & 9 & 3 \\
9 & 20 & 0 & 22 \\
23 & 0 & 3 & 0 \\
9 & 12 & 14 & 0
\end{array}
$$

Our final step depends on the obvious fact that, so long as our matrix consists of positive or zero elements, the total effectiveness cannot be negative for any assignment. Consequently, if we can choose an assignment that has a zero total, there cannot be an assignment with a lower total. In other words the total is certain to be minimum if all assignments can be made to positions where elements are zero.

Thus we make the following assignments:

A–I, B–III, C–II, D–IV

In view of the theorem these assignments will also minimize the total number of man-hours for the original matrix.

In the example above, the reduction of the effectiveness matrix by subtraction resulted in an obvious solution to the original problem. We cannot always count on being so fortunate; all we can be sure of, after performing the reduction, is that we will end up with a matrix possessing at least one zero in each row and at least one zero in each column. A complete assignment may not be present among the zeros at this stage; or, if it is present, it may be difficult to recognize if the matrix is of large dimensionality. Thus two questions remain:

1. Given a matrix with some zero and all non-negative elements, how do we look for the maximal existing assignment among the zeros?

2. If a complete assignment does not exist among the zeros, how can we further modify the matrix by additions (subtractions) to rows or columns so as to obtain more zeros?

Although algorithms exist which give a complete answer to the first question, they are too complex for inclusion here. For matrices of small dimensionality, the maximal existing assignment can usually be found by inspection or trial and error. With matrices of higher dimensionality, some degree of ingenuity or luck may be needed to find the maximal assignment in the absence of a formal algorithm. In all cases one would start by using the following rules:

(*a*) Examine rows successively until a row with exactly one unmarked zero is found. Mark (□) this zero, as an assignment will be made there. Mark (×) all other zeros in the same *column* to show that they cannot be used to make other assignments. Proceed in this fashion until all rows have been examined.

(*b*) Next, examine columns for single unmarked zeros, marking them (□) and also marking with an (×) any other unmarked zeros in their rows.

(*c*) Repeat (*a*) and (*b*) successively until one of two things occurs: (1) there are no zeros left unmarked, or (2) the remaining unmarked zeros lie at least two in each row and column.

In outcome (1) we have a maximal assignment. In outcome (2) we must use ingenuity and/or trial and error in order to build up to a maximal assignment if we are to avoid the use of a highly complex algorithm. Regardless of how the maximal assignment is obtained, we can say that, if it has an assignment in every row, this maximal assignment is a complete solution to the original problem. If it does not contain an assignment in every row, we are faced with the question of modifying the effectiveness matrix by addition or subtraction. Before we discuss this, we give an example of finding maximal assignments.

Example 2

Given an effectiveness matrix with zero elements in the positions shown, and positive non-zero elements elsewhere, show how to obtain a maximal assignment.

	0			
0	0			
0		0		0
0		0		0
		0	0	0

SOLUTION

Row 1 has a single zero in column 2. Make an assignment, and delete the second zero in column 2.

	[0]			
0	⌦			
0		0		0
0		0		0
		0	0	0

Row 2 now has a single zero in the first column. Make an assignment, and delete the remaining zeros in column 1.

	[0]			
[0]	⌦			
⌦		0		0
⌦		0		0
		0	0	0

All the remaining rows have at least two zeros left; so we now examine columns. Column 4 has a single zero in row 5; so we make an assignment and delete the remaining zeros in row 5.

Both the remaining rows and columns have two zeros. Make an assignment in the position (3, 3), and delete the remaining zeros in row 3 and column 3. This leaves one zero at (4, 5) and we make the last assignment.

We see there are no remaining zeros, and every row has an assignment. Since no two assignments are in the same column (they cannot be if the procedure has been correctly followed), the maximal assignment is a solution.

Two remarks should be made at this point, concerning the operation of this procedure in practice. First, there may be more than one maximal assignment. Second, it is not necessary in practice to rewrite the matrix repeatedly; this was done in the example only to give clarity to the presentation.

We now return to our other question: if the maximal assignment does not constitute a complete solution, how should we add further zeros? We will give the following rules, and hasten to add (without proof) that it can be shown that their repeated application must lead to an optimal assignment in a finite number of iterations. *Starting with a maximal assignment*:

(a) Mark all rows for which assignments have not been made.
(b) Mark columns not already marked which have *zeros* in marked rows.

(*c*) Mark rows not already marked which have *assignments* in marked columns.

(*d*) Repeat steps *b* and *c* until the chain of markings ends.

(*e*) Draw lines through all *unmarked rows* and through all *marked columns*.

[If the procedures have been carried out correctly, there should be as many lines as there were assignments in the maximal assignment, and every zero will have at least one line through it. Moreover, this method yields the minimum number of lines that will pass through all zeros.]

(*f*) Having drawn the set of lines in steps *a* through *e*, examine the elements that *do not* have a line through them. Select the smallest of these, and subtract it from all the elements that do not have a line through them. Add this smallest element to every element that lies at the intersection of *two* lines. Leave the remaining elements of the matrix unchanged.

Example 3

Show how to construct the minimum number of lines that will pass through all the zeros of the matrix below.

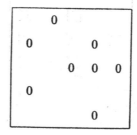

SOLUTION

We first mark the maximal assignment.

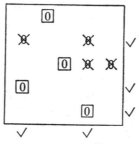

Then we mark row 2 as having no assignment and columns 1 and 4 as having zeros in row 2.

Next mark rows 4 and 5 because they contain assignments in marked columns. The procedure leads to no further marked rows or marked columns.

The minimum set of lines that will cover all zeros is the set through rows 1 and 3 (unmarked) and columns 1 and 4 (marked).

Example 4

Modify the matrix below so as to obtain a better maximal assignment.

$$
\begin{matrix}
5 & 0 & 8 & 10 & 11 \\
0 & 6 & 15 & 0 & 3 \\
8 & 5 & 0 & 0 & 0 \\
0 & 6 & 4 & 2 & 7 \\
3 & 5 & 6 & 0 & 8
\end{matrix}
$$

SOLUTION

The zeros are in the same position as in the previous example; so we already have the maximal assignment and the lines. These are as follows:

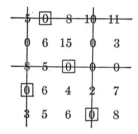

Select the smallest element not deleted by a line; in this matrix it is 3 in row 2, column 5; subtract this element from every element that does not have a line through it, and add it to every element that lies at an intersection of two lines.

The new matrix is:

$$
\begin{matrix}
8 & \boxed{0} & 8 & 13 & 11 \\
\cancel{0} & 3 & 12 & \cancel{0} & \boxed{0} \\
11 & 5 & \boxed{0} & 3 & \cancel{0} \\
\boxed{0} & 3 & 1 & 2 & 4 \\
3 & 2 & 3 & \boxed{0} & 5
\end{matrix}
$$

and we now find that we have a complete assignment in positions with zero elements [(1, 2); (2, 5); (3, 3); (4, 1); (5, 4)]. If the maximal assignment did not constitute a solution to the original problem, we would proceed to draw lines and continue to iterate until we finally obtained a solution.

It is not essential to follow the above procedures exactly in drawing lines. In fact so long as we can cover all zeros in an n-by-n matrix with fewer than n lines (horizontal or vertical) it can be shown that the maximal assignment is not yet a complete solution. The disposition of the zeros can always be improved by applying step f on page 190 (subtracting the minimum element) to any set of less than n lines covering all zeros. However, if it is possible to obtain a set with fewer lines, the final result may be obtained with fewer iterations.

No general statement can be made as to whether the extra work of finding the maximal assignment at each stage can be justified by the savings in iteration. It appears to be a matter of personal taste, and the reader who prefers may choose to draw any covering set of less than n lines (preferably as few as possible) and use them for step f instead of the minimum set.

It can be shown that, if it is impossible to cover the zeros with less than n lines, then a complete assignment among the zeros is possible at that stage.

Summarizing, we have the following rules for solving the assignment problem.

(a) Modify the effectiveness matrix by subtracting the minimum element of each row from all the elements of the row. Then modify the resulting matrix by subtracting the minimum element of each column from all the elements of the column, obtaining the first reduced matrix.

(b) Find a maximal assignment for the first reduced matrix. If this maximal assignment is a complete solution, the procedure ends at this point. If the maximal assignment is not a complete solution proceed to step c.

(c) Draw lines to cover all the zeros. Subtract the smallest element not covered by a line from all the elements not covered; and add this smallest element to all elements lying at the intersection of two lines, obtaining the second reduced matrix.

(d) Repeat steps b and c on the second reduced matrix, and so on until a complete solution is obtained.

PROBLEMS FOR SOLUTION

Set X

1. A national car-rental service has a surplus of one car in each of cities 1, 2, 3, 4, 5, 6, and a deficit of one car in each of cities 7, 8, 9, 10, 11, 12. The distances between cities with a surplus and cities with a deficit are displayed in the matrix below. How should the cars be dispatched so as to minimize the total mileage traveled?

		To					
		7	8	9	10	11	12
	1	41	72	39	52	25	51
	2	22	29	49	65	81	50
From	3	27	39	60	51	32	32
	4	45	50	48	52	37	43
	5	29	40	39	26	30	33
	6	82	40	40	60	51	30

2. A small airline, operating seven days a week, serves three cities (A, B, and C) according to the schedule shown in Table 1. The layover cost per stop is

TABLE 1

Flight no.	From	Time of departure	To	Time of arrival
1	A	9:00 AM	B	Noon
2	A	10:00 AM	B	1:00 PM
3	A	3:00 PM	B	6:00 PM
4	A	8:00 PM	C	Midnight
5	A	10:00 PM	C	2:00 AM
6	B	4:00 AM	A	7:00 AM
7	B	11:00 AM	A	2:00 PM
8	B	3:00 PM	A	6:00 PM
9	C	7:00 AM	A	11:00 AM
10	C	3:00 PM	A	7:00 PM

roughly proportional to the square of the layover time. How should planes be assigned to flights so as to minimize total layover cost?

3. Solve Example 1 of the text, by enumeration.

4. Prove the theorem quoted in the text: If in an assignment problem we add a constant to every element of a row in the effectiveness matrix, then

an assignment that minimizes the total effectiveness in one matrix also minimizes the total effectiveness in the other matrix.

5. A company has four territories open, and four salesmen available for assignment. The territories are not equally rich in their sales potential; it is estimated that a typical salesman operating in each territory would bring in the following annual sales:

Territory   I: $60,000.
Territory   II: 50,000.
Territory III: 40,000.
Territory IV: 30,000.

The four salesmen are also considered to differ in ability; it is estimated that, working under the same conditions, their yearly sales would be proportionately as follows:

Salesman A: 7.
Salesman B: 5.
Salesman C: 5.
Salesman D: 4.

If the criterion is maximum expected total sales, the intuitive answer is to assign the best salesman to the richest territory, the next best salesman to the second richest territory, and so on. Verify this answer by the assignment method.

[*Hint:* To find an assignment with maximum value, multiply each of the elements in the effectiveness matrix by -1, and solve the latter assignment problem in the usual way.]

6. Show that the procedure of subtracting the smallest element not covered by a line from all uncovered elements and adding the same element to all elements lying at an intersection of two lines results in a matrix with the same optimal assignments(s) as the original matrix. [*Hint:* Use the theorem quoted in problem 4 above.]

7. Show that the line-drawing procedure given just after Example 2 in the text results in a system of lines that pass through all the zeros, and with the property that every line passes through one and only one assignment. [*Hint:* If a row is unmarked, it has a line through it; if a row is marked, there are vertical lines through all its zeros. This establishes the first statement. To prove the second statement, note that each unmarked row has an assignment in an unmarked column, and hence that each horizontal line goes through an assignment. Assume that there is a vertical line which does not go through an assignment. By tracing the chain of markings back to the initial row markings, show that the present assignment is not maximal. This contradicts the assumption of a maximal assignment.]

THE TRANSPORTATION PROBLEM

The transportation problem can be regarded as a generalization of the assignment problem. It will be recalled that one interpretation of the assignment problem is that we have a number of origins each possessing one item, and the same number of destinations each requiring one item, and are asked to empty the origins and fill the destinations in such a way that the total effectiveness is optimized. In the transportation problem, we have m origins, with origin i possessing a_i items, and n destinations (possibly a different number from m), with destination j requiring b_j items, and with $\Sigma a_i = \Sigma b_j$. We are given the mn costs associated with shipping *one* item from any origin to any destination, and are asked to empty the origins and fill the destinations in such a way that the total cost is minimized.

The problem may be stated formally as follows. Given an m-by-n array of real numbers (c_{ij}), as well as two sets of positive integers $(a_1, a_2, \cdots, a_m)$ and $(b_1, b_2, \cdots, b_n)$ with

$$\sum_{i=1}^{m} a_i = \sum_{j=1}^{n} b_j$$

Determine, among all m-by-n arrays (x_{ij}) of non-negative integers that satisfy

$$\sum_{i=1}^{m} x_{ij} = b_j \qquad \text{for each } j$$

as well as

$$\sum_{j=1}^{n} x_{ij} = a_i \qquad \text{for each } i$$

that array (x_{ij}) for which the quantity

$$\sum_{i,j} x_{ij} c_{ij}$$

takes its minimum value. Here c_{ij} represents the cost associated with shipping one item from origin i to destination j, and x_{ij} represents the allocation from origin i to destination j.

The assignment problem, in this terminology, is seen to be a special case of the transportation problem in which $m = n$, all the a_i and b_j are unity, and each x_{ij} is limited to one of the two values 0 and 1. In these circumstances, exactly n of the x_{ij} can be non-zero, one in each row of the array and one in each column.

The iterative routine to be presented as the mode of solution of the transportation problem involves a succession of "feasible solutions" of gradually diminishing cost; eventually the minimum achievable cost is reached, and the corresponding feasible solution is optimal. By a "feasible solution" we mean a set of individual allocations which simultaneously removes all the existing surpluses and satisfies all the existing deficiencies. The next example shows ways of finding an initial feasible solution to be used as the starting point in the algorithm.

Example 5

A company has four warehouses and six stores. The warehouses altogether have a surplus of 22 units of a given commodity, divided among them as follows:

Warehouse	Surplus
1	5
2	6
3	2
4	9

The six stores altogether need 22 units of the commodity. Individual requirements are:

Store	Requirements
1	4
2	4
3	6
4	2
5	4
6	2

Costs of shipping one unit of the commodity from warehouse i to store j are displayed in the following matrix:

		Store				
	1	2	3	4	5	6
Warehouse 1	9	12	9	6	9	10
2	7	3	7	7	5	5
3	6	5	9	11	3	11
4	6	8	11	2	2	10

Find feasible (not necessarily optimal) solutions, and the cost associated with each.

The first step is to draw up a blank *m*-by-*n* matrix complete with row and column requirements, as follows:

Available

						5
						6
						2
						9

Required   4   4   6   2   4   2

We wish to put a set of allocations in the cells so that row totals and column totals will be as indicated.

One method is to start at the upper left-hand corner, which we may call cell (1, 1), and allocate as much as possible there: in other words 4. This satisfies the requirement for column 1, and leaves a surplus of 1 unit for row 1; so we allocate 1 to cell (1, 2). Now the allocations are complete for column 1 and row 1; and we have a remaining deficiency of 3 in column 2. Allocate 3 in position (2, 2); now we have columns 1 and 2 complete and a surplus of 3 in row 2. Continuing in this way, from left to right and top to bottom, we will eventually complete all the requirements by an allocation in the lower right-hand corner. The resulting feasible solution is:

Available

4	1					5
	3	3				6
		2				2
		1	2	4	2	9

Required   4   4   6   2   4   2

To obtain the cost for the feasible solution, we multiply each individual allocation by its corresponding unit cost, and add. The resulting cost is 139.

A better method of finding a feasible solution, in that it usually gives a lower beginning cost, is described next. We first write down the cost matrix, together with row and column identifications and row and column requirements:

Store

		1	2	3	4	5	6	Available
	1	9	12	9	6	9	10	5
Warehouse	2	7	3	7	7	5	5	6
	3	6	5	9	11	3	11	2
	4	6	8	11	2	2	10	9
Required		4	4	6	2	4	2	

The next step is to enter the difference between the smallest and second smallest elements in each column beneath the corresponding column, and the difference between the smallest and second smallest elements of each row to the right of the row. These differences are the numbers in parentheses in the matrix following this paragraph. The first individual allocation will be to the smallest cost of a row or the smallest cost of a column; we choose that one for which there is the greatest penalty for not choosing it. That is, we choose the minimum cost location in that row or column whose corresponding number in parentheses is the largest. As 5 is the largest number in parentheses, we choose column 6 as the line for the first individual allocation, and allocate as much as we can to location (2, 6), the minimum cost location in this column. Thus 2 units are allocated to location (2, 6) as indicated by the small numeral in the upper left corner of that cell; and this completes the allocations for column 6, so that the other allocations in this column are zero.

Store

	1	2	3	4	5	6	Available	
1	9	12	9	6	9	0 10	5 (3)	
2	7	3	7	7	5	2 5	6 (2)	Completes column 6
3	6	5	9	11	3	0 11	2 (2)	
4	6	8	11	2	2	0 10	9 (0)	
Required	4 (0)	4 (2)	6 (2)	2 (4)	4 (1)	2 (5)↑		

(Warehouse at left of rows)

The next step is to write down the shrunken cost matrix comprising the rows and columns whose allocations are not yet determined, including revised row and column totals which take into account the allocations already made. Now 4 is the largest unit penalty; this leads to an allocation in the corresponding minimum cost location in column 4: namely cell (4, 4). The maximum possible allocation is 2; so we allocate 2 units to cell (4, 4), and 0 units to the remaining cells in column 4.

Store

	1	2	3	4	5	Available	
1	9	12	9	0 6	9	5 (3)	
2	7	3	7	0 7	5	4 (2)	
3	6	5	9	0 11	3	2 (2)	Completes column 4
4	6	8	11	2 2	2	9 (0)	
Required	4 (0)	4 (2)	6 (2)	2 (4)↑	4 (1)		

(Warehouse at left of rows)

Next, we write down the new cost matrix with column 4 also deleted, and proceed as before. The successive resulting matrices are set down below.

Store

	1	2	3	5	Available	
1	9	12	9	⁰9	5 (0)	
2	7	3	7	⁰5	4 (2)	
Warehouse 3	6	5	9	⁰3	2 (2)	Completes column 5
4	6	8	11	⁴2	7 (4) ←	

Required 4   4   6   4
(0) (2) (2) (1)

Store

	1	2	3	Available	
1	9	12	9	5 (0)	
Warehouse 2	⁰7	⁰3	⁴7	4 (4) ←	Completes row 2 *
3	6	5	9	2 (1)	
4	6	8	11	3 (2)	

Required 4   4   6
(0) (2) (2)

Store

	1	2	3	Available	
1	9	12	9	5 (0)	
Warehouse 3	⁰6	²5	⁰9	2 (1)	Completes row 3
4	6	8	11	3 (2)	

Required 4   4   2
(0) (3) (0)
        ↑

* The reader may have noticed that the authors have failed to apply the rules correctly. The allocation of 4 should be in row 2, column 2. If this is done the solution obtained will be found to be optimal by the methods of example 6. However, a feasible solution has been obtained and, despite the error, is made optimal in example 6.

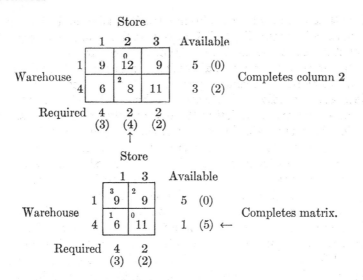

Copying the various positive allocations as they occur in the successive stages, we obtain as our feasible solution:

Store

	1	2	3	4	5	6
Warehouse 1	3		2			
2			4			2
3		2				
4	1	2		2	4	

The cost for this solution turns out to be 127.

The unit penalty method above appears to involve a lot of rewriting of the cost matrix; but much of the repetition was done for clarity of exposition rather than from necessity. In practice, a person can carry through the method if he wishes on the original cost matrix entirely, crossing out rows and columns as they become completed, and working with the remaining matrix after correcting the corresponding row sums, column sums, and unit penalties. In any case, the time saved in avoiding a long set of iterations more than justifies the extra time spent in obtaining the initial feasible allocation.

Now that we know how to obtain a feasible solution, how do we test this solution for optimality? Before we give the answer to this question, we must introduce the notion of "independence" for a set of cells in a rectangular matrix. A set of allocations comprising a feasible solution are said to be in "independent positions" if it is impossible to increase or decrease any individual allocation without either changing the positions of allocations or violating the row or column restrictions. Both feasible solutions obtained in the previous example have this property. For example, suppose that, in the feasible solution obtained by the first method, the allocation in cell (2, 2) is changed from 3 to 2. Then the allocation in cell (1, 2) must change from 1 to 2, to preserve the sum for column 2; the allocation in position (1, 1) must decrease from 4 to 3, because of the restriction on row 1; and finally an allocation in a new position in column 1 is required in order to satisfy the requirement for column 1. A simple criterion for independence is that it is impossible to travel from any allocation back to itself by a series of alternating horizontal and vertical jumps from one occupied cell to another, without a direct reversal of route. The occupied cells in the following matrix, for example, are not in independent positions because of the "loop" connecting cells (2, 2), (2, 3), (3, 3), and (3, 2).

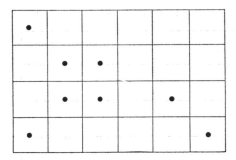

Non-independent positions

The optimality test of this section is applicable to any feasible solution of an m-by-n transportation problem which satisfies the following two conditions:

1. It consists of exactly $m+n-1$ individual allocations:
2. These allocations are in independent positions.

(Later we shall explain how any feasible solution can be modified to meet these conditions.)

The underlying motivation of the optimality test will be indicated briefly. We start with an arbitrary *empty* cell (one lacking an allocation) and allocate $+1$ unit to this cell. In order to keep the row and column sums fixed, this perturbation necessarily produces a change of -1 in some occupied cell of the same row, which in turn requires another change of $+1$ in another occupied cell of the corresponding column, and so on. If the feasible solution satisfies the two requirements above, this chain of events resulting from the allocation of one unit to an empty cell is *consistent* (i.e., we end up with a new feasible solution which satisfies the restrictions on row and column totals) and *unique* (i.e., one and only one such consistent cycle of changes is possible.) The net change in total cost resulting from the perturbation is called the *evaluation* for the empty cell in question; it may be regarded as a sort of first difference, analogous to the first derivative of the calculus. If the cell evaluation is positive, the perturbation would increase the cost; if it is negative, it would decrease the cost. Since there are $mn-(m+n-1)$, or $(m-1)(n-1)$ empty cells, there are $(m-1)(n-1)$ such cell evaluations which may be calculated. If all the cell evaluations turn out to be positive or zero, the feasible solution being tested must be optimal (minimal). Actually, it is not necessary to compute each cell evaluation individually; the optimality test routine set down below gives a method for calculating all of them simultaneously.

Optimality Test

Starting with a feasible solution consisting of $m+n-1$ allocations in independent positions:

1. Determine a set of $m+n$ numbers

$$u_i \qquad i = 1, 2, \cdots, m$$

$$v_j \qquad j = 1, 2, \cdots, n$$

such that, for each *occupied* cell (r, s),

$$c_{rs} = u_r + v_s$$

(Recall that c_{rs} is the individual cost associated with an allocation from origin r to destination s.) If the feasible solution has the demanded properties, this can easily be done by inspection as in Example 6 below.

2. Calculate the cell evaluations Δ_{rs} for each vacant cell (r, s) by

means of the formula

$$\Delta_{rs} = c_{rs} - (u_r + v_s)$$

(See Problem 3 of Set XI for a suggestion of the mode of proof of this formula.)

3. Examine the matrix of cell evaluations for negative entries. If none are negative, the solution under test is optimal. If none are negative and any are zero, other optimal solutions exist. If any are negative, the solution under test is not optimal.

Example 6

Test the lower-cost feasible solution obtained in Example 5 for optimality.

SOLUTION

The allocations for the feasible solution with cost 127 fall in the following positions:

•		•			
		•			•
	•				
•	•		•	•	

The positions are seen to be independent, and there are 9 of them $(m+n-1)$; so the optimality test routine is applicable. Since the u_i and v_j are to be determined by means of the unit costs in the occupied cells only, we write in the corresponding unit costs:

9		9			
		7			5
	5				
6	8		2	2	

We assign a u-value of any particular amount to any particular row; thus u_4 is taken as 0. Since we want $u_i + v_j$ to equal c_{ij} for occupied cells (i, j), this value for u_4 leads to $v_1 = 6$, $v_2 = 8$, $v_4 = 2$, and $v_5 = 2$; and we have

						u_i
9		9				
		7			5	
	5					
6	8		2	2		0
v_j 6	8		2	2		

The subset of the u_i and v_j already determined leads successively to $u_1 = 3$, $u_3 = -3$, $v_3 = 6$, $u_2 = 1$, $v_6 = 4$. Our complete set of u_i and v_j becomes

						u_i
9		9				3
		7			5	1
	5					-3
6	8		2	2		0
v_j 6	8	6	2	2	4	

(Our starting point could have been any particular value for any particular one of the u_i or v_j; it is slightly more convenient to start with zero for the row with the most allocations. No matter which row or column or which number we start with, the mn numbers $(u_i + v_j)$ will not change.)

To compute the matrix of cell evaluations, it is convenient to write down the matrix of the corresponding unit costs, and the matrix of the numbers $(u_i + v_j)$, and then subtract the latter matrix from the former:

•	12	•	6	9	10
7	3	•	7	5	•
6	•	9	11	3	11
•	•	11	•	•	10

Matrix of unit costs (empty cells only)

•	11	•	5	5	7
7	9	•	3	3	•
3	•	3	-1	-1	1
•	•	6	•	•	4

Matrix of $(u_i + v_j)$

•	1	•	1	4	3
0	-6	•	4	2	•
3	•	6	12	4	10
•	•	5	•	•	6

Matrix of cell evaluations

Since one of the cell evaluations turns out to be negative, we conclude that the feasible solution under test is not optimal. We show how to obtain an optimal solution in the following example.

Example 7

Obtain an optimal solution to the transportation problem stated in Example 5, using as a starting point the feasible solution tested in the previous example.

SOLUTION

For convenience we recopy the initial feasible solution:

Available

3		2				5	
	✓	4			2	6	Initial feasible solution
	2					2	—cost 127
1	2		2	4		9	

Required   4   4   6   2   4   2

The check mark indicates the position of the empty cell for which the corresponding evaluation turned out to be negative in the last example.

Recall that an evaluation of $-N$ for an empty cell means that an allocation of $+1$ unit to that cell will reduce the achieved cost by N. If it is possible to allocate $+2$ units to that cell without making any of the other allocations negative, the achieved cost will be reduced by $2N$, and so on. Since the aim of the iteration is to arrive at the minimum cost as quickly as possible, we shall allocate as much as possible to the empty cell with the negative evaluation (or, in general, to the empty cell with the highest negative evaluation).

To perform this re-allocation, we first identify the loop joining the empty cell to occupied cells, as indicated below. (Recall that a *loop* is a closed succession of horizontal and vertical jumps between cells in a matrix.)

3		2			
	✓	4			
1	2				

Loop joining cell (2, 2) to occupied cells

It is seen that we can allocate at most 2 units to cell (2, 2) and still satisfy the row-and-column-total and non-negativity restrictions on the allocations. (If we were to allocate 3 units to the empty cell, the net allocation to cell (4, 2) would have to be -1 if we are to preserve the totals for row 3 and column 2.) The effect of allocating 2 units to the empty cell is

1		4			
	2	2			
3	0				

Re-allocation among cells of loop

The four allocations which do not belong to the loop are carried forward without change, and the new feasible solution becomes

Available

1		4				5
	2	2			2	6 Second feasible solution
	2					2 —cost 115
3			2	4		9

Required   4   4   6   2   4   2

The cost for this new feasible solution is computed to be 115, which is 12 less than the cost for the initial solution; a reduction of this size is anticipated because we are allocating 2 units to a cell where each unit results in a cost change of −6.

The second feasible solution again has 9 allocations in independent positions, and the optimality test is applicable. The result is:

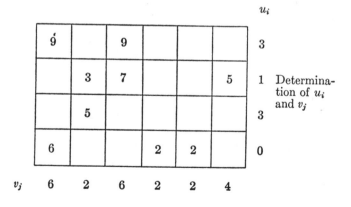

u_i

9		9				3
	3	7			5	1 Determination of u_i and v_j
	5					3
6			2	2		0

v_j 6   2   6   2   2   4

•	5	•	5	5	7
7	•	•	3	3	•
9	•	9	5	5	7
•	2	6	•	•	4

Matrix of $u_i + v_j$

•	7	•	1	4	3
0	•	•	4	2	•
−3	•	0	6	−2	4
•	6	5	•	•	6

Matrix of cell evaluations

The solution is still not optimal.

The steps for the next iteration, which turns out to yield an optimal solution, are:

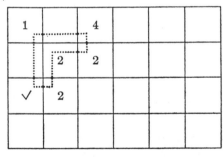

Loop joining cell (3, 1) to occupied cells

0		5			
	3	1			
1	1				

Re-allocation among cells of loop

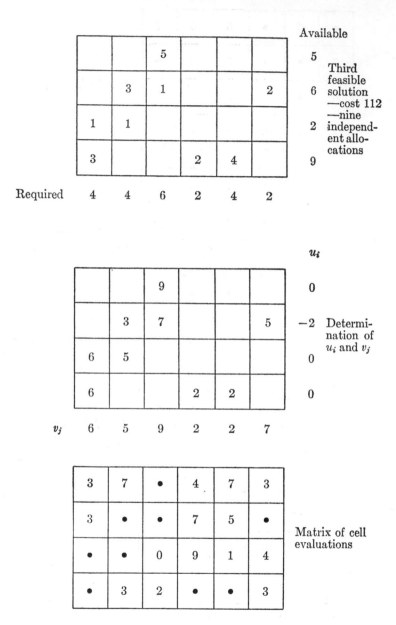

						Available	
		5				5	
	3	1			2	6	Third feasible solution —cost 112 —nine independent allocations
1	1					2	
3			2	4		9	
Required 4	4	6	2	4	2		

						u_i	
		9				0	
	3	7			5	−2	Determination of u_i and v_j
6	5					0	
6			2	2		0	
v_j 6	5	9	2	2	7		

3	7	•	4	7	3	
3	•	•	7	5	•	
•	•	0	9	1	4	Matrix of cell evaluations
•	3	2	•	•	3	

Since all the cell evaluations are non-negative, the third feasible solution is optimal, and 112 is the corresponding minimum cost.

In the above example, the iterative routine could be carried out without difficulty, because each successive feasible solution was "permissible"; i.e. it consisted of $m+n-1$ allocations in independent positions. The remainder of this section deals with the modifications which must be made when, as frequently happens, a feasible solution at some stage does not satisfy the required conditions.

If a feasible solution has allocations in positions which are not independent, there will be a loop (or loops) connecting occupied cells. Such loops can be eliminated by re-allocating among cells in the loop, as in Example 7; and the result will be a feasible solution in independent position. Once a feasible solution is put in independent position, later steps in the iteration will all result in solutions in independent positions. Thus the independence requirement is not hard to fulfill. But the requirement concerning the number of allocations is more difficult to meet, because, even if we start with a permissible solution, the number of allocations is likely to drop below $m+n-1$ at any stage of the iteration.

The following example gives a case where the number of allocations drops below the required number after the first stage of the iteration, and shows how one can proceed to an optimal solution.

Example 8

Obtain an optimal solution to the transportation problem stated in Example 5, using as a starting point the following feasible solution:

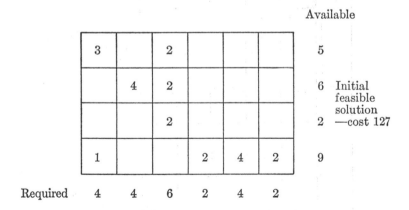

Available

3		2				5
	4	2				6 Initial feasible solution
		2				2 —cost 127
1			2	4	2	9

Required   4   4   6   2   4   2

SOLUTION

Since the initial solution has nine allocations in independent positions, we may proceed to test for optimality and iterate as before:

u_i

						u_i
9		9				3
	3	7				1
		9				3
6			2	2	10	0

| v_j | 6 | 2 | 6 | 2 | 2 | 10 |

Determination of u_i and v_j

•	7	•	1	4	−3
0	•	•	4	2	−6
−3	0	•	6	−2	−2
•	6	5	•	•	•

Matrix of cell evaluations

3		2			
		2			✓
1					2

Loop joining cell (2, 6) to occupied cells

1		4			
		0			2
3					0

Re-allocation among cells of loop

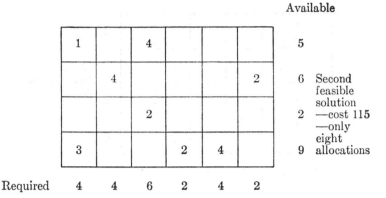

Available

						Available	
1		4				5	
	4				2	6	Second feasible solution
		2				2	—cost 115 —only eight
3			2	4		9	allocations

Required   4   4   6   2   4   2

A feasible solution with independence, but with fewer than the required number of individual allocations, is altered to become permissible in the following manner. First, the requisite number of vacant cells is chosen, so that (a) this number of cells plus the existing number of allocations is $m+n-1$, and (b) these $m+n-1$ cells are independent. (This can always be done if the solution we start with is in independent positions.) Then, an infinitesimal but positive allocation, of amount ϵ, is given to each of the chosen vacant cells. This fiction does not appreciably alter the physical nature of the original set of allocations, but will be found to suffice for carrying through the iterations.

In our example, we need to make but one infinitesimal allocation. One of the empty cells which would suffice for this is cell $(1, 2)$; we allocate ϵ to this cell, and note that the resulting set of nine allocations are in independent positions.

1		4			
ϵ	4				2
		2			
3			2	4	

Revised second feasible solution —cost 115

Now that we have a permissible set of allocations, we can apply the optimality test and iterate:

u_i

						u_i
9		9				3
7	3				5	1
		9				3
6			2	2		0

v_j : 6 2 6 2 2 4

Determination of u_i and v_j

Matrix of cell evaluations

•	7	•	1	4	3
•	•	0	4	2	•
−3	0	•	6	−2	4
•	6	5	•	•	6

Loop joining cell (1, 3) to occupied cells

1		4			
✓		2			

Re-allocation among cells of loop

0		5			
1		1			

Available

		5				5
ε	4				2	6
1		1				2
3			2	4		9

Required   4   4   6   2   4   2

Third feasible solution—cost 112—nine independent allocations

u_i

		9				0
7	3				5	1
6		9				0
6			2	2		0

v_j 6   2   9   2   2   4

Determination of u_i and v_j

3	10	•	4	7	6
•	•	−3	4	2	•
•	3	•	9	1	7
•	6	2	•	•	6

Matrix of cell evaluations

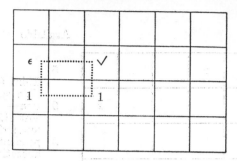

Loop joining cell (2, 3) to occupied cells

At this point we note that the maximum amount we can move into the designated cell is the infinitesimal amount ϵ. We do this, even though the new solution will have the same achieved cost as the old one, because it places us in a position to carry out later iterations if needed.

Re-allocation among cells of loop (ignore infinitesimal changes in non-infinitesimal allocations)

						Available
		5				5
	4	ϵ			2	6
1		1				2
3			2	4		9
Required 4	4	6	2	4	2	

Fourth feasible solution—cost 112—nine independent allocations

u_i

		9					u_i
		9				0	
	3	7			5	−2	Determi-nation of u_i and v_j
6		9				0	
6			2	2		0	
v_j 6	5	9	2	2	7		

3	7	•	4	7	3
3	•	•	7	5	•
•	0	•	9	1	4
•	3	2	•	•	3

Matrix of cell evaluations— indicates fourth feasible solution is optimal

Inasmuch as the infinitesimal quantity ϵ plays only an auxiliary role, it is removed when the optimum is reached, and our final answer is:

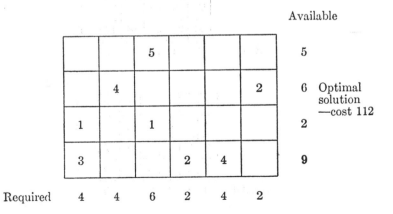

						Available	
		5				5	
	4				2	6	Optimal solution —cost 112
1		1				2	
3			2	4		9	
Required 4	4	6	2	4	2		

Note that the optimal solution is somewhat different from that reached in the previous example, though of course both achieve the same minimum cost.

It is quite possible that a feasible solution may degenerate to $m+n-3$ or even fewer independent allocations—compare any assignment problem, where any feasible solution consists of exactly n allocations. In such cases, if the transportation method of this section is to be used in solving the problem, two or more ϵ's must be used. The ϵ's placed in various independent locations are distinguished from each other by subscripts, and some convention is made about their relative magnitudes.

A rule that will suffice is to read across the rows from left to right, starting with the top row, and call the first ϵ encountered the smallest, the next one the second smallest, and so on.

PROBLEMS FOR SOLUTION

Set XI

1. Solve the following transportation problems. (Cell entries represent unit costs.)

(a)

					Available
73	40	9	79	20	8
62	93	96	8	13	7
96	65	80	50	65	9
57	58	29	12	87	3
56	23	87	18	12	5

Required   6   8   10   4   4

(b)

						Required
5	3	7	3	8	5	3
5	6	12	5	7	11	4
2	8	3	4	8	2	2
9	6	10	5	10	9	8

Available   3   3   6   2   1   2

Required

2	0	4	0	5	3	4
1	6	6	0	1	6	3
0	7	0	2	4	0	2
2	6	5	4	1	3	4
4	1	4	0	3	4	2

(c)

Available 5 2 3 1 2 2

2. A department store wishes to purchase the following quantities of ladies' dresses.

Dress type	A	B	C	D	E
Quantity	150	100	75	250	200

Tenders are submitted by 4 different manufacturers who undertake to supply not more than the quantities below (all types of dress combined).

Manufacturer	W	X	Y	Z
Total quantity	300	250	150	200

The store estimates that its profit per dress will vary with the manufacturer as shown in the matrix below. How should orders be placed?

Dress

Manufacturer		A	B	C	D	E
	W	2.75	3.50	4.25	2.25	1.50
	X	3.00	3.25	4.50	1.75	1.00
	Y	2.50	3.50	4.75	2.00	1.25
	Z	3.25	2.75	4.00	2.50	1.75

[*Hint:* Add a "dummy dress" for which there will be no profit, to represent unused capacity of manufacturers.]

3. Justify the formula given in the text for the simultaneous calculation of all the cell evaluations. That is, if we have a feasible solution consisting of $m+n-1$ independent allocations, and if we have the u_i and v_j satisfying

$$u_r + v_s = c_{rs} \qquad \text{for each filled cell } (r, s)$$

show that the evaluation Δ_{ij} corresponding to each empty cell (i, j) is given by

$$\Delta_{ij} = c_{ij} - (u_i + v_j)$$

[*Hint:* First verify the formula for the simple case where the empty cell is connected to filled cells by a square loop as below. This is done by allocating

$+1$ unit to cell (i, j), and -1 unit to the next cell occupying a corner of the loop, and so on, and computing the resulting change in cost.

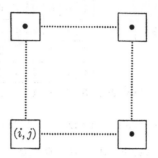

Then generalize your proof to the case of a loop of arbitrary shape connecting cell (i, j) to filled cells.]

THE LINEAR PROGRAMMING PROBLEM

In this type of problem we wish to maximize the linear function

$$(8.1) \qquad Z = C_1 x_1 + C_2 x_2 + \cdots + C_k x_k$$

over all those points in the region

$$(8.2) \qquad x_1 \geq 0, \quad x_2 \geq 0, \quad \cdots, \quad x_k \geq 0$$

which also satisfy the m linear inequalities

$$(8.3) \qquad \begin{aligned} a_{11} x_1 + a_{12} x_2 + \cdots + a_{1k} x_k &\leq b_1 \\ a_{21} x_1 + a_{22} x_2 + \cdots + a_{2k} x_k &\leq b_2 \\ &\vdots \\ a_{m1} x_1 + a_{m2} x_2 + \cdots + a_{mk} x_k &\leq b_m \end{aligned}$$

We can assume without loss of generality that the m expressions comprising the left-hand side in (8.3) are linearly independent, and also that each restriction is satisfied by some but not all points $(x_1, x_2, \cdots, x_k)$ with non-negative coordinates. The latter assumption means that, for each restriction (say, the rth), at least one coefficient a_{rj} has the same sign as b_r.

In this section and most of the next, we shall limit ourselves to the case where all the b_i are non-negative. Later, in Example 11, this limitation will be abandoned. Problem 3 of Set XII gives some discussion of the case where some of the restrictions are equations rather than inequalities.

If Z is a function of only one variable x, the problem of maximizing Z is trivial. In the cases where Z is a function of two or three variables, there is a geometric solution to the problem, which parallels the general algebraic method to be discussed in the next section. We present the geometric approach through a numerical example.

Example 9

Find the non-negative values of x, y, z that maximize the expression

$$Z = 3x + 5y + 4z$$

subject to the restrictions

$$2x + 3y \leq 8$$

(8.4)

$$2y + 5z \leq 10$$

$$3x + 2y + 4z \leq 15$$

SOLUTION

If we consider x, y, and z to be coordinates in three-dimensional space, the non-negativity restrictions mean that we are concerned only with the region consisting of points whose coordinates are all either positive or zero. However, we are not free to choose any point in this region because of the restrictions (8.4). In fact we are limited to points that lie within or on the boundary of the solid enclosed by the six planes, whose equations are

$$2x + 3y = 8 \qquad x = 0$$

$$2y + 5z = 10 \qquad y = 0$$

$$3x + 2y + 4z = 15 \qquad z = 0$$

This solid $[OABCDEFG]$ is shown in Figure 8.1. Now consider the plane whose equation is

(8.5)
$$\frac{3}{\sqrt{50}} x + \frac{5}{\sqrt{50}} y + \frac{4}{\sqrt{50}} z = p$$

It is shown in textbooks on analytical geometry that p is the perpendicular distance of the plane from the origin. Now $Z = p \sqrt{50}$, so that Z has the same value for any point of the plane (8.5). If we think

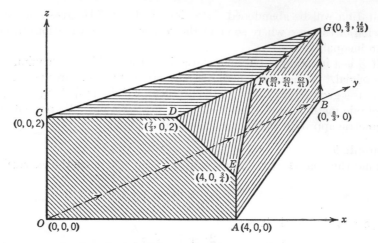

Figure 8.1. Region of admissible solutions in three dimensions (Example 9).

of p as a variable parameter, (8.5) will represent a family of parallel planes, and maximizing Z is equivalent to finding that member of the family which is furthest from the origin, while still having at least one point within or on the boundary of the solid $OABCDEFG$.

A little reflection will show that such a plane must pass through one of the corners of the solid $OABCDEFG$. Consider Figure 8.2, where P

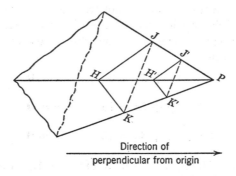

Direction of
perpendicular from origin

Figure 8.2. View of one vertex.

is any corner, and JHK is one plane of the family. It is clear that the parallel plane $J'H'K'$ still has points within the solid and that it is further from the origin. Thus, until we move $J'H'K'$ as far as P, there will be parallel planes further from the origin with points within the solid. Of course, there may be other parallel planes further from the origin and with a point within $OABCDEFG$, but the plane for which we are looking must pass through some corner. In other words, the *maximum value of Z is taken at one of the corners of the solid bounded by the restricting planes.* This result, or its algebraic analog, is the key theorem to all that follows.

Having decided that we can confine our search for the maximum Z to corners, we could first find all the corners (as in Figure 8.1) and then evaluate Z at each, until we found the maximum. Unfortunately finding all the corners is a long and tedious process, and we are led to wonder if a more systematic approach is possible. The most commonly used approach consists of four steps.

1. Find one corner as a starting point.

2. Examine each edge through the corner to see whether movement along it increases Z. If movement along no such edge increases Z, the corner maximizes Z. If movement along at least one edge increases Z, proceed to step 3.

3. Choose one of the edges along which movement increases Z, and move along it until the next corner is reached.

4. Repeat steps 1, 2, 3 until Z cannot be increased further.

In order to do this with reasonable algebraic simplicity we introduce the so-called *slack variables* u, v, w, defined by the equations

$$2x + 3y + u = 8$$

(8.6)
$$2y + 5z + v = 10$$

$$3x + 2y + 4z + w = 15$$

It will be realized that u, v, w are the deficiencies when the inequality signs hold in the original restrictions. Moreover, if x, y, z are to satisfy these restrictions, u, v, w must be non-negative.

If we rewrite (8.6) as

$$u = 8 - 2x - 3y$$

(8.6A)
$$v = 10 - 2y - 5z$$

$$w = 15 - 3x - 2y - 4z$$

we see that any two of the six equations $u = 0$, $v = 0$, $w = 0$, $x = 0$, $y = 0$, $z = 0$ represent together one of the edges of the solid $OABCDE-FG$. Now suppose we start at the origin which is clearly a corner of the solid. Thus we choose $x = y = z = 0$ and read off the corresponding values of u, v, w as 8, 10, 15.

The three edges through the origin are represented by the pairs of equations

$$x = 0 \atop y = 0 \Big\} \qquad x = 0 \atop z = 0 \Big\} \qquad y = 0 \atop z = 0 \Big\}$$

If we move along these lines, we increase z, y, x, respectively. Each unit increase in x, y, z increases Z by 3, 5, 4, respectively; so we decide to increase y as much as possible, and for the time being to leave x and z as zero.

Referring to (8.6A) we see that we can increase y by 8/3 without making u negative; we can increase y by 5 without making v negative, and we can increase y by 15/2 without making w negative. Thus the maximum increase in y is 8/3, and we move from the origin to the point $B(0, 8/3, 0)$. Next we re-arrange equations (8.6) so that we can read off the non-zero variables at B, just as previously we read off the non-zero variables at the origin. To do this we solve (8.6) for v, w, and y (the non-zero variables at B) in terms of x, z, and u (the zero variables at B). An easy way to do this is to solve the first equation of (8.6A) for y, and then substitute this expression for y in the other two equations of (8.6A). We obtain

$$\tfrac{2}{3}x + y + \tfrac{1}{3}u = \tfrac{8}{3}$$

$$-\tfrac{4}{3}x + 5z - \tfrac{2}{3}u + v = \tfrac{14}{3}$$

$$\tfrac{5}{3}x + 4z - \tfrac{2}{3}u + w = \tfrac{29}{3}$$

(8.7)   or

$$y = \tfrac{8}{3} - \tfrac{2}{3}x - \tfrac{1}{3}u$$

$$v = \tfrac{14}{3} + \tfrac{4}{3}x - 5z + \tfrac{2}{3}u$$

$$w = \tfrac{29}{3} - \tfrac{5}{3}x - 4z + \tfrac{2}{3}u$$

The edges through B are given by

$$x = 0 \atop z = 0 \Big\} BO \qquad x = 0 \atop u = 0 \Big\} BG \qquad z = 0 \atop u = 0 \Big\} BA$$

We have just moved along BO; so we consider moving along BG and BA.

If we move along BA, we will have to increase x, and from the first equation in (8.7) we see we will have to decrease y by 2/3 for every unit increase in x. Thus, for every unit increase in x, we will change Z by $3 \times 1 - 5 \times 2/3 = -1/3$. Thus we do not want to move along BA.

If we move along BG, we increase z, and we see from (8.7) that x and y do not change as z increases. Consequently, increasing z increases Z by 4 per unit. From the second of equations (8.7), we can increase z by as much as 14/15 without making v negative; and, from the third equation, we can increase z by as much as 29/12 without making w negative. Thus the maximum permissible increase in z is 14/15, and we move from B to G.

Again we express the non-zero variables (y, z, and w) in terms of the zero variables

$$\tfrac{2}{3}x + y + \tfrac{1}{3}u = \tfrac{8}{3}$$

$$-\tfrac{4}{15}x + z - \tfrac{2}{15}u + \tfrac{1}{5}v = \tfrac{14}{15}$$

$$\tfrac{41}{15}x - \tfrac{2}{15}u - \tfrac{4}{5}v + w = \tfrac{89}{15}$$

(8.8)   or

$$y = \tfrac{8}{3} - \tfrac{2}{3}x - \tfrac{1}{3}u$$

$$z = \tfrac{14}{15} + \tfrac{4}{15}x + \tfrac{2}{15}u - \tfrac{1}{5}v$$

$$w = \tfrac{89}{15} - \tfrac{41}{15}x + \tfrac{2}{15}u + \tfrac{4}{5}v$$

and repeat the operations, arriving at the point F with coordinates (89/41, 50/41, 62/41). Here we discover that movement in any direction decreases Z, and we conclude that Z takes its maximum at the vertex F.

The geometric method for the simplex has been described here in order to motivate the algebraic presentation which follows, and is *not* recommended as a calculational procedure even in the three-dimensional case. From here on, we will be thinking of the algebraic analog of the geometry already discussed, and will develop the simplex tableau which is used for calculation. (A geometric procedure which is practical for the two-dimensional case is sketched in problem 1 of Problem Set XII.)

THE SIMPLEX METHOD

The first step in the simplex method for solving the general problem posed at the beginning of this section is to convert the system of m linear inequalities (8.3) to a system of m linear equations. This is done by the insertion of the so-called "slack variables" $x_{k+1}, x_{k+2}, \cdots, x_{k+m}$, one for each of the displayed inequalities so that (8.3) becomes

$$a_{11}x_1 + a_{12}x_2 + \cdots + a_{1k}x_k + x_{k+1} = b_1$$
$$a_{21}x_1 + a_{22}x_2 + \cdots + a_{2k}x_k + x_{k+2} = b_2$$

(8.9)

$$a_{m1}x_1 + a_{m2}x_2 + \cdots + a_{mk}x_k + x_{k+m} = b_m$$

The linear programming problem may now be restated as follows: to find, among all sets of points $(x_1, x_2, \cdots, x_{k+m})$ satisfying (8.9) with each x_j non-negative, that point $(\bar{x}_1, \bar{x}_2, \cdots, \bar{x}_{k+m})$ which maximizes the linear function

(8.10) $$Z = C_1x_1 + C_2x_2 + \cdots + C_kx_k$$

Once the maximal $(\bar{x}_1, \bar{x}_2, \cdots, \bar{x}_{k+m})$ is found, the answer to the problem as originally stated is just the subset $(\bar{x}_1, \bar{x}_2, \cdots, \bar{x}_k)$. The slack variables are merely a device used in arriving at the optimal solution, and may or may not have physical meaning in individual problems.

The key theorem underlying the simplex approach says, in effect, that the set $(x_1, x_2, \cdots, x_{m+k})$ which maximizes (8.10) subject to (8.9) must necessarily possess k elements which are zero. If we knew which coordinates were zero at the optimum, we could insert their values in (8.9); the latter system would then be a set of m equations in m unknowns, and could be solved algebraically for the optimum. Without this knowledge, we must be content to proceed in a step-by-step fashion toward a solution. The procedure may be visualized as follows. We choose k of the $k+m$ coordinates, and assign them the value zero. Using these values, we then solve the restriction equations for the remaining m coordinates. If any of the coordinates are negative, we discard this solution as violating the non-negativity restriction, and try another set of k coordinates for the zero variables. If none of the coordinates are negative, we have what is called a *feasible solution*, which is the starting point of the iterative process. The simplex technique permits us to test the feasible solution for optimality, and, if it is non-optimal, to proceed directly to a different feasible solution with an improved Z. It can be shown that eventually the technique must take us to an optimal solution.

A feasible solution for the nth stage is related to the feasible solution for the $n+1$st stage in the following way. One of the zero coordinates for the nth stage becomes non-zero in the $n+1$st stage, and is called an *entering variable.* To compensate, one of the non-zero coordinates in the nth stage becomes zero in the $n+1$st stage, and is called a *departing variable.* The other zero coordinates remain zero; and the other non-zero coordinates in general remain non-zero (though their values may change).

In what follows, we shall use repeatedly the concept of a matrix representation of a system of linear equations, and shall also assume that the reader is acquainted with the procedure for manipulating rows of the matrix until a solution to the original system may be read off. The reader who is not familiar with these topics is advised to read Appendix III before proceeding further with this chapter.

The simplex routine is presented next. For definiteness, we shall give the tableau for the case of five original variables and four restrictions [$k = 5$, $m = 4$ in (8.9) and (8.10) above].

Step One

Convert the m restrictive inequalities to m equations, by the insertion of the non-negative slack variables x_{k+1}, x_{k+2}, $\cdots$, x_{k+m}, one to each of the m restrictions. Write this system of equations in matrix form. Mark each column in some way so as to designate which variable is served by that column of coefficients. (Below, we mark the column of coefficients of x_i by P_i, and use P_0 to designate the column of constant terms. Insert also a row C_j, where C_j is the coefficient of x_j in the objective function Z.

P_1	P_2	P_3	P_4	P_5	P_6	P_7	P_8	P_9	P_0
a_{11}	a_{12}	a_{13}	a_{14}	a_{15}	1	0	0	0	b_1
a_{21}	a_{22}	a_{23}	a_{24}	a_{25}	0	1	0	0	b_2
a_{31}	a_{32}	a_{33}	a_{34}	a_{35}	0	0	1	0	b_3
a_{41}	a_{42}	a_{43}	a_{44}	a_{45}	0	0	0	1	b_4

$C_j \rightarrow$ C_1 C_2 C_3 C_4 C_5 0 0 0 0

Step Two

Read off a feasible solution, and insert it as a row below the coefficient matrix. The feasible solution at any stage is read off by choosing the non-zero variables to be those whose columns consist of 1 and the rest zeros. Insert P-designations $P_{[i]}$ to the left of each row of the coefficient matrix, to indicate which non-zero coordinate value is read from that equation. Insert also a column of $C_{[i]}$, where $C_{[i]}$ is the coefficient of $x_{[i]}$ in Z.

If all the b_i are positive, a feasible solution is obviously $x_1 = x_2 = x_3 = x_4 = x_5 = 0$, $x_6 = b_1$, $x_7 = b_2$, $x_8 = b_3$, $x_9 = b_4$. The tableau becomes:

$C_{[i]}$	$P_{[i]}$		P_1	P_2	P_3	P_4	P_5	P_6	P_7	P_8	P_9	P_0
0	P_6		a_{11}	a_{12}	a_{13}	a_{14}	a_{15}	1	0	0	0	b_1
0	P_7		a_{21}	a_{22}	a_{23}	a_{24}	a_{25}	0	1	0	0	b_2
0	P_8		a_{31}	a_{32}	a_{33}	a_{34}	a_{35}	0	0	1	0	b_3
0	P_9		a_{41}	a_{42}	a_{43}	a_{44}	a_{45}	0	0	0	1	b_4

$$C_j \rightarrow \quad C_1 \quad C_2 \quad C_3 \quad C_4 \quad C_5 \quad 0 \quad 0 \quad 0 \quad 0$$

Solution $\quad 0 \quad 0 \quad 0 \quad 0 \quad 0 \quad b_1 \quad b_2 \quad b_3 \quad b_4$

(If not all the b_i are positive, some preliminary manipulation is necessary before the feasible solution can be read off. See Example 11, page 234.)

Step Three

Test the solution for optimality. This is done by computing an "evaluation" Δ_j for each zero variable x_j, by the formula

(8.11) $$\Delta_j = C_j - \sum_{i=1}^{m} a_{ij} C_{[i]}$$

If one or more of the evaluations Δ_j are positive, the solution is non-optimal, and we proceed to step four. If $\Delta_j \leq 0$ for each j, the solution is optimal. (Note: If none of the evaluations is positive, but if any are zero, other optimal solutions exist, with the same value for Z. If all the evaluations are less than zero, the achieved optimal solution is unique.)

The interpretation of the evaluations is as follows. Let Z_0 be the value of Z for the feasible solution under test, and let $Z_0^{(j)}$ be the value of Z that would result if the feasible solution were altered viz.: Increase the zero coordinate x_j from 0 to 1, retain the other zero coordinates as zero, and adjust the non-zero coordinates so that the restriction equations remain satisfied. Then

(8.12) $$\Delta_j = Z_0^{(j)} - Z_0$$

The proof of (8.12) is left to the reader as an exercise.

The tableau has now grown to:

$C_{[i]}$	$P_{[i]}$		P_1	P_2	P_3	P_4	P_5	P_6	P_7	P_8	P_9	P_0
0	P_6		a_{11}	a_{12}	a_{13}	a_{14}	a_{15}	1	0	0	0	b_1
0	P_7		a_{21}	a_{22}	a_{23}	a_{24}	a_{25}	0	1	0	0	b_2
0	P_8		a_{31}	a_{32}	a_{33}	a_{34}	a_{35}	0	0	1	0	b_3
0	P_9		a_{41}	a_{42}	a_{43}	a_{44}	a_{45}	0	0	0	1	b_4

$$C_j \rightarrow \quad C_1 \quad C_2 \quad C_3 \quad C_4 \quad C_5 \quad 0 \quad 0 \quad 0 \quad 0$$

Solution $\quad 0 \quad 0 \quad 0 \quad 0 \quad 0 \quad b_1 \; b_2 \; b_3 \; b_4$

$\Delta_j \qquad \Delta_1 \quad \Delta_2 \quad \Delta_3 \quad \Delta_4 \quad \Delta_5 \quad - \; - \; - \; -$

(At this stage, and indeed at any stage of a problem where the set of non-zero variables is just the set of slack variables, it is seen that $\Delta_j = C_j$ for each j. But such a relationship will not hold for later iterations.)

Step Four

Determine the entering variable x_r. Recall that the entering variable is that zero variable in the feasible solution which is to become non-zero in the next iteration. An entering variable x_j must have the following properties:

(i)   It is zero in the present tableau.
(ii) $\Delta_j \geq 0$.
(iii) At least one of the a_{ij} in the column for x_j must be greater than zero.*

Any variable x_j with these properties could be used, in the sense that the resulting feasible solution in the next iteration will produce a value of Z at least as great as that in the present tableau. The following empirical rule for choosing the entering variable has been found to produce quick convergence. Choose from among the possible entering variables that zero coordinate x_j for which Δ_j is largest.

Step Five

Determine the departing variable x_s. The departing variable is that non-zero coordinate $x_{[i]}$ which is to become zero in the next iteration.

* Any variable x_j which has no element a_{ij} in its column greater than zero may be increased indefinitely without violating the original restrictions. If such a variable also has a *positive* Δ_j, Z may be increased indefinitely merely by increasing z_j. Such cases can hardly arise in models of physical problems.

The choice of departing variable is, in general, determined by the choice of the entering variable, together with the non-negativity restrictions on the coordinates. If x_r is the entering variable, the rule is: s will be that $[i]$ for which the quotient b_i/a_{ir} takes its smallest non-negative value; and x_s will be the departing variable. (*Note:* Since we assumed earlier that the problem has been put into such a form that all the b_i are positive, we are really selecting from among positive a_{ir} in the rth column.)

We now have all the information we need to complete the simplex tableau for this stage of the iteration. For definiteness, let the entering variable be x_3 and the departing variable be x_7.

$C_{[i]}$	$P_{[i]}$		P_1	P_2	P_3	P_4	P_5	P_6	P_7	P_8	P_9	P_0
0	P_6		a_{11}	a_{12}	a_{13}	a_{14}	a_{15}	1	0	0	0	b_1
0	P_7		a_{21}	a_{22}	a_{23}	a_{24}	a_{25}	0	1	0	0	b_2
0	P_8		a_{31}	a_{32}	a_{33}	a_{34}	a_{35}	0	0	1	0	b_3
0	P_9		a_{41}	a_{42}	a_{43}	a_{44}	a_{45}	0	0	0	1	b_4

$$C_j \rightarrow \quad C_1 \quad C_2 \quad C_3 \quad C_4 \quad C_5 \quad 0 \quad 0 \quad 0 \quad 0$$

Solution: $\quad 0 \quad 0 \quad 0 \quad 0 \quad 0 \quad b_1 \quad b_2 \quad b_3 \quad b_4$

$$\Delta_j \quad \Delta_1 \quad \Delta_2 \quad \Delta_3 \quad \Delta_4 \quad \Delta_5 \quad - \quad - \quad - \quad -$$

Entering variable x_r ↑   Departing variable x_s ↓

The reason for distinguishing the element in the column labeled P_r and the row labeled P_s will become apparent in the next step.

Step Six

Calculate the new coefficient matrix by means of suitably chosen row operations on the old coefficient matrix. The new coefficient matrix is to have unity in the position distinguished in step five, and zero elsewhere in that column. When this is accomplished, the new matrix will be such that the new feasible solution can be read off immediately.

Computationally, we proceed as follows. Divide all elements of the distinguished row by the distinguished element of that row, thus obtaining unity in the distinguished position. Then subtract appropriate multiples of this new row from the other $m-1$ rows, so as to obtain zeros in the remaining positions of the distinguished column.

If we use a'_{ij}, b'_i to denote the elements of the new coefficient matrix, the new matrix will be:

P_1	P_2	P_3	P_4	P_5	P_6	P_7	P_8	P_9	P_0
a'_{11}	a'_{12}	0	a'_{14}	a'_{15}	1	a'_{17}	0	0	b'_1
a'_{21}	a'_{22}	1	a'_{24}	a'_{25}	0	a'_{27}	0	0	b'_2
a'_{31}	a'_{32}	0	a'_{34}	a'_{35}	0	a'_{37}	1	0	b'_3
a'_{41}	a'_{42}	0	a'_{44}	a'_{45}	0	a'_{47}	0	1	b'_4

The b'_i will all be non-negative, because of the way the entering and departing variables were chosen.

Step Seven

Repeat steps one through six as needed, until an optimum is finally attained in step three.

The steps are performed, of course, on the new coefficient matrix, so that for example (8.11) becomes

$$\Delta'_j = C_j - \sum_{i=1}^{m} a'_{ij} C_{[i]},$$

and so on. The complete second tableau, before entering and departing variables are chosen, is given below.

$C_{[i]}$	$P_{[i]}$	P_1	P_2	P_3	P_4	P_5	P_6	P_7	P_8	P_9	P_0
0	P_6	a'_{11}	a'_{12}	0	a'_{14}	a'_{15}	1	a'_{17}	0	0	b'_1
C_3	P_3	a'_{21}	a'_{22}	1	a'_{24}	a'_{25}	0	a'_{27}	0	0	b'_2
0	P_8	a'_{31}	a'_{32}	0	a'_{34}	a'_{35}	0	a'_{37}	1	0	b'_3
0	P_9	a'_{41}	a'_{42}	0	a'_{44}	a'_{45}	0	a'_{47}	0	1	b'_4

$$C_j \rightarrow \quad C_1 \quad C_2 \quad C_3 \; C_4 \quad C_5 \quad 0 \quad 0 \quad\quad 0 \quad 0$$

Solution $\quad 0 \quad\quad 0 \quad\quad b'_2 \; 0 \quad\quad 0 \quad\quad b'_1 \; 0 \quad\quad b'_3 \; b'_4$

$\Delta_j \quad\quad \Delta'_1 \quad \Delta'_2 \quad - \; \Delta'_4 \quad \Delta'_5 \quad - \; \Delta'_7 \quad - \; -$

Example 10

Rework Example 9 (the geometric example) by the simplex method.

SOLUTION

To agree with the notation of the simplex routine presented above, we rename the variables x, y, z as x_1, x_2, x_3, and call the slack variables x_4, x_5, x_6. Then the problem becomes one of maximizing

$$Z = 3x_1 + 5x_2 + 4x_3$$

subject to the restrictions

$$2x_1 + 3x_2 \qquad + x_4 = 8$$

$$2x_2 + 5x_3 + x_5 = 10$$

$$3x_1 + 2x_2 + 4x_3 + x_6 = 15$$

The first tableau becomes

$C_{[i]}$	$P_{[i]}$	P_1	P_2	P_3	P_4	P_5	P_6	P_0
0	P_4	2	3	0	1	0	0	8
0	P_5	0	2	5	0	1	0	10
0	P_6	3	2	4	0	0	1	15

$$C_j \rightarrow \quad 3 \quad 5 \quad 4 \quad 0 \quad 0 \quad 0$$

		P_1	P_2	P_3	P_4	P_5	P_6	
Solution		0	0	0	8	10	15	$(Z = 0)$
Δ_j		3	5	4	—	—	—	
$b_i/a_{i,2}$		—	—	—	$\frac{8}{3}$	$\frac{10}{2}$	$\frac{15}{2}$	

$$\uparrow \qquad\qquad \downarrow$$

Enter-   Depart-
ing   ing *
variable   variable

To obtain the second tableau, we first calculate the intermediate coefficient matrix

$\frac{2}{3}$	1	0	$\frac{1}{3}$	0	0	$\frac{8}{3}$
0	2	5	0	1	0	10
3	2	4	0	0	1	15

* Recall that the entering variable x_2 is determined by the largest Δ_j, and the departing variable x_4 is determined by the smallest $b_i/a_{i,2}$.

and by row operations we get the coefficient matrix for the second tableau:

$$
\begin{array}{cccccc|c}
\frac{2}{3} & 1 & 0 & \frac{1}{3} & 0 & 0 & \frac{8}{3} \\[4pt]
-\frac{4}{3} & 0 & 5 & -\frac{2}{3} & 1 & 0 & \frac{14}{3} \\[4pt]
\frac{5}{3} & 0 & 4 & -\frac{2}{3} & 0 & 1 & \frac{29}{3}
\end{array}
$$

In this example, it turns out that four tableaus are needed before an optimum is reached. The second, third, and fourth are obtained in the manner described, and are set down below.

SECOND TABLEAU

$C_{[i]}$	$P_{[i]}$	P_1	P_2	P_3	P_4	P_5	P_6	P_0
5	P_2	$\frac{2}{3}$	1	0	$\frac{1}{3}$	0	0	$\frac{8}{3}$
0	P_5	$-\frac{4}{3}$	0	5	$-\frac{2}{3}$	1	0	$\frac{14}{3}$
0	P_6	$\frac{5}{3}$	0	4	$-\frac{2}{3}$	0	1	$\frac{29}{3}$

	C_j	3	5	4	0	0	0	0
	Solution	0	$\frac{8}{0}$	0	0	$\frac{14}{3}$	$\frac{29}{3}$	
	Δ_j	$-\frac{1}{3}$	—	4	$-\frac{5}{3}$	—	—	
	b_i/a_{ir}	—	∞	—	—	$\frac{14}{15}$	$\frac{29}{12}$	

$(Z = \frac{40}{3})$

Entering variable ↑ (P_3 column)   Departing variable ↓ (P_6 row)

Entering   Departing
variable   variable

THIRD TABLEAU

$C_{[i]}$	$P_{[i]}$	P_1	P_2	P_3	P_4	P_5	P_6	P_0
5	P_2	$\frac{2}{3}$	1	0	$\frac{1}{3}$	0	0	$\frac{8}{3}$
4	P_3	$-\frac{4}{15}$	0	1	$-\frac{2}{15}$	$\frac{1}{5}$	0	$\frac{14}{15}$
0	P_6	$\frac{41}{15}$	0	0	$-\frac{2}{15}$	$-\frac{4}{5}$	1	$\frac{89}{15}$

	$C_j \rightarrow$	3	5	4	0	0	0
	Solution	0	$\frac{8}{3}$	$\frac{14}{15}$	0	0	$\frac{89}{15}$
	Δ_j	$\frac{11}{15}$	—	—	$-\frac{17}{15}$	$-\frac{4}{5}$	
	b_i/a_{ir}	—	4	$-\frac{7}{2}$	—	—	$\frac{89}{41}$

$(Z = \frac{256}{15})$

Entering
variable ↑

Departing
variable ↓

FOURTH TABLEAU

$C_{[i]}$	$P_{[i]}$	P_1	P_2	P_3	P_4	P_5	P_6	P_0
5	P_2	0	1	0	$\frac{15}{41}$	$\frac{8}{41}$	$-\frac{10}{41}$	$\frac{50}{41}$
4	P_3	0	0	1	$-\frac{6}{41}$	$\frac{5}{41}$	$\frac{4}{41}$	$\frac{62}{41}$
3	P_1	1	0	0	$-\frac{2}{41}$	$-\frac{12}{41}$	$\frac{15}{41}$	$\frac{89}{41}$

$$C_j \rightarrow \quad 3 \quad 5 \quad 4 \qquad 0 \qquad 0 \qquad 0$$

Solution $\quad \frac{89}{41} \quad \frac{50}{41} \quad \frac{62}{41} \qquad 0 \qquad 0 \qquad 0 \qquad (Z = \frac{765}{41})$

$\Delta_j \qquad — \quad — \quad — \quad -\frac{45}{41} \quad -\frac{24}{41} \quad -\frac{11}{41}$

Since all the Δ_j are non-positive, the fourth tableau yields an optimum. The optimal solution is (89/41, 50/41, 62/41), giving a Z of 765/41.

It has already been pointed out that the routine given above cannot even start if some of the constant terms b_i are negative. The reason is that, if a b_i is negative, the solution read off from the original coefficient matrix contains the negative coordinate $x_i(= b_i)$, and is therefore not feasible. Once a feasible solution is obtained, by ruse or inspiration, the simplex routine can proceed as given.

The following example illustrates how a feasible solution can be obtained when some of the b_i are negative.

Example 11

Obtain a first feasible solution in the case where some linear function $Z(x_1, x_2, x_3)$ is to be maximized subject to the restrictions

(8.13)
$$x_1 + x_2 + x_3 \leq 8$$
$$-x_1 - 2x_2 + x_3 \leq -2$$

SOLUTION

If we merely introduced the slack variables x_4 and x_5, so that the restrictions became

$$x_1 + x_2 + x_3 + x_4 = 8$$
$$-x_1 - 2x_2 + x_3 + x_5 = -2$$

the solution read off would be $(0, 0, 0, 8, -2)$, which is not feasible. But, if we also introduce a so-called "artificial variable" x_6, understood to be positive and not greater than x_5, the restrictions (8.13) can be rewritten as

$$x_1 + x_2 + x_3 + x_4 = 8$$
$$-x_1 - 2x_2 + x_3 + x_5 - x_6 = -2$$

or better

$$x_1 + x_2 + x_3 + x_4 = 8$$

$$x_1 + 2x_2 - x_3 - x_5 + x_6 = 2$$

The first tableau becomes

$P_{[i]}$	P_1	P_2	P_3	P_4	P_5	P_6	P_0
P_4	1	1	1	1	0	0	8
P_6	1	2	-1	0	-1	1	2

Solution   0   0   0   8   0   2

The solution consists of non-negative coordinates, but is not yet feasible, since $x_6 > x_5$, and the second restriction in (8.13) is violated.

We now transform the equations as in the simplex routine, using the artificial variable x_6 as the departing variable. We choose as an entering variable one of the original variables x_1, x_2, x_3, being careful to choose one that will yield a transformed matrix with a non-negative constant column. In this example, we may choose x_2 if we wish as the entering variable. The next tableau becomes

P_1	P_2	P_3	P_4	P_5	P_6	P_0
$\frac{1}{2}$	0	$\frac{3}{2}$	1	$\frac{1}{2}$	$-\frac{1}{2}$	7
$\frac{1}{2}$	1	$-\frac{1}{2}$	0	$-\frac{1}{2}$	$\frac{1}{2}$	1

Solution   0   1   0   7   0   0

The solution $(0, 1, 0, 7, 0, 0)$ is feasible, since it consists of non-negative coordinates which satisfy the restrictions (8.13). The artificial variable x_6 has served its purpose, and is dropped from the problem. To maximize $Z(x_1, x_2, x_3)$, we would start with the 2-by-5 tableau:

P_1	P_2	P_3	P_4	P_5	P_0
$\frac{1}{2}$	0	$\frac{3}{2}$	1	$\frac{1}{2}$	7
$\frac{1}{2}$	1	$-\frac{1}{2}$	0	$-\frac{1}{2}$	1

Solution   0   1   0   7   0

(If there were more than one negative b_i, a corresponding number of artificial variables would be introduced. Then the artificial variables would be removed one at a time and replaced by the original and slack variables.)

Since the arithmetic of the simplex method is fairly lengthy, it may be advisable to perform certain checks on a tableau before proceeding to the next tableau. One obvious check is that the Z value obtained for a tableau should not be less than the Z value for the previous tableau. A more precise check relies on the fact (not proved here) that the row of evaluations Δ_j may be obtained from the Δ_j row of the previous tableau, in the same way that the rows of the coefficient matrix are obtained from the previous coefficient matrix. That is, to obtain the new row of evaluations we subtract from the old evaluation row the product of Δ_r times the distinguished row divided by the distinguished element of that row. [This procedure could have been used to compute the new Δ_j; then the check would consist of the application of equation (8.11).]

The discussion of the text has been confined to problems where Z is to be *maximized* subject to restrictions, each requiring a linear function of the x_j to be *less than or equal to* some constant. However, this is no real limitation. If Z is to be minimized, we merely regard the problem as one of maximizing $(-Z)$. Further, any restriction of the form

$$\Sigma k_j x_j \geq b_j$$

can be rewritten as

$$\Sigma(-k_j)x_j \leq -b_j$$

APPLICATIONS OF LINEAR PROGRAMMING

Although the arithmetic technique used in linear programming problems is long and tedious, it is essentially a mechanical repetition of a sequence of precisely defined steps. The real task for the operations research worker is to recognize that his problem can be solved by linear programming and to formulate a model that will lead to a useful solution. In this section we will give some illustrative examples of problems that can be solved with the simplex technique.

Example 12

A company makes two kinds of leather belts. Belt A is a high-quality belt, and belt B is of lower quality. The respective profits are $0.40 and $0.30 per belt. Each belt of type A requires twice as much time as a belt of type B, and, if all belts were of type B, the company could make 1000 per day. The supply of leather is sufficient for only

800 belts per day (both A and B combined). Belt A requires a fancy buckle, and only 400 per day are available. There are only 700 buckles a day available for belt B. Set up the linear programming equations for the problem.

SOLUTION

Suppose the company makes x_1 belts of type A and x_2 belts of type B each day.

From the restrictions on the number of buckles available we have

$$x_1 \leq 400$$

$$x_2 \leq 700$$

From the availability of leather we have

$$x_1 + x_2 \leq 800$$

and from the limitation on time

$$2x_1 + x_2 \leq 1000$$

Introducing the slack variables x_3, x_4, x_5 and x_6, we can write the restrictions as

$$x_1 + x_0 = 400$$

$$x_2 + x_4 = 700$$

$$x_1 + x_2 + x_5 = 800$$

$$2x_1 + x_2 + x_6 = 1000$$

The profit will be

$$Z = 0.40x_1 + 0.30x_2$$

and we wish to maximize Z over non-negative values of x_1, x_2, $\cdots$, x_6 subject to the above restrictions.

Example 13

A blender of whiskey imports three grades A, B, and C. He mixes them according to recipes which specify the maximum or minimum percentages of grades A and C in each blend. These are shown in Table 2.

TABLE 2. SPECIFICATIONS OF BLENDS

Blend	Specification	Price per fifth
Blue Dot	Not less than 60% of A Not more than 20% of C	$6.80
Highland Fling	Not more than 60% of C Not less than 15% of A	$5.70
Old Frenzy	Not more than 50% of C	$4.50

Supplies of the three basic whiskeys together with their costs are shown in Table 3.

TABLE 3. AVAILABILITY AND COSTS OF INGREDIENTS

Whiskey	Maximum quantity available, fifths per day	Cost per fifth
A	2000	$7.00
B	2500	5.00
C	1200	4.00

Show how to obtain the first matrix in a simplex computation of a production policy that will maximize profits.

SOLUTION

It is clear that, if there were no limitations on supplies, the blender would use the maximum quantities of the cheaper of the whiskeys that the specifications allow. In Old Frenzy he would use 50% C and 50% B. The average cost per fifth of the mixture would be $4.50, and at this price there would be no profit. Any other blend meeting the specification would result in a loss, and we may conclude that Old Frenzy will not be made. We can thus reduce the problem to the blends Blue Dot and Highland Fling only.

We will use the following notation.

x_{11} = quantity of A used for Blue Dot
x_{12} = quantity of B used for Blue Dot
x_{13} = quantity of C used for Blue Dot
x_{21} = quantity of A used for Highland Fling
x_{22} = quantity of B used for Highland Fling
x_{23} = quantity of C used for Highland Fling

An amount $x_{11} + x_{12} + x_{13}$ of Blue Dot will be produced and sold for $6.80(x_{11} + x_{12} + x_{13})$. An amount $x_{21} + x_{22} + x_{23}$ of Highland Fling will be produced and sold for $5.70(x_{21} + x_{22} + x_{23})$. The total amounts of each ingredient used will be $(x_{11} + x_{21})$ of A, $(x_{12} + x_{22})$ of B, and $(x_{13} + x_{23})$ of C.

Hence the total profit Z is given by

$$Z = 6.80(x_{11} + x_{12} + x_{13}) + 5.70(x_{21} + x_{22} + x_{23})$$
$$-7.00(x_{11} + x_{21}) - 5.00(x_{12} + x_{22}) - 4.00(x_{13} + x_{23})$$

So $Z = -0.20x_{11} + 1.80x_{12} + 2.80x_{13} - 1.30x_{21} + 0.70x_{22} + 1.70x_{23}$.

Thus we wish to maximize Z, subject to the limitations imposed by the specifications and the availability.

From the availability

$$(8.14) \qquad\qquad x_{11} + x_{21} \leq 2000$$

$$(8.15) \qquad\qquad x_{12} + x_{22} \leq 2500$$

$$(8.16) \qquad\qquad x_{13} + x_{23} \leq 1200$$

From the specifications for Blue Dot,

$(8.17) \quad x_{11} \geq 0.60(x_{11} + x_{12} + x_{13})$ or $3x_{12} + 3x_{13} - 2x_{11} \leq 0$

$(8.18) \quad x_{13} \leq 0.20(x_{11} + x_{12} + x_{13})$ or $4x_{13} - x_{11} - x_{12} \leq 0$

From the specifications of Highland Fling,

$(8.19) \quad x_{23} \leq 0.60(x_{21} + x_{22} + x_{23})$ or $2x_{23} - 3x_{21} - 3x_{22} \leq 0$

$(8.20) \quad x_{21} \geq 0.15(x_{21} + x_{22} + x_{23})$ or $3x_{22} + 3x_{23} - 17x_{21} \leq 0$

We now introduce the slack variables $x_1 \cdots x_7$ into the inequalities (8.14) through (8.20) and obtain the first tableau given below.

$C_j \rightarrow$		0	0	0	0	0	0	0	-0.20	1.80	2.80	-1.30	0.70	1.70
	P_0	P_1	P_2	P_3	P_4	P_5	P_6	P_7	P_{11}	P_{12}	P_{13}	P_{21}	P_{22}	P_{23}
P_1	2000	1							1			1		
P_2	2500		1							1			1	
P_3	1200			1							1			1
P_4	0				1				-2	3	3			
P_5	0					1			-1	-1	4			
P_6	0						1					-3	-3	2
P_7	0							1				-17	3	3
Solution		2000	2500	1200	0	0	0	0	0	0	0	0	0	0
Δ_j		–	–	–	–	–	–	–	-0.20	1.80	2.80	-1.30	0.70	1.70

Example 14

A steel mill produces three types of coils, each made of a different alloy. The process flow chart looks like Figure 8.3. The problem is to determine the amounts of each alloy to produce, within the limitations of sales and machine capacities, so as to maximize profits.

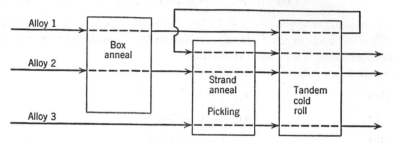

Figure 8.3. Flow chart for Example 14.

Data on capacities and profits are given in Tables 4 and 5.

TABLE 4

Machine	No. of machines	8-hour Shifts per week	Down time, %
Box anneal	4	21	5
Strand anneal	1	20	10
Tandem roll	1	12	0

TABLE 5

Alloy	Operation	Machine rate	Sales potential	Profit per ton
1	Box anneal	28 hr per 10 tons	1250 tons	$25
	Tandem roll (1)	50 ft per min	per month	
	Strand anneal	20 ft per min		
	Tandem roll (2)	25 ft per min		
2	Box anneal	35 hr per 10 tons	250 tons	$35
	Strand anneal	20 ft per min	per month	
	Tandem roll	25 ft per min		
3	Strand anneal	16 ft per min	1500 tons	$40
	Tandem roll	20 ft per min	per month	

Coils for each alloy are 400 feet long and weigh 4 tons. Set up the objective function and the restrictions, from which a simplex solution to the manufacturer's problem might be obtained.

SOLUTION

Let x_i ($i = 1, 2, 3$) be the number of tons of alloy i produced each month. We wish to maximize

$$C = 25x_1 + 35x_2 + 40x_3$$

subject to limitations imposed by the available machine capacity and sales potential.

We first compute the machine capacity in hours per month (Table 6).

TABLE 6

Machine	No. of machines	Shifts per week	% useful time	Capacity, hr per month
Box anneal	4	21	95	$4 \times 21 \times 8 \times 4\frac{1}{3} \times 0.95 = 2766.2$
Strand anneal	1	20	90	$1 \times 20 \times 8 \times 4\frac{1}{3} \times 0.90 = 624$
Tandem roll	1	12	100	$1 \times 12 \times 8 \times 4\frac{1}{3} \quad = 416$

We next translate the various machine rates into tons per hour (Table 7).

TABLE 7

Alloy	Operations	Machine rate
1	Box anneal	28 hr per 10 tons = 0.357 ton per hr
	Tandem roll (1)	50 ft/min $= \dfrac{50 \times 60 \times 4}{400} = 30$ tons per hr
	Strand anneal	20 ft/min = 12 tons per hr
	Tandem roll (2)	25 ft/min = 15 tons per hr
2	Box anneal	35 hr per 10 tons = 0.286 ton per hr
	Strand anneal	20 ft/min $= \dfrac{20 \times 60 \times 4}{400} = 12$ tons per hr
	Tandem roll	25 ft/min $= \dfrac{25 \times 60 \times 4}{400} = 15$ tons per hr
3	Strand anneal	16 ft/min $= \dfrac{16 \times 60 \times 4}{400} = 9.6$ tons per hr
	Tandem roll	20 ft/min = 12 tons per hr

We now compute the machine times required for x_1, x_2, x_3 tons of alloy 1, 2, 3, and use these machine times for a formal statement of the capacity restrictions:

For box anneal:

(8.21)
$$\frac{x_1}{0.357} + \frac{x_2}{0.286} \leq 2766.2$$

For tandem roll:

(8.22) $\dfrac{x_1}{30} + \dfrac{x_1}{15} + \dfrac{x_2}{12} + \dfrac{x_3}{12} \leq 416$ or $\dfrac{x_1}{10} + \dfrac{x_2}{12} + \dfrac{x_3}{12} \leq 416$

For strand anneal:

(8.23)
$$\frac{x_1}{12} + \frac{x_2}{12} + \frac{x_3}{9.6} \leq 624$$

In addition we have the limitations imposed by the sales potential.

(8.24) $x_1 \leq 1250$

(8.25) $x_2 \leq 250$

(8.26) $x_3 \leq 1500$

Examination of the restrictions (8.21) through (8.26) shows that (8.24) is redundant, since, even if $x_2 = 0$, the restriction (8.21) implies that

$$x_1 \leq 987.5 < 1250$$

Thus we wish to maximize

$$C = 25x_1 + 35x_2 + 40x_3$$

subject to the restrictions (8.21), (8.22), (8.23), (8.25), (8.26).

Example 15

The strategic bomber command receives instructions to interrupt the enemy's tank production. The enemy has four key plants located in separate cities, and destruction of any one plant will effectively halt the production of tanks. There is an acute shortage of fuel, which limits the supply to 48,000 gallons for this particular mission. Any bomber sent to any particular city must have at least enough fuel for the round trip plus a reserve of 100 gallons.

The number of bombers available to the commander and their descriptions are listed in the following table.

Bomber type	Description	Miles per gallon	Number available
1	Heavy	2	48
2	Medium	3	32

Information about the location of the plants and their vulnerability to attack by a medium bomber and a heavy bomber is given below.

Plant	Distance from base, miles	Probability of destruction by a heavy bomber	a medium bomber
1	450	0.10	0.08
2	480	0.20	0.16
3	540	0.15	0.12
4	600	0.25	0.20

How many of each type of bomber should be dispatched, and how should they be allocated among the four targets, in order to maximize the probability of success? (Assume that no damage is inflicted on a plant by a bomber that fails to destroy it.)

SOLUTION

Let x_{ij} be the number of bombers of type i sent to city j:

$$i = 1, 2; \qquad j = 1, 2, 3, 4$$

We wish to maximize the probability of destroying at least one plant, and this is equivalent to minimizing the probability of not destroying any plant. We will use Q to denote this probability. So

$$Q = (1 - 0.10)^{x_{11}}(1 - 0.20)^{x_{12}}(1 - 0.15)^{x_{13}}(1 - 0.25)^{x_{14}}$$

$$(1 - 0.08)^{x_{21}}(1 - 0.16)^{x_{22}}(1 - 0.12)^{x_{23}}(1 - 0.20)^{x_{24}}$$

We now have to impose the restrictions on the x_{ij} due to availability of fuel and aircraft.

Fuel

$$\frac{2 \times 450}{2} x_{11} + \frac{2 \times 480}{2} x_{12} + \frac{2 \times 540}{2} x_{13} + \frac{2 \times 600}{2} x_{14}$$

$$+ \frac{2 \times 450}{3} x_{21} + \frac{2 \times 480}{3} x_{22} + \frac{2 \times 540}{3} x_{23} + \frac{2 \times 600}{3} x_{24}$$

$$+ 100(x_{11} + x_{12} + x_{13} + x_{14} + x_{21} + x_{22} + x_{23} + x_{24}) \leq 48,000$$

Thus

(8.27) $\quad 550x_{11} + 580x_{12} + 640x_{13} + 700x_{14} + 400x_{21}$

$$+ 420x_{22} + 460x_{23} + 500x_{21} \leq 48,000$$

Aircraft

(8.28) $$x_{11} + x_{12} + x_{13} + x_{14} \leq 32$$

(8.29) $$x_{21} + x_{22} + x_{23} + x_{24} \leq 48$$

Now, although the restrictions on the x_{ij} are linear, the function Q is not linear. However, minimizing Q is equivalent to minimizing $\log Q$, and $\log Q$ is linear in the x_{ij}. Moreover minimizing $\log Q$ is equivalent to maximizing $-\log Q = \log (1/Q)$. Any convenient base of logarithms will do, and we will use a base 10, as $\log_{10}$ is readily available in tables. Thus we wish to maximize

$$\log \frac{1}{Q} = 0.0457x_{11} + 0.09691x_{12} + 0.07041x_{13} + 0.12483x_{14}$$
$$+ 0.03623x_{21} + 0.06558x_{22} + 0.05538x_{23} + 0.09691x_{24}$$

subject to the restrictions (8.27) through (8.29).

Example 16

The sales forecasts for a certain product, by months, are given below.

January	2,000	July	10,000
February	3,000	August	6,000
March	4,000	September	4,000
April	6,000	October	3,000
May	8,000	November	2,000
June	10,000	December	2,000

It costs \$1.00 per unit to increase production from one month to the next, and \$0.50 per unit to decrease production. Production scheduled for the month of December in the current year is 2000 units, and it is estimated that the inventory level on January 1 will be 1000 units. Storage capacity is limited to 5000 units at any one time.

Show how to obtain a production schedule for the coming year that will minimize the cost of changing production rates, while at the same time insuring that sufficient stock will be available to meet the sales forecast at all times. (Assume that production scheduled during a month becomes available for shipment just in time to meet the current month's sales demand.)

SOLUTION

Let q_i denote the production scheduled for the ith month, where $i = 0$ for this December, $i = 1$ for January, and so on. Then, if $q_i \geq q_{i+1}$, the change in production rate will cost $0.50 \, (q_i - q_{i+1})$, and, if $q_{i+1} \geq q_i$, the change will cost $1.00(q_{i+1} - q_i)$.

We introduce new variables u_i, v_i defined by

(8.30)

$$u_i = \begin{cases} q_i - q_{i+1} & \text{if} \quad q_i > q_{i+1} \\ 0 & \text{if} \quad q_i \le q_{i+1} \end{cases}$$

$$v_i = \begin{cases} 0 & \text{if} \quad q_i > q_{i+1} \\ q_{i+1} - q_i & \text{if} \quad q_i \le q_{i+1} \end{cases}$$

For any production schedule $q_1, q_2, \cdots, q_{12}$, the series u_i and v_i are each uniquely defined, are non-negative variables, and have the further property that

$$q_i - q_{i+1} = u_i - v_i$$

for all i.

A given production schedule $q_1, q_2, \cdots, q_{12}$ will involve relevant costs equal to

(8.31)
$$\sum_{i=0}^{11} (0.50u_i + 1.00v_i) = \sum_{i=0}^{11} \left(\frac{u_i}{2} + v_i \right)$$

Since all sales forecasts are to be met, the sum of the initial inventory and the cumulated production must at all times exceed the cumulated sales. If we use S_i to denote sales in month i, this gives the restrictions

(8.32)
$$1000 + \sum_{j=1}^{i} q_j \ge \sum_{j=1}^{i} S_j \qquad i = 1, 2, \cdots, 12$$

We also have the restriction that inventory at any time cannot exceed 5000:

(8.33)
$$1000 + \sum_{j=1}^{i} q_j - \sum_{j=1}^{i} S_j \le 5000 \qquad i = 1, 2, \cdots, 12$$

We next express the restrictions (8.32) and (8.33) in terms of the new variables u_j and v_j. Since

$$q_i = q_0 + \sum_{j=0}^{i-1} (q_{j+1} - q_j)$$

we have

(8.34)
$$q_i = q_0 - \sum_{j=0}^{i-1} (u_j - v_j)$$

Thus

$$\sum_{j=1}^{i} q_j = iq_0 - \sum_{j=1}^{i} \sum_{k=0}^{j-1} (u_k - v_k)$$

The latter equality reduces to

$$(8.35) \qquad \sum_{j=1}^{i} q_j = iq_0 - \sum_{j=0}^{i-1} (i - j)(u_j - v_j)$$

and the restrictions (8.32) and (8.33) become

$$(8.36) \qquad 1000 + iq_0 - \sum_{j=0}^{i-1} (i - j)(u_j - v_j) \geq \sum_{j=1}^{i} S_j$$

$$iq_0 - \sum_{j=0}^{i-1} (i - j)(u_j - v_j) - \sum_{j=1}^{i} S_j \leq 4000$$

Since i ranges from 1 to 12, there are 24 restrictions in all included in (8.36). Twelve more restrictions arise from the fact that each $q_i \geq 0$; from (8.34), the statement in terms of the new variables is

$$(8.37) \qquad \sum_{j=0}^{i-1} (u_j - v_j) \leq q_0$$

We can now state the scheduling problem as a linear programming problem. Given [see (8.31)] the linear form

$$C = \sum_{i=0}^{11} \left[\frac{u_i}{2} + v_i \right]$$

Find, among all non-negative u_i and v_i satisfying the 36 restrictions (8.36) and (8.37), that set $(u_0 \cdots u_{11} v_0 \cdots v_{11})$ which minimizes C.

In order for the optimal solution so obtained to be of any practical use, we must use the relation (8.34) to go from the u_i and v_i to the corresponding q_i. But (8.34) is based on the assumption that at least one of each pair (u_i, v_i) is zero. Apparently this is a defect in the solution, but actually it is not. In all 36 restrictions, the coefficient of any u_i is minus the coefficient of the corresponding v_i; and there is a theorem in linear programming which implies that, in such a situation, u_i and v_i (fixed i) cannot both be non-zero in a feasible solution.

PROBLEMS FOR SOLUTION

Set XII

1. Find values of x and y that maximize

$$Z = 2x + 5y$$

subject to the conditions

$$0 \leq x \leq 400$$

$$0 \leq y \leq 300$$

$$x + y \leq 600$$

Work in two ways.   [*Ans.* $x = y = 300.$]

[*Hint:* Draw the region defined by the restrictions in the xy plane. Superpose on this region the lines of the family $2x + 5y = Z$, where Z is regarded as a parameter. The line furthest from the origin which still intersects the region will determine the optimal solution (x, y). A second method of solution is the algebraic simplex routine.]

2. Use the simplex method to maximize $Z = 5x - 2y + 3z$, where x, y, z are non-negative variables subject to the restrictions

$$2x + 2y - z \geq 2$$

$$3x - 4y \qquad \leq 3$$

$$y + 3z \leq 5$$

[*Hint:* Use the method of Example 11 to obtain a first feasible solution.]

3. Use the simplex method to maximize

$$Z = 6x + 5y - 3z - 4w$$

where x, y, z, w are non-negative variables subject to the following restrictions:

$$2x + 3y + 2z - 4w = 24$$

$$x + 2y \qquad \leq 10$$

$$x + y + 2z + 3w \leq 15$$

$$y + z + w \leq 8$$

[*Hint:* Since one of the restrictions is in the form of an equality, some modification of the methods given thus far is needed. The temptation in such problems is to use the equality to eliminate one variable (say x) from the problem and solve for the optimum in terms of the remaining variables y, z, w. The flaw in this procedure is that, at the resulting optimum, x may turn out to be negative. The suggested method is to write the simplex array with four rows, introducing only *three* slack variables (one for each inequality), and treat one of the original variables (say x) as if it were a slack variable. If we choose x, we divide the first row by 2 and subtract suitable multiples of the result from the remaining rows, so as to yield an array in which x has a coefficient of unity in the first row and zero in the others. There is now a negative element (-2) in the P_0 column, second row. In order to obtain a feasible solution, use the methods of Example 11 of the text.]

4. A ship has three cargo holds, forward, aft, and center. The capacity limits are:

Forward	2000 tons	100,000 cubic feet
Center	3000 tons	135,000 cubic feet
Aft	1500 tons	30,000 cubic feet

The following cargoes are offered; the shipowners may accept all or any part of each commodity:

Commodity	Amount, tons	Volume per ton, cu ft	Profit per ton, $
A	6,000	60	6
B	4,000	50	8
C	2,000	25	5

In order to preserve the trim of the ship, the weight in each hold must be proportional to the capacity in tons. How should the cargo be distributed so as to maximize profit? (Note: Since the restrictions will contain an equality, the approach suggested in the previous problem may be needed in order to obtain a numerical answer.)

5. A trucking company with $400,000 to spend on new equipment is contemplating three types of vehicle. Vehicle A has a 10-ton payload and is expected to average 35 miles per hour. It costs $8000. Vehicle B has a 20-ton payload and is expected to average 30 miles per hour. It costs $13,000. Vehicle C is a modified form of B; it carries sleeping quarters for one driver, and this reduces its capacity to 18 tons and raises the cost to $15,000.

Vehicle A requires a crew of one man, and, if driven on three shifts per day, could be run for an average of 18 hours per day. Vehicles B and C require a crew of two men each, but, whereas B would be driven 18 hours per day with three shifts, C could average 21 hours per day. The company has 150 drivers available each day and would find it very difficult to obtain further crews. Maintenance facilities are such that the total number of vehicles must not exceed 30. How many vehicles of each type should be purchased if the company wishes to maximize its capacity in ton-miles per day?

6. A plant makes two products, A and B, which are routed through four processing centers, 1, 2, 3, 4, as shown by the solid lines in Figure 8.4. If

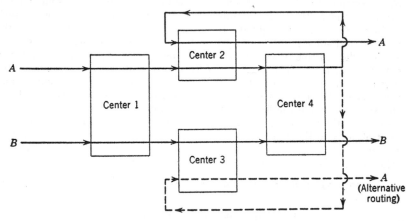

Figure 8.4. Routing of products A and B in problem 6. Each center can handle only one pass of one product at a time.

there is spare capacity in center 3, it is possible to route product *A* through 3 instead of going through 2 twice, but this is more expensive.

Given the information below, how should production be scheduled so as to maximize profits? [By a "production schedule" is meant the specification of the following three amounts: (1) the daily amount of raw material used for *A*, regular route, (2) the daily amount of raw material used for *A*, optional route, (3) the daily amount of raw material used for *B*. Assume that sufficient storage capacity is available at no additional cost.]

TABLE 8

Product	Center	Input, gals per hr	% recovery	Running cost per hr, $
	1	300	90	150
	2 (1st pass)	450	95	200
A	4	250	85	180
	2 (2nd pass)	400	80	220
	3	350	75	250
	1	500	90	300
B	3	480	85	250
	4	400	80	240

Product	Raw material cost per gal	Sales price per finished gal	Maximum daily sales, gal of finished product
A	5	20	1700
B	6	18	1500

Centers 1 and 4 run up to 16 hours a day; centers 2 and 3 run up to 12 hours a day. A final restriction is furnished by shipping facilities, which limit the daily output of *A* and *B* to a total of 2500 gallons.

REFERENCES

Charnes, A., W. W. Cooper, and A. Henderson, *An Introduction to Linear Programming*, John Wiley & Sons, New York, 1953.

Churchman, C. W., R. L. Ackoff, and E. L. Arnoff, *Introduction to Operations Research*, John Wiley & Sons, New York, 1957.

Dorfman, R., P. A. Samuelson, and R. M. Solow, *Linear Programming and Economic Analysis*, McGraw-Hill Book Co., New York, 1958.

Koopmans, Tjalling C., ed., *Activity Analysis of Production and Allocation*, John Wiley & Sons, New York, 1951.

Rohde, F. Virginia, "Bibliography on Linear Programming," *Operations Research*, Vol. 5, no. 1 (Feb. 1957). See also a supplement to this bibliography by H. M. Wagner in *Operations Research*, Vol. 5, no. 4 (Aug. 1957).

Vajda, S., *The Theory of Games and Linear Programming*. John Wiley & Sons, New York, 1956.

CHAPTER

NINE

Sequencing

In sequencing we are concerned with a situation where the effectiveness measure is a function of the order or sequence in which a series of tasks are performed. Problems fall into two broad groups. In the first group we have n tasks to perform, each of which requires processing on some or all of m different machines. The effectiveness for any given sequence of the tasks at each machine can be measured, and we wish to select from the $(n!)^m$ theoretically possible sequences:

(a) those that are *technologically feasible:* i.e. those which satisfy the restrictions (if any) on the order in which each task must be processed through the m machines.

(b) one (or several) of the technologically feasible sequences which optimizes the effectiveness measure.

In theory, a solution by enumeration is always possible, but, in practice, the computation of effectiveness for a given sequence can be quite involved, and the number of cases for enumeration makes this approach prohibitive even for moderate values of m and n.

[If $m = 5$ and $n = 5$, there are $(5!)^5 = 25,000,000,000$ cases to enumerate.]

In the second type of problem, we have a job shop with a number of machines and a list of tasks to perform. Each time a machine completes the task on which it is engaged we have to decide on the next task to be started. One of the characteristics of the situation is that the list of tasks will change as fresh orders are received.

Unfortunately both types of problem seem to be intrinsically difficult, and at present solutions are known only for some special cases of the first type. At the time of writing, there appears to be no mathematical theory for the second type of problem, but some empirical rules have been tested with moderate success by simulation on computers.

PROCESSING EACH OF n JOBS THROUGH m MACHINES

There are n jobs $(1, 2, \cdots, n)$, each of which have to be processed one at a time at each of m machine centers $(A, B, \cdots)$. The order of processing each job through the machine centers is given (for example, job 1 is processed in centers A, C, B in this order). We are also given the time that each job must spend at each machine center. The problem is to find a sequence for processing the jobs so that the total elapsed time for all the jobs will be a minimum.

Symbolically, let

A_i = time for job i on machine A
B_i = time for job i on machine B; etc.
T = time from start of first job to completion of the last job

We wish to determine for each machine a sequence, $(i_1, i_2, \cdots, i_n)$, where $(i_1, i_2, \cdots, i_n)$ is a permutation of the integers $(1, 2, \cdots, n)$, which will minimize T.

Satisfactory solutions are available at present only for three special cases:

(1) n jobs and two machines A and B; all jobs processed in the order AB.

(2) n jobs and three machines A, B, and C; all jobs processed in the order ABC; other limitations as described below.

(3) two jobs and m machines; each job to be processed through the machines in a prescribed order which is not necessarily the same for both jobs.

These three cases are described in more detail in later subsections, which also give methods of solution and some examples.

Example 1

Suppose that we have four jobs 1, 2, 3, 4 which must be processed through machines A, B, C, D in the following order.

Job 1: $ABCD$
Job 2: $ACBD$
Job 3: $BCDA$
Job 4: $BCDA$

Each individual task (processing one job on one machine) takes one hour.

(a) Show that the following job sequence, selected from among the $(4!)^4$ possible job sequences, is not feasible.

Machine A: 1342
Machine B: 3412
Machine C: 1423
Machine D: 4321

(b) Find a feasible job sequence, and compute the corresponding elapsed time T from the start of the first job started to the completion of the last job finished.

SOLUTION

We first set down the two arrays, one representing the prescribed machine order for each job, and the other representing the suggested job order in each machine.

1	A	B	C	D
2	A	C	B	D
3	B	C	D	A
4	B	C	D	A

A	1	3	4	2
B	3	4	1	2
C	1	4	2	3
D	4	3	2	1

An individual task is feasible at any particular instant provided the machine is idle, the job is idle, the machine is next for the job, and the job is next for the machine. Thus, at time zero, the tasks $(A, 1)$ and $(B, 3)$ are feasible; we indicate the completion of these two operations by circles about each machine and job, as below.

1	Ⓐ	B	C	D
2	A	C	B	D
3	Ⓑ	C	D	A
4	B	C	D	A

A	①	3	4	2
B	③	4	1	2
C	1	4	2	3
D	4	3	2	1

Now $(B, 4)$ is feasible; and we continue circling completed operations until we reach the following situation.

1	Ⓐ	Ⓑ	Ⓒ	D
2	A	C	B	D
3	Ⓑ	C	D	A
4	Ⓑ	Ⓒ	Ⓓ	A

A	①	3	4	2
B	③	④	①	2
C	①	④	2	3
D	④	3	2	1

At this point we can proceed no further, and conclude that the job sequence under test is not feasible.

We can modify the given sequence in such a way that it becomes feasible, by starting with the completed portion of the tasks:

A	1			
B	3	4	1	
C	1	4		
D	4			

and then filling in the blank boxes so as to be compatible with the prescribed machine order array. A resulting feasible sequence is

    Machine A: 1342
    Machine B: 3412
    Machine C: 1432
    Machine D: 4132

To compute the elapsed time for this feasible job sequence, we recall that each individual task is assumed to require one hour, and proceed to construct a time-table.

Hour	Tasks
1	$(A, 1)$ $(B, 3)$
2	$(B, 4)$
3	$(B, 1)$
4	$(C, 1)$
5	$(C, 4)$
6	$(D, 4)$
7	$(C, 3)$ $(D, 1)$
8	$(D, 3)$
9	$(A, 3)$
10	$(A, 4)$
11	$(A, 2)$
12	$(C, 2)$
13	$(B, 2)$
14	$(D, 2)$

The elapsed time is 14 hours. This answer can also be obtained graphically, by means of a Gantt chart of the sort illustrated on page 262.

Note that we have not really solved the sequencing problem of this example; all we have done is to find a feasible sequence and compute the corresponding T. No mathematical method (besides enumeration) is available at present for finding the optimal sequence in problems of this dimensionality.

Processing n Jobs through Two Machines

This sequencing problem, for which a solution is available, is more completely described as follows:

(a) Only two machines are involved, A and B.
(b) Each job is processed in the order AB.
(c) The exact or expected processing times $A_1, A_2, \cdots, A_n, B_1, B_2, \cdots, B_n$ are known.

The problem is to minimize T, the elapsed time from the start of the first job to the completion of the last job.

It can be shown that the sequences that minimize T are the same for both machines. The method of computation, given here without proof, is due to S. M. Johnson.*

1. Select the smallest processing time occurring in the list $A_1 \cdots A_n$, $B_1 \cdots B_n$. If there is a tie, select either smallest processing time.

2. If the minimum processing time is A_r, do the rth job first. If it is B_s, do the sth job last. Note that this decision will apply to *both* machines A and B.

3. There are now $n-1$ jobs left to be ordered. Apply steps 1 and 2 to the *reduced* set of processing times obtained by deleting the two machine processing times corresponding to the job already assigned.

4. Continue in this manner until all jobs have been ordered. The resulting ordering will minimize T.

Example 2

We have five jobs, each of which must go through the two machines A and B in the order AB. Processing times are given in the table below:

PROCESSING TIME, HR

Job	Machine A	Machine B
1	5	2
2	1	6
3	9	7
4	3	8
5	10	4

Determine a sequence for the five jobs that will minimize the elapsed time T.

SOLUTION

Applying the routine of the text, we see that the smallest processing time is 1 hour for job 2 on machine A. Thus we schedule job 2 first:

2				

---

*S. M. Johnson, "Optimal Two- and Three-Stage Production Schedules with Setup Times Included." *Naval Research Logistics Quarterly*, Vol. 1, no. 1 (Mar. 1954).

The reduced set of processing times is

Job	A	B
1	5	2
3	9	7
4	3	8
5	10	4

The smallest processing time, 2, is B_1. So we schedule job 1 last

2				1

Continuing, we have

Job	A	B
3	9	7
4	3	8
5	10	4

leading to

2	4			1

Job	A	B
3	9	7
5	10	4

yielding

2	4		5	1

so that the optimal sequence is

2	4	3	5	1

We may calculate the elapsed time corresponding to the optimal ordering, using the individual processing times given in the statement of the problem. The details are given in the following table.

Job	Machine A		Machine B	
	Time in	Time out	Time in	Time out
2	0	1	1	7
4	1	4	7	15
3	4	13	15	22
5	13	23	23	27
1	23	28	28	30

Thus the minimum elapsed time is 30 hours. Idle time is 3 hours for machine B, and 2 hours for machine A.

Processing n Jobs through Three Machines

No solution is available at present for the general sequencing problem of n jobs, three machines A, B, and C, prescribed order ABC for each job, and no passing. However, the method of the previous subsection can be extended to cover the special cases where either or both of the following conditions hold:

(*a*) The smallest processing time for machine A is at least as great as the largest processing time for machine B.

(*b*) The smallest processing time for machine C is at least as great as the largest processing time for machine B.

The method, stated here without proof, is to replace the problem with an equivalent problem involving n jobs and *two* machines. We denote the fictitious machines by G and H, and define the corresponding processing times G_i and H_i by

$$G_i = A_i + B_i$$

$$H_i = B_i + C_i$$

We work the new problem, with prescribed ordering GH, by the method of the last subsection. The resulting optimal sequence will also be optimal for the original problem.

Example 3

We have five jobs, each of which must go through the machines A, B, and C in the order ABC. Processing times are:

Job	A	B	C
1	4	5	8
2	9	6	10
3	8	2	6
4	6	3	7
5	5	4	11

Determine a sequence for the five jobs that will minimize the elapsed time T.

SOLUTION

Here min $A_i = 4$, max $B_i = 6$, min $C_i = 6$. Since max $B_i \leq$ min C_i, we are justified in applying the method of this subsection. The equivalent problem becomes

PROCESSING TIMES

Job	G	H
1	9	13
2	15	16
3	10	8
4	9	10
5	9	15

Because of ties, there are several optimal orderings. They are

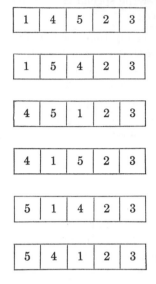

Any of these orderings may be used to sequence the jobs through machines A, B, and C; and they will all yield a minimum elapsed time of 51 hours.

Processing Two Jobs through m Machines

In this subsection, we consider the following situation:

(a) There are m machines, denoted by $A, B, C, \cdots, K$.

(b) Only two jobs are to be performed: job 1 and job 2.

(c) The technological ordering of each of the two jobs through the m machines is prescribed in advance. This technological ordering need not be the same for both jobs.

(d) The exact or expected processing times $A_1, B_1, \cdots, K_1, A_2, B_2, \cdots, K_2$ are known.

The problem again is to minimize T, the elapsed time from the start of the first job to the completion of the last job.

The method will be presented by means of an example. Let us suppose that we have two jobs which are to be processed through four machines, $A, B, C,$ and D. The prescribed technological orderings are:

Job 1: $ABCD$
Job 2: $DBAC$

Processing times are given in the following table.

	Machine *A*	Machine *B*	Machine *C*	Machine *D*
Job 1	2	4	5	1
Job 2	2	5	3	6

It is obvious that at time zero we should put either job 1 on machine *A* or job 2 on machine *D*. It is not so obvious, however, that we should start both jobs together. Something might be gained by starting one job first and keeping the other machine idle for a time. The same sort of problem will recur at later stages of the schedule: should we start a job through its next process as soon as the machine becomes available, or should we wait? With a little thought the reader can see that the sequencing problem is to determine, for each machine, whether the jobs shall be processed in the order 1, 2, or 2, 1. Such a set of *m* decisions will be called a *program*. The first step in the solution is to prepare a table showing all possible programs. [There are 2^m possible programs; here, with $m = 4$, there are 16 programs.]

To abbreviate the notation for the programs, we resort to a symbolic device. Let

a = the decision{job 1 before job 2 on machine A}
$\bar{a}$ = the decision {job 2 before job 1 on machine A}

and similarly for the other machines. With this notation, we obtain the following table displaying the 16 possible programs for the case of two jobs and four machines.

Program No.

1	2	3	4	5	6	7	8	9	10	11	12	13	14	15	16
$\bar{a}$	a	$\bar{a}$	a	$\bar{a}$	a	$\bar{a}$	a	$\bar{a}$	a	$\bar{a}$	a	$\bar{a}$	a	$\bar{a}$	a
$\bar{b}$	$\bar{b}$	b	b	$\bar{b}$	$\bar{b}$	b	b	$\bar{b}$	$\bar{b}$	b	b	$\bar{b}$	$\bar{b}$	b	b
$\bar{c}$	$\bar{c}$	$\bar{c}$	$\bar{c}$	c	c	c	c	$\bar{c}$	$\bar{c}$	$\bar{c}$	$\bar{c}$	c	c	c	c
$\bar{d}$	$\bar{d}$	$\bar{d}$	$\bar{d}$	$\bar{d}$	$\bar{d}$	$\bar{d}$	$\bar{d}$	d	d	d	d	d	d	d	d

[Such a table can be generated by filling the first $2^{(k-1)}$ spaces on the *k*th row with barred letters, and then completing the row with alternate blocks of $2^{(k-1)}$ letters without bars and with bars. For example, row 3 starts with $2^{(3-1)} = 4\bar{c}$'s; then $4c$'s; etc.] Note that the programs give the ordering of the two jobs on a given machine, but say nothing about the (technological) ordering of the machines for a given job. Thus $\bar{a}\bar{b}\bar{c}\bar{d}$ (program 1) merely says "do job 2 on each machine before job 1," and could just as well be written as $\bar{b}\bar{a}\bar{c}\bar{d}$ or $\bar{b}\bar{c}\bar{d}\bar{a}$, etc.

The next step is to delete all programs that are not technologically feasible, in that they are not consistent with the two prescribed technological orderings.

Rule

Suppose that machine X must precede machine Y for job 1, and machine Y must precede machine X for job 2. Then no program that contains both the decision $\bar{x}$ and the decision y is technologically feasible.

The rule is easily proved. Technologically, we must have the following time relationships between events.

$$[1 \text{ on } X] \quad \text{precedes} \quad [1 \text{ on } Y]$$

$$[2 \text{ on } Y] \quad \text{precedes} \quad [2 \text{ on } X]$$

A program containing the decisions $\bar{x}$ and y says, in part:

$$[2 \text{ on } X] \quad \text{precedes} \quad [1 \text{ on } X]$$

$$[1 \text{ on } Y] \quad \text{precedes} \quad [2 \text{ on } Y]$$

The first, second, and fourth statements imply

$$[1 \text{ on } X] \quad \text{precedes} \quad [2 \text{ on } X]$$

which violates the third statement.

In applying this rule, we first identify all machine pairs that appear in reverse order for the two jobs. In the example, these pairs are

$$AB \quad AD \quad BD \quad CD$$

where the given order of a pair is as for job 1. By the rule, all programs containing $\bar{a}b$, $\bar{a}d$, $\bar{b}d$, or $\bar{c}d$ are not technologically feasible. Thus we eliminate programs 3, 7, 9, 10, 11, 12, 13, 14, 15 and are left with

Program No.

1	2	4	5	6	8	16
$\bar{a}$	a	a	$\bar{a}$	a	a	a
$\bar{b}$	$\bar{b}$	b	$\bar{b}$	$\bar{b}$	b	b
$\bar{c}$	$\bar{c}$	$\bar{c}$	c	c	c	c
$\bar{d}$	$\bar{d}$	$\bar{d}$	$\bar{d}$	$\bar{d}$	$\bar{d}$	d

Next, we operate with the reduced set of programs and delete those that cannot be optimal. The rules for performing this operation are stated here without proof (Table 1); the proofs may be found in the original reference by Akers and Friedman.* (Dots indicate the pos-

TABLE 1

Rule	Technological orderings		Delete programs containing
	Job 1	Job 2	
I	$X \cdots Y$	$Y \cdots$	xy
II	$X \cdots Y \cdots$	$\cdots XY \cdots$	$\bar{x}y$
III	$\cdots X \cdots Y$	$\cdots XY \cdots$	$\bar{x}y$
IV	$\cdots XY \cdots$	$X \cdots Y \cdots$	$x\bar{y}$
V	$\cdots XY \cdots Z \cdots$	$\cdots X \cdots YZ \cdots$	$x\bar{y}z$
VI	$\cdots X \cdots YZ \cdots$	$\cdots XY \cdots Z \cdots$	$\bar{x}y\bar{z}$

sibility of other machines occupying the corresponding position in the technological ordering.)

In our example, where the technological orderings are $ABCD$ and $DBAC$, we see that rule I ($A \cdots D$ vs. $D \cdots$) eliminates programs containing ad; thus program 16 is eliminated from the reduced set. Using rule II ($A \cdots C \cdots$ vs. $\cdots AC \cdots$), we eliminate program 5 which contains $\bar{a}c$. Rules III, IV, V, VI do not apply to the given technological orderings. We are left with

Program No.

1	2	4	6	8
$\bar{a}$	a	a	a	a
$\bar{b}$	$\bar{b}$	b	$\bar{b}$	b
$\bar{c}$	$\bar{c}$	$\bar{c}$	c	c
$\bar{d}$	$\bar{d}$	$\bar{d}$	$\bar{d}$	$\bar{d}$

We are thus left with five programs which are technologically feasible and which do not violate the rules for optimality. The last step is to calculate the elapsed times for each of the remaining programs, and to choose that program for which the elapsed time is the smallest. The simplest method is probably the Gantt chart, as shown in Figure 9.1.

* S. B. Akers, Jr., and J. Friedman, "ANon-Numerical Approach to Production Scheduling Problems," *Operations Research*, Vol. 3, no. 4 (Nov. 1955).

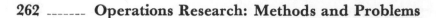

$$T = 22$$

Figure 9.1. Gantt chart for program 4 ($ab\bar{c}d$). Technological Orderings: $ABCD$ for job 1, $DBAC$ for job 2.

The reader should verify that program 8, requiring 16 hours, is the optimal program.

There is also a graphical approach to the two-job m-machine problem, which is rather simple to apply and usually leads to good (though not necessarily optimal) results. The first step in the procedure is to draw a set of axes, where the horizontal axis represents processing time on job 1, and the vertical axis processing time on job 2. (See Figure 9.2.) The machine times for the two jobs are laid out on the corresponding axes, in the given technological order. The coordinates of any point on the grid represent a possible state of completion of the two jobs; thus point Q in Figure 9.2 denotes an instant when job I is 1/3 completed and job II is 1/4 completed. A program involves starting with point Q at the origin and moving Q through various states of completion (i.e. points) until Q reaches the point marked "Finish." Physically, the path taken by Q is limited to a series of segments which are horizontal, or vertical, or diagonal with slope 1. Movement to the right means that job I is proceeding while job II is idle, movement upward means that job II is proceeding while job I is idle, and movement diagonally means that both jobs are proceeding simultaneously.

A further proscription on the movement of Q is that both jobs cannot be processed simultaneously on the same machine. This prohibition is translated to graphical form by taking the "Cartesian product" of A-horizontal and A-vertical, and agreeing that diagonal movement through this blocked-out area is forbidden; and similarly for the other machines. In our problem, the result is that diagonal movement through the shaded areas of the figure is prohibited.

An optimal path (program) is one that minimizes idle time for job I (horizontal movement). Equivalently, an optimal path is one that minimizes idle time for job II (vertical movement).   Evidently we want to choose a path with as much travel on the diagonal as possible.

A good path, according to this criterion, is chosen by eye, and drawn on the chart (see line with arrows).   The elapsed time is obtained by adding the idle time for either job to the processing time for that job.

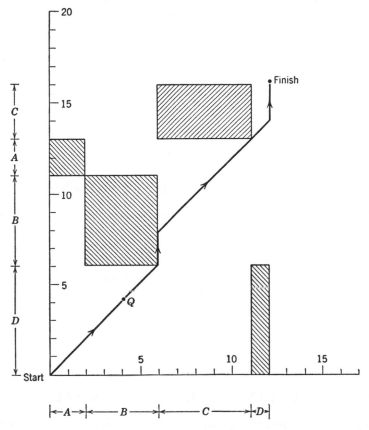

Figure 9.2.   Graphical solution for the two-job *m*-machine sequencing problem.

Idle time for the chosen path is seen to be 4 for job 1, and zero for job 2. Elapsed time $= 12 + 4 = 16 = 16 + 0$.   Note that the graphical approach happens to yield the same answer as the rigorous reduced-enumerative approach used earlier.

So far we have confined our discussions to situations where a given set of jobs had to be performed and we wished to determine a sequence that would best meet certain criteria. There is another type of situation which occurs frequently in practice, and about which even less is known.

In a job shop, orders arrive daily, each of which requires given amounts of time on various machines, and each of which may have a promised completion date. The shop foreman has to decide, each time he has an idle machine, which job shall be put on the machine next. He has a number of possible objectives to meet in making his decision:

(a) Minimize the average amount of time by which promised dates are missed.

(b) Minimize the maximum amount by which promised dates are missed.

(c) Minimize setup costs.

(d) Maximize production.

(e) Meet certain priorities assigned by management.

(f) Minimize production costs.

(g) Spread the work load uniformly over the available machines.

In addition, there are all the problems associated with inventory policies.

So far the only approach to problems involving criteria of this sort seems to be to simulate various possible decision rules on a computer and to measure the extent to which each rule meets the criteria. It is hardly possible to give a discussion of such simulation in a book of this type. Examples of rules whose efficacy can be tested by simulation are: Start production of the job that has the earliest promise date. Or start production of that job which, if started now, would be finished latest before its promise date.

THE TRAVELING SALESMAN PROBLEM

The problem faced by the traveling salesman is to select a route that will minimize the total distance traveled in visiting n cities and returning to his starting point. Here we prefer to state this problem in an equivalent form. Suppose that n products are to be made in some order on a continuing basis, and the setup cost for each depends on the preceding product made. Given the setup cost when product A_i is followed by A_j, denoted by c_{ij}, we wish to determine the sequence of products that will minimize the total setup cost. We arrange the individual setup costs in a square matrix, with the leading diagonal blank.

To

	A_1	A_2	A_3		A_n
A_1	—	c_{12}	c_{13}		c_{1n}
A_2	c_{21}	—	c_{23}		c_{2n}
A_n	c_{n1}	c_{n2}	c_{n3}		—

From

Each non-diagonal element shows the cost of changing from the product listed to the left of its row to the product listed at the top of its column. Since changing from a product to itself involves no setup costs, the leading diagonal is blank.

Our problem is to choose a set of n elements, one in each row and one in each column, so as to minimize the sum of the elements chosen. Thus far the problem is identical with the assignment problem of Chapter Eight; however there are two further restrictions on our choice of elements, one of which makes the problem considerably more difficult. Clearly we cannot choose an element along the diagonal, and this can be avoided by agreeing to fill the leading diagonal with infinitely large elements. The second restriction is that, having produced product A_i say, we do not wish to produce it again until we have made all the other products. For example with five products $A_1, \cdots, A_5$, a solution comprising the elements $c_{12}, c_{21}, c_{34}, c_{45}, c_{53}$ would not be acceptable, because it corresponds to a situation where we start with A_1, make A_2, and then make A_1 again, before making A_3, A_4, A_5. All known methods for obtaining a solution to the traveling salesman problem involve resorting to enumeration at some stage. At the present time the best available procedure is to solve the problem as if it were an assignment problem, and, if the solution obtained does not satisfy all the requirements, to modify it "by hand" until a solution is obtained that does.

Before illustrating the problem with an example, we give a formal statement of the problem.

Given a square matrix $[c_{ij}]$ of size n and with $c_{ii} = \infty$ for each i, find a subset of n elements $c_{pq}, c_{qr}, c_{rs}, \cdots, c_{uv}, c_{vp}$, where $p, q, \cdots,$ u, v are some permutation of the integers, 1, 2, $\cdots, n$, such that the sum of the elements of the subset shall be a minimum.

It will be realized that there are $n!$ permutations of the numbers $1, \cdots, n$; but, from any given subset we could form n equivalent subsets, merely by starting partway through the given subset and listing the elements omitted in order at the tail end. There are thus $(n-1)!$ subsets among which we must search for the solution.

Example 4

Given the matrix of setup costs below, show how to sequence production so as to minimize setup cost per cycle.

To

A_1 A_2 A_3 A_4 A_5

	A_1	A_2	A_3	A_4	A_5
A_1	∞	2	5	7	1
A_2	6	∞	3	8	2
From A_3	8	7	∞	4	7
A_4	12	4	6	∞	5
A_5	1	3	2	8	∞

SOLUTION

We commence by treating the problem as an assignment problem: Subtract minimum element from each row and column.

To

A_1 A_2 A_3 A_4 A_5

	A_1	A_2	A_3	A_4	A_5
A_1	∞	1	3	6	[0]
A_2	4	∞	[0]	6	0
From A_3	4	3	∞	[0]	3
A_4	8	[0]	1	∞	1
A_5	[0]	2	0	7	∞

The zeros of this particular matrix provide a solution to the assignment problem, shown by distinguished elements. However, this is not a solution of the traveling salesman problem, because it tells us to go from A_1 to A_5 and then back to A_1.

We examine the matrix for some of the "next best" solutions to the assignment problem, and try to find one that satisfies the additional restrictions. The smallest non-zero element is 1; so we try the effect of putting such an element in the solution.

∞	[1]	3	6	0
4	∞	[0]	6	0
4	3	∞	[0]	3
8	0	1	∞	[1]
[0]	2	0	7	∞

∞	1	3	6	0
4	∞	0	6	0
4	3	∞	0	3
8	0	[1]	∞	1
0	2	0	7	∞

We start with the element (1, 2) and delete row 1 and column 2. In the remaining 4-by-4 matrix, there is no solution to the assignment problem among the zeros, but it is easy to see the best solution lies in the distinguished elements. Moreover, this is also a feasible solution of the traveling salesman problem; the "cost" in the reduced matrix is 2. We now know that any solution where the "cost" exceeds 2 is not optimum; we need only examine solutions containing the element 1 (row 4, column 3) not so far used to see if a better solution exists. On deleting row 4 and column 3 we see that the remaining 4-by-4 matrix does not have a solution among the zeros, and we conclude that the minimum "cost" for the reduced matrix is 2.

Thus the best cycle is

$$A_5 \rightarrow A_1 \rightarrow A_2 \rightarrow A_3 \rightarrow A_4 \rightarrow A_5$$

and the setup costs will total $1 + 2 + 3 + 4 + 5 = 15$.

PROBLEMS FOR SOLUTION

Set XIII

1. A bookbinder has one printing press, one binding machine, and the manuscripts of a number of different books. The times required to perform the printing and binding operations for each book are known. We wish to determine the order in which books should be processed, in order to minimize the total time required to turn out all the books.

Book	Printing time	Binding time
1	30	80
2	120	100
3	50	90
4	20	60
5	90	30
6	110	10

2. An additional operation is added to the process: finishing. What should the order of the books be?

Book	Printing time	Binding time	Finishing time
1	30	80	20
2	120	100	40
3	50	90	60
4	20	60	120
5	90	30	70
6	110	10	30

[*Hint:* Do not seek a rigorous optimum, as the methods of the text are not applicable to this problem. Do try to find an economical solution.]

3. A machine shop has six machines: A, B, C, D, E, and F. Two jobs must be processed through each of these machines. The times spent on each machine and the necessary sequence of the jobs through the shop are given below.

Order	1	2	3	4	5	6
Job I	A—20	C—10	D—10	B—30	E—25	F—15
Job II	A—10	C—30	B—15	D—10	F—15	E—20

In what order should the jobs be done on each of the machines, in order to minimize the total time necessary to finish the jobs?

(Do in two ways.)

4. A machine operator processes five types of items on his machine each week, and must choose a sequence for them. The main costs involved are setup costs and priority. The setup cost per change depends on the item presently on the machine and the setup to be made, according to the following table:

		To item				
		A	B	C	D	E
From item	A	∞	4	7	3	4
	B	4	∞	6	3	4
	C	7	6	∞	7	5
	D	3	3	7	∞	7
	E	4	4	5	7	∞

In addition, there is a priority rating among the items, A and B having a higher priority than C, D, E. This may be interpreted as adding an additional cost of 5 when any high-priority item immediately follows a low-priority item.

If he processes each type of item once and only once each week, how should he sequence the items on his machine?

REFERENCES

Churchman, C. W., R. L. Ackoff, and E. L. Arnoff, *Introduction to Operations Research*, John Wiley & Sons, New York, 1957.

Vazsonyi, Andrew, *Scientific Programming in Business and Industry*, John Wiley & Sons, New York, 1958.

CHAPTER

TEN

Dynamic
programming

Dynamic programming is a newly developed mathematical technique which is useful in many types of decision problems. In most of the situations we have discussed in this book, where a series of consecutive decisions have to be made, the optimal over-all policy could be arrived at by considering the effects of each decision separately. In the inventory area, for example, there are some situations where a policy of producing each month so as to minimize inventory cost for the month immediately affected will minimize the inventory cost for the whole year. In many other problems, however, it is by no means clear that the over-all return from a procedure of optimizing over each individual period is the best that can be attained. It might be, for example, that a bit of a sacrifice in January's return might place us in a much stronger position in relation to February, and so on. Dynamic programming is a method for investigating such possibilities.

The subject owes much of its development to Richard Bellman and his associates at the Rand Corporation; the reader interested in a more complete treatment is referred to the book by Bellman cited in the references at the end of this chapter.

PROBLEMS WITH A FINITE NUMBER OF CONSECUTIVE DECISIONS

The method of dynamic programming is based on the mathematical notion of recursion. We will start by discussing a purely mathematical example to illustrate the method, and then give a more complicated decision-type problem.

Example 1

A positive quantity c is to be divided into n parts in such a way that the product of the n parts is to be a maximum. Use recursion to obtain the optimal subdivision.

SOLUTION

Let $f_n(c)$ denote the maximum attainable product regarded as a function of c (the given positive quantity) and n (the number of parts into which the quantity is to be divided).

If we regard c as fixed, and let n vary over the positive integers, $f_n(c)$ becomes a function of the discrete variable n. We may define $f_1(c) = c$, and we then have, for $n = 2$,

$$f_2(c) = \text{the maximum value of } y\, f_1(c - y)$$

or
$$f_2(c) = \text{the maximum value of } y(c - y)$$

subject to the restriction

$$0 \leq y \leq c$$

We may abbreviate the notation by writing this as

$$(10.1) \qquad f_2(c) = \underset{0 \leq y \leq c}{\text{Max}} \{y(c - y)\}$$

By simple calculus, we find that the function $y(c-y)$ attains its maximum for $y = c/2$, and this value of y certainly satisfies the restriction. Thus, for $n = 2$ we have

$$\text{Optimal policy} \quad (c/2,\ c/2)$$
$$(10.2)$$
$$f_2(c) = c^2/4$$

Now suppose that we have solved the problem [that is, we know $f_n(c)$] for $n = 2, 3, \cdots, m$, and inquire into the solution for $n = m+1$. If we take the first of the $m+1$ parts as y, we have an amount $c-y$ to be divided into m further parts. To proceed further, we make use of

Bellman's *principle of optimality*, which states:

An optimal policy has the property that, whatever the initial state and initial decision are, the remaining decisions must constitute an optimal policy with respect to the state resulting from the first decision.

If the initial state is c, and the first decision is y, then the state just preceding the second decision is $c - y$. By definition of f_m, the maximum achievable product for $c - y$ divided into m parts is $f_m(c - y)$. Then the conditional maximum product for c divided into $m+1$ parts, given the initial choice of y, is

$$y\, f_m(c - y)$$

By the principle of optimality, we therefore have

(10.3) $$f_{m+1}(c) = \operatorname*{Max}_{0 \le y \le c} \{y\, f_m(c - y)\}$$

Since the function $f_m(x)$ is known by our assumption, the quantity in braces in (10.3) is a known function of the single variable y. The maximizing $\bar{y}$ can be obtained, and we will have

(10.4)
$$f_{m+1}(c) = \bar{y}\, f_m(c - \bar{y})$$
Optimal policy: $(\bar{y} + m\text{-part policy for } c - \bar{y})$

The explicit solution for $n = 2$ has already been given in (10.2). For $n = 3$, (10.3) specializes to

$$f_3(c) = \operatorname*{Max}_{0 \le y \le c} \left\{ y\, \frac{(c - y)^2}{4} \right\}$$

yielding a $\bar{y}$ of $c/3$. Since $f_2(2c/3) = 4c^2/36 = c^2/9$, we have, for $n = 3$:

(10.5)
Optimal policy $(c/3, c/3, c/3)$
$$f_3(c) = c^3/27$$

With (10.2) and (10.5) as a guide, we may conjecture that the solution for general n is:

(10.6)
Optimal policy $(c/n, c/n, \cdots, c/n)$
$$f_n(c) = (c/n)^n$$

This result is readily established by induction. Assuming that (10.6) holds for n, we have, from (10.3),

$$f_{n+1}(c) = \operatorname*{Max}_{0 \le y \le c} \left\{ y \left[\frac{(c - y)}{n} \right]^n \right\}$$

This yields $\bar{y} = c/(n + 1)$. The optimal n-part policy for $[n/(n + 1)]c$, by the induction assumption, is

$$[c/(n + 1), c/(n + 1), \cdots, c/(n + 1)]$$

Thus

$$f_{n+1}(c) = [c/(n + 1)]^{n+1}$$

The problem has been solved in this manner in order to introduce the notion of recursion. A more direct approach would be to use the method of Lagrangian multipliers, as follows. Let C be divided into n parts $x_1, x_2, \cdots, x_n$, so that we have to maximize the function

$$y = x_1 x_2 \cdots x_n$$

subject to the constraints

$$\sum_{i=1}^{n} x_i = C; \quad x_1 \geq 0; \quad x_2 \geq 0; \quad \cdots; \quad x_n \geq 0$$

Let

$$Y = x_1 x_2 \cdots x_n + \lambda[C - \sum_{i} x_i]$$

The maximum value of y, for admissible values of x_i, either occurs at the subset $(x_1, \cdots, x_n)$ of the solution $(x_1, \cdots, x_n, \lambda)$ of the system

$$\frac{\partial Y}{\partial x_i} = 0 \quad i = 1, 2, \cdots, n$$

$$\frac{\partial Y}{\partial \lambda} = 0$$

or conceivably it could occur on one of the bounding planes $x_i = 0$. The solution of the system of equations is readily found to be

$$x_i = \frac{c}{n} \quad \text{for each } i$$

yielding

$$y = \left(\frac{c}{n}\right)^n$$

These values for x_i satisfy all the constraints and yield a value for y

larger than the value when any x_i is zero; so together they constitute the optimal subdivision of c.

An essential difference between the two methods is that the recursive (dynamic programming) approach changes one problem in n variables into n problems, each in one variable. In more complicated examples, the simultaneous equations resulting from the classical calculus approach may be extremely difficult to solve; and, if more than one solution exists, we must ascertain which solution yields the absolute maximum. Worse still, the calculus approach will not necessarily reveal the maximum, subject to constraints, if it lies on the boundary of the admissible region or if we are dealing with non-differentiable functions. (In the previous example, calculus will not reveal a *minimizing* subdivision of c, which is any subdivision for which at least one of the x_i is taken as zero.) We thus would have to examine the values of the function on the boundaries in order to be sure that the "maximum" (if any) revealed by calculus is not exceeded on them. We may even have to use a "search technique" to examine the function numerically over the entire admissible region. With a large number of variables and complex boundaries, this can become a far more difficult task than n iterations of a one-variable problem with comparatively simple boundaries.

The advantage of the dynamic programming approach to such problems is heightened when the function we are attempting to maximize does not possess partial derivatives at all points in the region of interest. The ordinary approach is to compute functional values at sequentially chosen points in n-space, eventually locating the maximum either exactly or, more likely, within some small interval. Roughly speaking, the amount of computation increases exponentially with the number of variables. When it is possible to reformulate the n-variable problem as a series of n problems each in one variable, the computational labor is much reduced.

Example 2

A man is engaged in buying and selling identical items, each of which required considerable storage space. He operates from a warehouse which has a capacity of 500 items. He can order on the 15th of each month, at the prices shown below, for delivery on the first of the following month. During a month he can sell any amount up to his total stock on hand, at the market prices given below. If he starts the year with 200 items in stock, how much should he plan to purchase and sell each month in order to maximize his profits (cash receipts minus cash expenditures) for the year? (Decision problems of this type are often referred to as "warehouse problems.")

Cost prices $[c_i]$		Sales prices $[p_i]$	
January 15	150	January	165
February 15	155	February	165
March 15	165	March	185
April 15	160	April	175
May 15	160	May	170
June 15	160	June	155
July 15	155	July	155
August 15	150	August	155
September 15	155	September	160
October 15	155	October	170
November 15	150	November	175
December 15	150	December	170

SOLUTION

Let us call January month 1, February month 2, etc., and introduce the following notation:

x_i = amount to be sold during month i
y_i = amount to be ordered on the 15th of month i
p_i = sales price during month i
c_i = purchase price on the 15th of month i
s_i = stock level on the 1st of month i
H = warehouse capacity

Each month we must decide on the values of x_i and y_i. As a basis for these two decisions, we have future cost prices and sales prices, the existing inventory level s_i, and the restriction that no future s_i can exceed the warehouse capacity H. (An additional restriction is, of course, that no x_i, y_i, or s_i can be negative.)

Following the notation of the previous problem, we define

$f_n(s)$ = maximum achievable return during the remaining n months, if the existing stock level is s

Thus, f_{12} refers to January, f_{11} to February, etc.

On the first day of December, the final month, we have

$$f_1(s_{12}) = \max_{x_{12}, y_{12}} \{p_{12}x_{12} - c_{12}y_{12}\}$$

where x_{12} and y_{12} are subject to the restrictions

$$0 \leq x_{12} \leq s_{12}$$
$$0 \leq y_{12} \leq H - [s_{12} - x_{12}]$$

The solution for December is clearly

(10.7)
$$f_1(s_{12}) = p_{12}s_{12}$$
$$\text{Policy: Take } x_{12} = s_{12}; \; y_{12} = 0$$

On November 1, there are two months left and the existing stock level is s_{11}. Thus

(10.8) $$f_2(s_{11}) = \underset{x_{11}, y_{11}}{\text{Max}} \{p_{11}x_{11} - c_{11}y_{11} + f_1(s_{11} + y_{11} - x_{11})\}$$

subject to

(10.9) $$0 \le x_{11} \le s_{11}, \qquad 0 \le y_{11} \le H - [s_{11} - x_{11}]$$

We know from solution (10.7) that $f_1(s_{11} + y_{11} - x_{11})$ has the value

$$p_{12}(s_{11} + y_{11} - x_{11})$$

Thus we have explicitly

(10.10) $$f_2(s_{11}) = \underset{x_{11}, y_{11}}{\text{Max}} \{[p_{11} - p_{12}]x_{11} + [p_{12} - c_{11}]y_{11} + p_{12}s_{11}\}$$

subject to the same restrictions on x_{11} and y_{11}.

Since the expression in brackets in (10.10) is linear in x_{11} and y_{11}, and the restrictions on x_{11} and y_{11} are also linear, we know from the

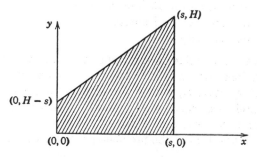

Figure 10.1. **Restrictions on sales and purchases during a month starting with stock level s.**

simplex discussion in Chapter Eight that the solution will be at one of the corners of the area satisfying all of the restrictions (10.9). The restrictions are: $x_{11} \ge 0$, $y_{11} \ge 0$, $x_{11} \le s_{11}$, $-x_{11} + y_{11} \le H - s_{11}$.

Figure 10.1 shows the area including all feasible decisions. The four corners representing possible optima are, for the situation in (10.10), $(0, 0)$, $(0, H - s_{11})$, (s_{11}, H), $(s_{11}, 0)$. The actual optimum is obtained by enumeration, yielding a solution for x_{11} and y_{11} in terms of s_{11}. Further, since $s_{12} = s_{11} + y_{11} - x_{11}$, the policy (10.7) for December can also be stated in terms of s_{11}. Another iteration would give the policies for October, November, and December in terms of s_{10}, and so on, until finally we would have the policies for all the months stated in terms of the known initial stock level s_1.

A complete algebraic solution for general values of c_i, p_i, H, s_1 is extremely cumbersome, and will not be given here. Instead, we work out the numerical solution to the problem as stated.

The general relationship is

$$f_{n+1}(s) = \underset{\substack{0 \leq x \leq s \\ 0 \leq y \leq H - s + x}}{\text{Max}} \{p_{12-n}x - c_{12-n}y + f_n(s + y - x)\}$$

Notice that, as $f_1(s)$ is linear in s, each successive $f_n(s)$ is also linear in s. Hence the expression to be minimized is linear in x and y.

Repeated application of this equation yields the following:

December 1:   Maximize $170x_{12} - 150y_{12}$
Policy: $x_{12} = s_{12}, y_{12} = 0$
$f_1(s_{12}) = 170s_{12}$

November 1:   Maximize $5x_{11} + 20y_{11} + 170s_{11}$
Policy: $x_{11} = s_{11}, y_{11} = H$
$f_2(s_{11}) = 175s_{11} + 20H$

October 1:   Maximize $-5x_{10} + 20y_{10} + 175s_{10} + 20H$
Policy: $x_{10} = s_{10}, y_{10} = H$
$f_3(s_{10}) = 170s_{10} + 40H$

September 1:   Maximize $-10x_9 + 15y_9 + 170s_9 + 40H$
Policy: $x_9 = s_9, y_9 = H$
$f_4(s_9) = 160s_9 + 55H$

August 1:   Maximize $-5x_8 + 10y_8 + 160s_8 + 55H$
Policy: $x_8 = s_8, y_8 = H$
$f_5(s_8) = 155s_8 + 65H$

July 1:   Maximize $155s_7 + 65H$
Policy: Any feasible (x_7, y_7)
$f_6(s_7) = 155s_7 + 65H$

June 1:   Maximize $-5y_6 + 155s_6 + 65H$
Policy: $y_6 = 0$, any feasible x_6
$f_7(s_6) = 155s_6 + 65H$

May 1:   Maximize $15x_5 - 5y_5 + 155s_5 + 65H$
Policy: $x_5 = s_5, y_5 = 0$
$f_8(s_5) = 170s_5 + 65H$

April 1:   Maximize $5x_4 + 10y_4 + 170s_4 + 65H$
             Policy: $x_4 = s_4, y_4 = H$
             $f_9(s_4) = 175s_4 + 75H$

March 1:   Maximize $10x_3 + 10y_3 + 175s_3 + 75H$
             Policy: $x_3 = s_3, y_3 = H$
             $f_{10}(s_3) = 185s_3 + 85H$

February 1: Maximize $-20x_2 + 30y_2 + 185s_2 + 85H$
             Policy: $x_2 = s_2, y_2 = H$
             $f_{11}(s_2) = 165s_2 + 115H$

January 1:   Maximize $-10x_1 + 25y_1 + 165s_1 + 115H$
             Policy: $x_1 = s_1, y_1 = H$
             $f_{12}(s_1) = 165s_1 + 130H$

Here $s_1 = 200$, $H = 500$. Thus the maximum achievable return $f_{12}(200)$ is $(165)(200) + (130)(500) = 98,000$. This is achieved by means of the optimal policy summarized in Table 1.

TABLE 1

Month	Initial stock (s)	Sell (x)	Buy (y)
January	200	200	500
February	500	500	500
March	500	500	500
April	500	500	500
May	500	500	0
June	0	0	0
July	0	0	$y(\leq 500)$
August	y	y	500
September	500	500	500
October	500	500	500
November	500	500	500
December	500	500	0

Before leaving this problem we mention that Stuart Dreyfus * has discussed it in greater detail than we have here. He has been able to show that:

1. The optimal n-period return is a linear function of the initial stock with coefficients dependent on the cost and selling prices.

---

* See "An Analytic Solution of the Warehouse Problem," by Stuart E. Dreyfus, *Management Science*, Vol. 4, no. 1 (Oct. 1957).

2. The optimal policy at any stage is independent of the initial stock at that stage.

3. There is an optimal policy with the following structure: Do nothing for k periods (k may be zero), and then oscillate between a full and an empty warehouse.

4. The policy and return can be calculated from recurrence relationships between the coefficients of the linear return function.

PROBLEMS FOR SOLUTION

Set XIV

1. A sector of a circle $P_0 O P_n$ of unit radius subtends an angle α at the center. A set of $n-1$ points $P_1, P_2, \cdots, P_{n-1}$ is chosen along the arc. Show that the length of the broken segment $P_0 P_1 P_2 \cdots P_n$ is

$$2 \sum_{i=1}^{n} \sin \frac{\theta_i}{2}$$

where θ_i is the angle between $O P_{i-1}$ and $O P_i$.

If $f_n(\alpha)$ is the maximum length of $P_0 P_1 P_2 \cdots P_n$ show that

$$f_n(\alpha) = \underset{0 \le \theta \le \alpha}{\text{Max}} \left\{ 2 \sin \frac{\theta}{2} + f_{n-1}(\alpha - \theta) \right\}$$

Hence, show inductively that

$$f_n(\alpha) = 2n \sin \frac{\alpha}{2n}$$

and deduce that the polygon of n sides with the largest perimeter, which can be inscribed in a given circle, is the equiangular polygon. (See Figure 10.2.)

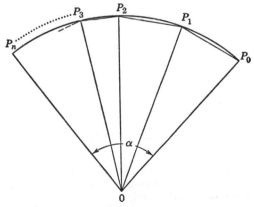

Figure 10.2. Diagram for Problem 1.

2. The manufacturing process for a perishable commodity is such that the cost of changing the level of production from one month to the next is twice the square of the difference in production levels. Any production not sold by the end of the month is wasted at a cost of $20 per unit. Given the sales forecast below, which must be met, determine a production schedule to minimize costs. Assume that December production was 200 units.

Month	January	February	March	April
Sales forecast	210	220	195	180

[*Hint:* Let $f_n(p)$ be the minimum achievable cost when last month's production was p and there are n months to go. Show that

$$f_n(p) = \underset{x \geq s}{\text{Min}} \{2(x - p)^2 + 20(x - s) + f_{n-1}(x)\}$$

where s = sales forecast for the current month
x = production for the current month

Use this formula for successive months starting with $f_1(p)$ for April and working backward to $f_4(p)$ for January.]

[*Ans:* January   February   March   April
210   220   210   205]

3. (A replacement problem.) A machine which produces light bulbs has one part that is liable to failure, in a manner that is a function of the number of bulbs made since the part was replaced. If the part fails in service, no bulb is produced and there is a cost c_f associated with wasted time, material and replacement. If the part is replaced before failure, there is a cost $c_r(< c_f)$. The probability of failure on the next bulb, when m bulbs have been made, is p_m.

After each bulb is produced, we have the choice of replacing the part or trying to make the next bulb with the existing part. The decision to replace or not will depend on the relative costs. Let $f_n(m)$ be the least expected cost of producing n more bulbs when the part has already made m bulbs.

Show that

$$f_n(m) = \min \{f_n(0) + c_r; (1 - p_m) f_{n-1}(m + 1) + p_m[c_f + f_n(0)]\}$$

and that

$$f_n(0) = f_{n-1}(1) + \frac{p_0}{1 - p_0} c_f$$

$$f_1(0) = \frac{p_0}{1 - p_0} c_f$$

Given

$$p_0 = 0, \quad p_1 = 0.1, \quad p_2 = 0.2, \quad p_3 = 0.4, \quad p_4 = 0.6, \quad p_5 = 1.0,$$
$$c_f = 3, \quad c_r = 1$$

compute successively $f_1(m), f_2(m), \cdots, f_6(m)$ for $m = 0, 1, 2, 3, 4, 5$. What do your results suggest about a replacement policy when the number of bulbs to be produced is increased indefinitely?

[*Ans.* For large $n, f_n(m)$ is minimized by replacing whenever $m \geq 3$.]

4. You are playing a game in which you are allowed to make as many as 10 successive draws from a normal distribution with mean zero and standard deviation unity. You are allowed to stop the game at the end of any draw, and are paid an amount equal to the result of that draw. At each step, the decision of whether or not to continue clearly depends on (1) the value just drawn, and (2) the stage of the game. Determine a strategy that will maximize your expected gain.

PROBLEMS WITH AN INDEFINITE NUMBER OF CONSECUTIVE DECISIONS

So far we have assumed that the number of consecutive decisions to be made is a known integer: e.g., $n = 12$ in the warehouse problem. In many situations, however, the number of decision periods over which we should attempt to optimize is not obvious. Whether the decision maker should consider only the following year, or the following five years, or the following fifty years is a fundamental problem in value theory; and it is not our purpose to attempt such an analysis. We can observe, however, that business operations are seldom designed to terminate at a specific point in time; usually it is an implicit intention of management to continue in business indefinitely. Thus management may wish to minimize total expected costs over the indefinite future.

Unfortunately, so long as some substantial non-zero costs are to be expected for each decision period, *all* policies will result in an unlimited cost if we consider a long enough time in the future. It is meaningless to talk of choosing a policy that will minimize a sum, divergent for all policies. Nevertheless, management regularly chooses policies whose results are to be measured over the indefinite future, and often operations research workers must assist in such decisions.

There are two ways out of the difficulty. The first is to discount costs to be incurred in the future. If decisions are to be made (and costs incurred) infrequently, say less often than once a year, this makes sense both intuitively and economically. Intuitively, one feels that costs to be incurred this year should have more influence on our decisions than those to be incurred next year, and so on. Economically, the postponement of expenditure is to be desired as the savings can presumably be invested elsewhere.

If the discount factor is less than one, and if costs each year are the same order of magnitude, the sum of discounted costs will converge, and it is meaningful to seek a policy that minimizes the sum of *all* future discounted costs.

There is one disadvantage to the use of a discount factor. If decisions are to be made frequently, say once a week, the idea of discounting over a week (even with a discount factor very nearly equal to unity) is difficult to reconcile with our intuitive notions of business and economics. This dilemma is avoided by the second of the two expedients referred to above. We have already seen (Example 3 of Chapter Five) that, for any series of future payments, there is an equivalent series of equal payments with the same present worth as the original series, and that, as the discount factor tends to one, the equal payments approach the average of the original series. Thus, if the decisions are to be made so frequently that the discount factor is effectively one, we can endeavor to choose a policy that minimizes the average cost per decision as the number of decisions tends to infinity.

In most practical problems, conditions are such that the total of the discounted costs over the indefinite future is finite, and the average cost per decision converges as the number of decisions approaches infinity. Moreover, the policy that minimizes long-term average cost will be the limiting case, as the discount factor tends to unity, of the policy that minimizes the total of the discounted costs. Proofs of convergence are not given here; but we note that proof of convergence is usually easier for the total of discounted costs, and that, in general, when total discounted costs converge, so does the average cost.

It sometimes happens that a policy that minimizes long-term average costs leads to the same individual decisions as a policy that aims only at minimizing cost during the period immediately affected by the decision. The following example illustrates a situation where this happens, and also gives the procedure for finding the long-term average cost associated with an optimal policy.

Example 3

A dealer places an order with his wholesaler on the first of each month, and obtains delivery one month later. The cost of holding inventory is C_1 per unit per month, and the cost of shortage is C_2 per unit per month—shortages being carried over from one month to the next. If the monthly demand x is a random variable with density function $p(x)$, find the policy that minimizes the long-term average costs per month, and show that it is the same as the policy that minimizes the expected cost during the month following delivery.

SOLUTION

The situation here is very similar to that of Example 7 in Chapter Four, which dealt with the recruitment of airline hostesses. The main difference is that we are now working with continuous quantities instead of discrete.

Let s = stock on hand (including the delivery just received) on the first day of the month in question

z = size of order to be placed

$S = s + z$

Since s is known at the time the decision is made, it is immaterial whether we regard z or S as the decision variable. For convenience in presentation, we shall use S. A policy is some function S of s, and an optimal policy is a function $S(s)$ which minimizes the long-term average monthly cost. It will be noted that, if there is no way of reducing stocks, apart from sales, we are restricted to policies for which $S(s) \geq s$.

Now let x = demand in current month

v = discount factor for one month $(v < 1)$

$I(s)$ = expected cost for current month [note that $I(s)$ is independent of our policy—it is defined for both positive and negative s]

$f_n(s)$ = total discounted cost (expected) over n months, when we use an optimal policy $S(s)$

The following month will start with a stock level $s - x + z = S - x$, and we will have, by the principle of optimality,

$$(10.11) \qquad f_n(s) = \operatorname*{Min}_{S \geq s} \left\{ I(s) + v \int_0^\infty f_{n-1}(S - x)\, p(x)\, dx \right\}$$

If we assume (as can be proved) that the sequence of functions $f_n(s)$ tends to a limiting function $f(s)$ as n tends to infinity, then $f(s)$ must satisfy the functional equation:

$$(10.12) \qquad f(s) = \operatorname*{Min}_{S \geq s} \left\{ I(s) + v \int_0^\infty f(S - x)\, p(x)\, dx \right\}$$

The first term in braces, $I(s)$, is clearly the same for all S. The second term is a function of S, which we may call $g(S)$, and may be interpreted as the present value of the return from an optimal policy starting a month hence (in a situation conditioned by the fact that $S - s$ is the order placed now). It is reasonable to suppose that this term graphed as a function of S should have roughly the form shown in Figure 10.3.

The value S_0 which minimizes the plotted function is independent of the present stock level s. If S_0 exceeds s, then S_0 is the minimizing S in (10.12), and our decision today should be to order $S_0 - s$. If S_0 is less than s, then the best we can do (see Figure 10.3) is to order nothing this month.

The discussion up to this point does not furnish a means for actually calculating S_0, since the function $g(S)$ is defined in terms of the undetermined function f. We can, however, obtain S_0 from the known function I as part of the following argument. Assuming that an optimizing

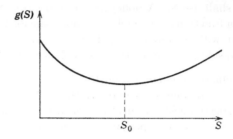

Figure 10.3.   Concavity of variable term in equation (10.12).

value S_0 exists; then, for $s \leq S_0$, we have

$$f(s) = I(s) + g(S_0)$$

$$= I(s) + v \int_0^\infty [I(S_0 - x) + g(S_0)]\, p(x)\, dx$$

$$= I(s) + v \int_0^\infty I(S_0 - x)\, p(x)\, dx + v\, g(S_0)$$

Equating $I(s) + g(S_0)$ to the last line and transposing, we obtain

(10.13) $$g(S_0) = \frac{v}{1 - v} \int_0^\infty I(S_0 - x)\, p(x)\, dx$$

Hence, for $s \leq S_0$,

$$f(s) = I(s) + \frac{v}{1 - v} \int_0^\infty I(S_0 - x)\, p(x)\, dx$$

Thus $f(s)$ is the present worth of a series of monthly payments

$$(1 - v)\, f(s) = (1 - v)\, I(s) + v \int_0^\infty I(S_0 - x)\, p(x)\, dx$$

[Recall the present worth of a payment X each month for an indefinite period is $X/(1-v)$.]

In the limit as v tends to unity these payments become the long-term average cost, which is therefore

$$(10.14) \qquad \int_0^\infty I(S_0 - x)\, p(x)\, dx$$

If we were to start at a point in time where s exceeded S_0, the same result would apply. For, we would order nothing until stocks fell to some point s' below S_0, and repeat the analysis from that point. Since the result (10.14) is independent of the initial stock level s, the long-term average from that point on will coincide with (10.14). The costs incurred up to the point where the stock level falls below S_0 make no contribution to the long-term average cost; and so (10.14) will apply from the present time on as well.

If the policy were to order $S_1 - s$ each month, where $S_1 \neq S_0$, then the long-term average monthly cost would be, after a calculation similar to the above,

$$(10.15) \qquad \int_0^\infty I(S_1 - x)\, p(x)\, dx$$

Since S_0 describes the optimal policy, (10.15) must exceed (10.14). The conclusion is that S_0 is that value of S which minimizes the known function

$$(10.16) \qquad \int_0^\infty I(S - x)\, p(x)\, dx$$

In this problem, the function $I(s)$, the expected cost for the present month starting with stock level s, is readily computed by the methods of Chapter Four. There are two different expressions for $I(s)$, depending on whether $s \geq 0$ or $s < 0$ (back orders).

$$(10.17) \quad I(s) = \int_0^s C_1\left(s - \frac{x}{2}\right) p(x)\, dx$$

$$+ \int_s^\infty \left[\frac{C_1 s^2}{2x} + \frac{C_2(s - x)^2}{2x}\right] p(x)\, dx \qquad s \geq 0$$

$$I(s) = C_2 \int_0^\infty \left(\frac{x}{2} - s\right) p(x)\, dx \qquad s < 0$$

$$(10.18)$$

$$= C_2\left(\frac{\bar{x}}{2} - s\right) \qquad \text{where} \quad \bar{x} = \text{average monthly demand}$$

To obtain the value S_0 that minimizes (10.16), we shall require $I'(s)$. Differentiation of the above expressions for $I(s)$ yields, after simplification,

$$I'(s) = (C_1 + C_2)\int_0^s p(x)\,dx$$

(10.19)
$$+ s(C_1 + C_2)\int_s^\infty \frac{p(x)}{x}\,dx - C_2 \qquad s \geq 0$$

$$I'(s) = -C_2 \qquad s < 0$$

Differentiating (10.16) with respect to S and putting the result equal to zero gives

$$\int_0^\infty I'(S_0 - x)\,p(x)\,dx = 0$$

For use with (10.19), we write this as

$$\int_0^{S_0} I'(S_0 - x)\,p(x)\,dx + \int_{S_0}^\infty I'(S_0 - x)\,p(x)\,dx = 0$$

and obtain

$$\int_0^{S_0}\left[(C_1 + C_2)\int_0^{S_0 - x} p(y)\,dy\right.$$

$$\left. + (S_0 - x)(C_1 + C_2)\int_{S_0 - x}^\infty \frac{p(y)}{y}\,dy - C_2\right] p(x)\,dx$$

$$+ \int_{S_0}^\infty (-C_2)\,p(x)\,dx = 0$$

This may be rewritten as

(10.20)
$$\frac{C_2}{C_1 + C_2} = \int_0^{S_0} p(x)\left\{\int_0^{S_0 - x} p(y)\,dy + (S_0 - x)\int_{S_0 - x}^\infty \frac{p(y)}{y}\right\}dx$$

From this equation, the optimal value S_0 may be obtained numerically.

The reader can verify, using the methods of Chapter Four, that this equation for S_0 is precisely the equation that S_0 satisfies if we set out to minimize expected costs in the month after delivery of the order we are about to place. Hence in this situation the optimal short-term and long-term policies coincide. The reason for this is that the stock level immediately after a delivery is made depends only on the S chosen for that particular delivery and is independent of all previous S.

Example 4

A plant manager has to schedule regular-time production on the 15th of each month for the coming month. To make his decision, he has at his disposal the following data:

(i)   the inventory level s on the 1st of the following month.
(ii)   the probability density $p(x)$ for the monthly demand x.
(iii)   the cost of holding inventory, c per unit per month.
(iv)   the cost of regular-time production, a per unit.
(v)   the cost of overtime production, $b(>a)$ per unit.

By the time the first of the month comes, he knows exactly what the demand x will be, and schedules just enough overtime, if necessary, so that all orders will be filled.

Both regular and overtime production as well as the demand can be considered as taking place uniformly during the month. How much regular production should be scheduled on the 15th, so as to minimize the long-term average monthly cost?

SOLUTION

Let q be the amount of production scheduled for regular time. If the demand x is less than $s+q$, inventory at time t during the month (t ranging from 0 to 1) will be

$$s + qt - xt$$

If the demand x is greater than $s+q$, an amount $x - (s+q)$ will be produced during overtime; and inventory at time t will be

$$s + qt - xt + [x - (s + q)]t = s(1 - t)$$

By integration with respect to t, we find that the average inventory levels during the month will be

$$s + \tfrac{1}{2}(q - x) \quad \text{if} \quad x \le s + q$$

$$\frac{s}{2} \quad\quad\quad \text{if} \quad x > s + q$$

If we write $S = s + q$, the average inventory is

$$\tfrac{1}{2}(S + s - x) \quad \text{if} \quad x \le S$$

$$\frac{s}{2} \quad\quad\quad \text{if} \quad x > S$$

Hence, denoting the expected cost during the following month by $I(s, S)$, we have

$$(10.21) \quad I(s, S) = \frac{c}{2} \int_0^S (S + s - x) \, p(x) \, dx + \frac{c}{2} \int_S^\infty s \, p(x) \, dx$$

$$+ a(S - s) + b \int_S^\infty (x - S) \, p(x) \, dx$$

The first two terms in (10.21) are inventory holding costs; the third term is the cost of regular production; and the last term is the cost of overtime production.

If we were concerned only with costs during one month, we would choose $S = \hat{S}$, where $\hat{S}$ minimizes $I(s, S)$ in the range $s \leq S < \infty$. To determine $\hat{S}$, we find the absolute minimum of $I(s, S)$ for the given s by calculus, and see whether the minimizing S exceeds s. If so, we would take the minimizing S as $\hat{S}$; otherwise, we would take $\hat{S} = s$. By use of the formulas of Appendix II, we find that

$$\frac{\partial I}{\partial S} = \frac{c}{2} \int_0^S p(x) \, dx + a - b \int_S^\infty p(x) \, dx$$

which may be rewritten as

$$(10.22) \qquad \frac{\partial I}{\partial S} = \left(\frac{c}{2} + b \right) \int_0^S p(x) \, dx + a - b$$

The condition on S for $I(s, S)$ to be a minimum becomes

$$(10.23) \qquad \int_0^S p(x) \, dx = \frac{b - a}{b + c/2}$$

It may be verified that (10.23) yields a minimum for $I(s, S)$. Thus our policy would be to produce $\hat{S} - s$ in regular time if $\hat{S}$ exceeds s, and nothing in regular time if $\hat{S}$ is less than s. We will now show that this policy does not minimize the long-term average monthly cost.

Let $f_n(s)$ be the minimum achievable discounted cost (expected) for n months, when we start with an inventory s, and costs are discounted by a factor v (<1) each month. Then $f_n(s)$ must satisfy

$$(10.24) \quad f_n(s) = \underset{S \geq s}{\text{Min}} \left\{ I(s, S) + v \int_0^S f_{n-1}(S - x) \, p(x) \, dx \right.$$

$$\left. + v \int_S^\infty f_{n-1}(0) \, p(x) \, dx \right\}$$

The first term in braces is the expected cost for the first month; the second term is the portion of the discounted cost in the remaining $(n-1)$ months ascribable to the possibility $x \leq S$. If $x > S$, then overtime will insure that the following month starts with zero inventory; hence the third term.

If we assume (as can be proved) that the sequence of functions $f_n(s)$ tends to a limit function $f(s)$ as n tends to infinity, then $f(s)$ must satisfy the following functional equation:

(10.25)

$$f(s) = \operatorname*{Min}_{S \geq s} \left\{ I(s, S) + v \int_0^S f(S - x) \, p(x) \, dx + v \int_S^\infty f(0) \, p(x) \, dx \right\}$$

As in the previous example, we shall obtain the minimizing value $S_0(s)$ by a somewhat devious argument.

We first differentiate the expression in braces with respect to S and set the result equal to zero:

$$\frac{\partial I}{\partial S} + v \int_0^S f'(S - x) \, p(x) \, dx = 0$$

Since $\partial I/\partial S$ is independent of s, as is the second term above, we deduce that, for sufficiently small s, the optimizing S_0 is independent of s.

Returning to (10.25), we have

(10.26) $\quad f(s) = I(s, S_0) + v \int_0^{S_0} f(S_0 - x) \, p(x) \, dx + v \int_{S_0}^\infty f(0) \, p(x) \, dx$

for $s < S_0$. From (10.21), we find that $I(s, S)$ may be broken down into the sum of $[c/2 - a]s$ and a function of S. Specifically, for $S = S_0$,

(10.27) $\quad I(s, S_0) = \left[\frac{c}{2} - a \right] s + S_0 \left\{ \left(\frac{c}{2} + b \right) \int_0^{S_0} p(x) \, dx + a - b \right\}$

$$- \frac{c}{2} \int_0^{S_0} x \, p(x) \, dx + b \int_{S_0}^\infty x \, p(x) \, dx$$

Symbolically, we write (10.26) as

(10.28) $\qquad\qquad f(s) = \left(\frac{c}{2} - a \right) s + g(S_0)$

where $g(S_0)$ is the sum of the last two terms on the right side of (10.26) and the last three terms on the right side of (10.27). From (10.28), we have

$$f(S_0 - x) = \left(\frac{c}{2} - a\right)(S_0 - x) + g(S_0)$$

(10.29)

$$f(0) = g(S_0)$$

Substituting (10.27) and (10.29) in the right side of (10.26) gives

$$f(s) = \left(\frac{c}{2} - a\right)s + S_0\left[\left(\frac{c}{2} + b\right)\int_0^{S_0} p(x)\,dx + a - b\right]$$

$$- \frac{c}{2}\int_0^{S_0} x\,p(x)\,dx + b\int_{S_0}^{\infty} x\,p(x)\,dx$$

$$+ v\int_0^{S_0}\left[\left(\frac{c}{2} - a\right)(S_0 - x) + g(S_0)\right]p(x)\,dx$$

$$+ v\int_{S_0}^{\infty} g(S_0)\,p(x)\,dx$$

This can be reduced to

(10.30)

$$f(s) = \left(\frac{c}{2} - a\right)s + S_0\left[\frac{c}{2}(1 + v) - av + b\right]\int_0^{S_0} p(x)\,dx$$

$$+ S_0(a - b) - \left[\frac{c}{2}(1 + v) - av\right]\int_0^{S_0} x\,p(x)\,dx$$

$$+ b\int_{S_0}^{\infty} x\,p(x)\,dx + v\,g(S_0)$$

Equating (10.28) and (10.30), we may solve specifically for $g(S_0)$:

(10.31)

$$g(S_0) = \frac{F(S_0)}{1 - v}$$

where

(10.32) $\quad F(S_0) = S_0\left[\frac{c}{2}(1 + v) - av + b\right]\int_0^{S_0} p(x)\,dx + S_0(a - b)$

$$- \left[\frac{c}{2}(1 + v) - av\right]\int_0^{S_0} x\,p(x)\,dx + b\int_{S_0}^{\infty} x\,p(x)\,dx$$

Writing $1/(1 - v)$ as $1 + v + v^2 + \cdots$, we can write (10.28) as

$$f(s) = \left(\frac{c}{2} - a \right) s + F(S_0) + v\, F(S_0) + v^2\, F(S_0) + \cdots$$

Thus the long-term average monthly cost, using an optimal policy S_0, is just $F(S_0)$.

If we were to use any other fixed value S_1 as a policy, so that each month we scheduled regular production of $S_1 - s$, we would find in exactly the same way that the long-term average monthly cost would be $F(S_1)$. Since S_0 is optimal, $F(S_0) \leq F(S_1)$; and we conclude that S_0 minimizes $F(S)$. Differentiating $F(S)$ with respect to S, and setting the result equal to zero yields, as our condition for S_0,

(10.33)
$$\int_0^{S_0} p(x)\, dx = \frac{b - a}{\dfrac{c}{2}(1 + v) - av + b}$$

Equation (10.33) should be compared with equation (10.23) for $\hat{S}$. The equations coincide for $v = 0$; this is to be expected, because, when $v = 0$, we take no account of costs incurred after the first month. As v approaches 1, the policy approaches the solution S_0 of the equation

$$\int_0^{S_0} p(x)\, dx = \frac{b - a}{b + c - a}$$

If s exceeds the solution S_0 of (10.33), the optimal policy is to schedule no regular production this month. Eventually, following the optimal policy, the stock will fall below S_0, and remain below. The long-term average monthly cost, as in the previous example, is not affected by whether s is initially greater than or less than S_0.

As we have noted in both this example and the last one, it is a fairly simple matter to deduce the average monthly cost for any policy involving a fixed S, say S_1, independent of s. Having done so, we can easily choose S_1 so as to minimize the average monthly cost. However, it is not obvious that the optimal policy has this form unless we establish this fact, as we have done in Examples 3 and 4. Unless we can prove the opposite for a particular situation, we have to regard the optimal S as an undetermined function of s, rather than an undetermined constant.

PROBLEMS FOR SOLUTION

Set XV

1. In the situation of Example 4, show that, with a policy of having a constant value of S, say S', each month, the average inventory at the end of each month will be

$$\int_0^{S'} (S'-x) \ p(x) \ dx$$

Hence show that the average monthly cost will be

$$S'(b + c - a)\int_0^{S'} p(x) \ dx - S'(b - a) + (a - c)\int_0^{S'} x \ p(x) \ dx + b\int_{S'}^{\infty} x \ p(x) \ dx$$

Deduce that the policy of minimizing costs in the month following the decision about S leads to an average cost per month of

$$S_0 \frac{(b - a)(c/2 - a)}{(b + c/2)} + (a - c)\int_0^{S_0} x \ p(x) \ dx + b\int_{S_0}^{\infty} x \ p(x) \ dx$$

where S_0 is the value of S which satisfies equation 10.23.

2. In an inventory situation, orders are placed monthly, and the costs during the month after each order are

$$I(s, S) = I_1(s) + I_2(S)$$

where s is the inventory immediately before the order is placed and $S-s$ is the quantity ordered. [$I_1(s)$ is independent of S, and $I_2(S)$ is independent of s.]

If $f(s)$ is the minimum expected discounted total of all future costs, and $p(x)$ is the probability density function for monthly demand, show that the optimal value $\hat{S}$ of S satisfies

$$I'_2(S) + v\int_0^{\infty} I'_1(S - x) \ p(x) \ dx = 0$$

and that the minimum expected cost is given by

$$f(s) = I_1(s) + \frac{1}{1 - v} [I_2(\hat{S}) + v\int_0^{\infty} I_1(\hat{S} - x) \ p(x) \ dx]$$

provided $s \leq \hat{S}$.

Deduce the equation satisfied by the S that minimizes the average monthly cost, and obtain an expression for this cost. [*Hint:* Reason as in Examples 3 and 4.]

3. A purchasing agent makes decisions about orders every month. If he decides to place an order, there are ordering costs of amount C. The cost of holding inventory is C_1 per unit per month, and shortages cost C_2 per unit per month. The probability density function for monthly demand x is $p(x)$. Demand can be assumed to take place continuously during the month, and

the backlog from one month is filled as soon as next month's shipments are received. If the agent places an order it is filled immediately.

The following notation will be used:

s = inventory level immediately before a decision on ordering is made

S = inventory level immediately after a shipment is received

$f_n(s)$ = minimum total expected cost during a period of n months, which starts with an inventory s

$I(S)$ = expected cost of inventory and shortage during a month which starts with an inventory S

Show that

(a) $f_1(s) = \min \{\underset{S \geq s}{\text{Min}} [I(S) + C]; I(s)\}$

(b) If costs are to be minimized over one month, an order will be placed for an amount $S_1 - s$, provided $s < s_1$, where

(1) S_1 satisfies $\partial I / \partial S = 0$.

(2) $I(S_1) + C = I(s_1)$; $s_1 < S_1$. If $s > s_1$, no order will be placed.

(c) For $n > 1$,

$$f_n(s) = \min \{\underset{S \geq s}{\text{Min}} [I(S) + C + \int_0^\infty f_{n-1}(S - x)\, p(x)\, dx];$$
$$I(s) + \int_0^\infty f_{n-1}(s - x)\, p(x)\, dx\}$$

(d) If costs are to be minimized over n months, an order will be placed for an amount $S_n - s$, provided $s < s_n$, where

(1) S_n satisfies

$$\frac{\partial I}{\partial S} + \int_0^\infty \frac{\partial f_{n-1}}{\partial S} (S - x)\, p(x)\, dx = 0$$

and

(2) s_n satisfies

$$I(S_n) + C + \int_0^\infty f_{n-1}(S_n - x)\, p(x)\, dx = I(s_n) + \int_0^\infty f_{n-1}(s_n - x)\, p(x)\, dx$$

(e) Determine the form of $I(S)$ in terms of C_1, C_2, and $p(x)$.

(f) Sketch the graph of $f_1(s)$.

Note: The equations in (d) would have to be solved iteratively by mechanical methods. Such iterative numerical solutions are usually needed in dynamic programming; only in exceptional situations can an explicit solution be obtained in terms of commonly tabulated functions.

REFERENCES

Bellman, Richard, *Dynamic Programming*, Princeton University Press, Princeton, 1957.

Vazsonyi, Andrew, *Scientific Programming in Business and Industry*, John Wiley & Sons, New York, 1958.

Finite
differences

The use of the calculus of finite differences can lead to a simplification of notation in many numerical processes. Many of the results are directly analogous to those of the infinitesimal calculus; and, in fact, many formulas of the latter can be derived in a simple manner from the corresponding formulas of the finite-difference calculus.

DEFINITION OF THE DIFFERENCE OPERATOR Δ

We shall be concerned with functions $f(n)$ defined only for integral values of the argument n.

The "first difference" of $f(n)$ is denoted by $\Delta f(n)$ and is defined by the formula

$$(\text{I.1}) \qquad \Delta f(n) = f(n + 1) - f(n)$$

Second and subsequent differences of $f(n)$ are defined by

$$(\text{I.2}) \qquad \Delta^{r+1} f(n) = \Delta\{\Delta^r f(n)\}$$

(The expression $\Delta f(n)$ is read as "delta $f(n)$" and $\Delta^r f(n)$ is read as "delta to the r of $f(n)$.")

It is readily verified that

(I.3) $$\Delta^{r+1}f(n) = \Delta^r\{\Delta f(n)\} = \Delta^r f(n+1) - \Delta^r f(n)$$

Equation (I.3) becomes true for all integral $r \geq 0$ if we make the conventions $\Delta^0 =$ identity operator, $\Delta^1 = \Delta$.

CONDITIONS FOR A MINIMUM OF $f(n)$

The function $f(n)$ will have a "local minimum" at n_0 provided both the following conditions are satisfied:

$f(n_0 + 1) > f(n_0)$; i.e. $\Delta f(n_0) > 0$.
$f(n_0 - 1) > f(n_0)$; i.e. $\Delta f(n_0 - 1) < 0$.

Thus $f(n)$ will have a local minimum at n_0 if

(I.4) $$\Delta f(n_0 - 1) < 0 < \Delta f(n_0)$$

The function $f(n)$ is said to have an *absolute minimum* at n_0 if $f(n_0) \leq f(n)$ for all n. Sufficient conditions for $f(n)$ to have an absolute minimum at n_0 are that (I.4) be satisfied, and also that

(I.5) $$\Delta^2 f(n) \geq 0 \qquad \text{for all } n$$

The conditions for $f(n)$ to assume a maximum at n_0 are analogous. (These conditions are sufficient for a minimum; however, they are not necessary. A precise statement of necessary conditions is more involved, and will not be given here.)

FIRST DIFFERENCES OF COMBINATIONS OF FUNCTIONS

If $f(n)$ and $g(n)$ are any two functions of n, then it is readily verified that

(I.6) $$\Delta\{f(n) + g(n)\} = \Delta f(n) + \Delta g(n)$$

(I.7) $$\Delta\{f(n)\,g(n)\} = f(n+1)\,\Delta g(n) + g(n)\,\Delta f(n)$$

(I.8) $$\Delta\left\{\frac{f(n)}{g(n)}\right\} = \frac{g(n)\,\Delta f(n) - f(n)\,\Delta g(n)}{g(n+1)\,g(n)}$$

Also, for any function $f(n)$,

(I.9) $$\Delta\{k\,f(n)\} = k\,\Delta f(n) \qquad \text{for } k \text{ a constant}$$

(I.10) $$\Delta\left\{\frac{1}{f(n)}\right\} = -\frac{\Delta f(n)}{f(n+1)\,f(n)}$$

A formula analogous to the formula in calculus for differentiating x^r results if we define

$$n_{[r]} = n(n-1) \cdots (n-r+1) \qquad r \text{ factors}$$

Then

(I.11) $\Delta n_{[r]} = r n_{[r-1]}$ for fixed r

Other formulas that are helpful in differencing particular functions are

(I.12) $\Delta\{n\} = 1$

(I.13) $\Delta\{C_{n,r}\} = C_{n,r-1}$ r fixed

(I.14) $\Delta\{a^n\} = a^n(a-1)$ a fixed

SUMMATION OF SERIES

We are interested in obtaining a closed form for an expression of the type

$$\sum_{n=a}^{b} f(n) = f(a) + f(a+1) + \cdots + f(b)$$

The formula obtained will be analogous to the fundamental theorem of the integral calculus, which evaluates

$$\int_a^b f(x)\, dx$$

as $F(b) - F(a)$, where $F(x)$ is an antiderivative of $f(x)$.

Let us call $F(n)$ an "antidifference" of $f(n)$ provided

(I.15) $\Delta F(n) = f(n)$

Then $$\sum_{n=a}^{b} f(n) = \sum_{n=a}^{b} \Delta F(n)$$

$$= F(b+1) - F(b)$$
$$+ F(b) \qquad - F(b-1)$$
$$\vdots$$
$$+ F(a+2) - F(a+1)$$
$$+ F(a+1) - F(a)$$
$$= F(b+1) - F(a)$$

Thus, if $F(n)$ is an antidifference of $f(n)$,

$$(I.16) \qquad \sum_{n=a}^{b} f(n) = [F(n)]_a^{b+1} = F(b+1) - F(a)$$

Note that the upper limit, unlike in integration, is $b+1$ and not b.

SUMMATION BY PARTS

In calculus, a definite integral of the form

$$\int_a^b f(x) \, dg(x)$$

is often more easily evaluated by integration by parts, viz.:

$$\int_a^b f(x) \, dg(x) = f(b) \, g(b) - f(a) \, g(a) - \int_a^b g(x) \, df(x)$$

In finite differences, we have an analogous formula which follows readily from (I.7):

$$(I.17) \quad \sum_{n=a}^{b} f(n) \, \Delta g(n)$$

$$= f(b+1) \, g(b+1) - f(a) \, g(a) - \sum_{n=a}^{b} g(n+1) \, \Delta f(n)$$

As an example, suppose we wish to compute

$$\sum_{n=1}^{k} n x^n$$

We cannot apply (I.16) directly, since we see no easy way to anti-difference the function nx^n. But we can antidifference x^n, since

$$x^n = \Delta \left\{ \frac{x^n}{x-1} \right\}$$

Applying (I.17) with $f(n) = n$, $g(n) = x^n/(x-1)$, we have

$$\sum_{n=1}^{k} n x^n = \frac{(k+1)x^{k+1}}{x-1} - \frac{x}{x-1} - \sum_{n=1}^{k} \frac{x^{n+1}}{x-1}$$

$$= \frac{(k+1)x^{k+1}}{x-1} - \frac{x}{x-1} - \frac{x^{k+2}}{(x-1)^2} + \frac{x^2}{(x-1)^2}$$

where the last step follows from (I.16).

DIFFERENCING UNDER A SUMMATION SIGN

In inventory applications where the stock level z is regarded as a discrete variable, we often run into the necessity for computing the first difference of some function $C(z)$ of the form

$$C(z) = \sum_{x,y,\cdots,u} f(x, y, \cdots, u; z)$$

If $f(x, y, \cdots, u; z)$ has the same functional form throughout the region of summation, and if the boundary of this region does not depend on z, then we can apply (I.6) to each term separately, and obtain

$$\Delta C(z) = \sum_{x,y,\cdots,u} \Delta f(x, y, \cdots, u; z)$$

where the differences on the right are with respect to z. However, if f has different functional forms in different sectors of the region of summation, or if the boundary of the region depends on z, the computation of $\Delta C(z)$ is usually more complicated.

Let us first consider the one-dimensional case where

$$C(z) = \sum_{x=a(z)}^{b(z)} f(x, z)$$

Then

$$C(z+1) = \sum_{x=a(z+1)}^{b(z+1)} f(x, z+1)$$

$$= \sum_{x=a(z)}^{b(z)} f(x, z+1) + \sum_{x=b(z)+1}^{b(z+1)} f(x, z+1) - \sum_{a(z)}^{a(z+1)-1} f(x, z+1)$$

and

$$(I.18) \quad \Delta C(z) = \sum_{a(z)}^{b(z)} \Delta f(x, z) + \sum_{b(z)+1}^{b(z+1)} f(x, z+1) - \sum_{a(z)}^{a(z+1)-1} f(x, z+1)$$

[We are assuming that $a(z)$, $b(z)$ are increasing functions of z; if this is not so some modification is required].

Now suppose that $f(x, z)$ is defined by

$$f(x, z) = \begin{cases} f_1(x, z) & \text{for } x \text{ in the interval } 0 \leq x \leq b(z) \\ f_2(x, z) & \text{for } x > b(z) \end{cases}$$

and that we wish to difference

$$C(z) = \sum_{x=0}^{\infty} f(x, z)$$

We have

$$C(z) = \sum_{x=0}^{b(z)} f_1(x, z) + \sum_{x=b(z)+1}^{\infty} f_2(x, z)$$

Applying (I.18) to both sums, we obtain

$$\Delta C(z)$$

$$= \sum_{x=0}^{b(z)} \Delta f_1(x, z) + \sum_{x=b(z)+1}^{\infty} \Delta f_2(x, z) + \sum_{b(z)+1}^{b(z+1)} [f_1(x, z+1) - f_2(x, z+1)]$$

Thus we have our final result for single sums:

$$\Delta C(z) = \sum_{x=0}^{\infty} \Delta f(x, z)$$

provided that $f_1(x, z+1)$ equals $f_2(x, z+1)$ for all x in the interval $b(z) + 1 \le x \le b(z + 1)$.

We now wish to extend these results to double sums. Suppose $C(z)$ is defined by

$$C(z) = \sum_{y=a(z)}^{b(z)} \sum_{x=u(y,z)}^{v(y,z)} f(x, y, z)$$

and that we wish to find $\Delta C(z)$.

Let us define $g(y, z)$ by

$$g(y, z) = \sum_{x=u(y,z)}^{v(y,z)} f(x, y, z)$$

Then

$$C(z) = \sum_{y=a(z)}^{b(z)} g(y, z)$$

and, applying (I.18), we obtain

$$\Delta C(z) = \sum_{y=a(z)}^{b(z)} \Delta g(y, z) + \sum_{b(z)+1}^{b(z+1)} g(y, z+1) - \sum_{a(z)}^{a(z+1)-1} g(y, z+1)$$

Then applying (I.18) to $g(y, z)$ yields

$$\Delta g(y, z) = \sum_{x=u(y,z)}^{v(y,z)} \Delta f(x, y, z) + \sum_{v(y,z)+1}^{v(y,z+1)} f(x, y, z+1)$$

$$- \sum_{u(y,z)}^{u(y,z+1)-1} f(x, y, z+1)$$

where all differences are with respect to z.   Hence

{I.19}
$$\Delta C(z) = \sum_{y=a(z)}^{b(z)} \sum_{x=u(y,z)}^{v(y,z)} \Delta f(x, y, z)$$

$$+ \sum_{a(z)}^{b(z)} \sum_{v(y,z)+1}^{v(y,z+1)} f(x, y, z+1)$$

$$- \sum_{a(z)}^{b(z)} \sum_{u(y,z)}^{u(y,z+1)-1} f(x, y, z+1)$$

$$+ \sum_{b(z)+1}^{b(z+1)} \sum_{u(y,z+1)}^{v(y,z+1)} f(x, y, z+1)$$

$$- \sum_{a(z)}^{a(z+1)-1} \sum_{u(y,z+1)}^{v(y,z+1)} f(x, y, z+1)$$

(Again we are assuming that the boundary functions a, b, u, v are increasing functions of z.)

Now let $f(x, y, z)$ be defined (see Figure I.1) as

$f_1(x, y, z)$ in the region $[0 \leq x \leq u(y, z); 0 \leq y \leq b(z)]$
$f_2(x, y, z)$ in the region $[u(y, z) < x; 0 \leq y \leq b(z)]$
$f_3(x, y, z)$ in the region $[0 \leq x \leq v(y, z); b(z) < y]$
$f_4(x, y, z)$ in the region $[v(y, z) < x; b(z) < y]$

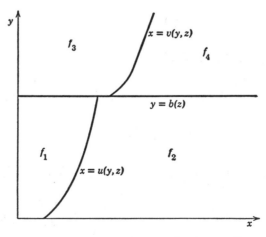

Figure I.1. Subregions of region of summation in two-dimensional case.

Then

$$C(z) = \sum_0^\infty \sum_0^\infty f(x, y, z)$$

$$= \sum_0^b \sum_0^u f_1 + \sum_0^b \sum_{u+1}^\infty f_2 + \sum_{b+1}^\infty \sum_0^v f_3 + \sum_{b+1}^\infty \sum_{v+1}^\infty f_4$$

Applying (I.19) to $C(z)$ yields

$$\Delta C(z) = \sum_0^b \sum_0^u \Delta f_1 + \sum_0^b \sum_{u+1}^\infty \Delta f_2 + \sum_{b+1}^\infty \sum_0^v \Delta f_3 + \sum_{b+1}^\infty \sum_{v+1}^\infty \Delta f_4$$

$$+ \sum_0^b \sum_{u+1}^{u(y,z+1)} [f_1(x, y, z+1) - f_2(x, y, z+1)]$$

$$+ \sum_{b+1}^\infty \sum_{v+1}^{v(y,z+1)} [f_3(x, y, z+1) - f_4(x, y, z+1)]$$

$$+ \sum_{b+1}^{b(z+1)} \left[\sum_0^{u(y,z+1)} f_1(x, y, z+1) + \sum_{u(y,z+1)+1}^\infty f_2(x, y, z+1) \right.$$

$$\left. - \sum_0^{v(y,z+1)} f_3(x, y, z+1) - \sum_{v(y,z+1)+1}^\infty f_4(x, y, z+1) \right]$$

It is possible for f_1, f_2, f_3, f_4 to be such that all terms except the first four cancel out. However, we cannot state sufficient conditions for this to happen in as simple a manner as we did for single summations. In practical cases, where we have to obtain differences in order to minimize some expected value, and where in the continuous analog the function being averaged is itself continuous, we may suspect that the first difference of the expected value in the discrete case will contain only four terms. It is usually worth checking such problems to see if such simplification is possible.

Example

Obtain $\Delta C(z)$, where

$$C(z) = \sum_{y=0}^z \sum_{x=0}^{z-y} C_1 \left(z - y - \frac{x}{2} \right) g(x)\, h(y)$$

$$+ \sum_{y=0}^z \sum_{x=z-y+1}^\infty \frac{1}{2x} [C_1(z - y)^2 + C_2(x + y - z)^2]\, g(x)\, h(y)$$

$$+ \sum_{y=z+1}^\infty \sum_{x=0}^\infty C_2 \left(\frac{x}{2} + y - z \right) g(x)\, h(y)$$

(This is the cost function of Example 7, Chapter 4.)

SOLUTION

The summation is over the first quadrant of the xy plane, divided into sectors as shown in Figure I.2.

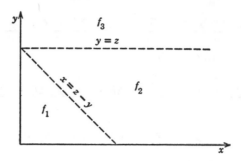

Figure I.2. Subregions in the example.

In the notation of this section, we have

$$f_* = C_1 \left(z - y - \frac{x}{2} \right) g(x)\, h(y)$$

$$f_\sim = \frac{1}{2x} [C_1(z - y)^2 + C_2(x + y - z)^2]\, g(x)\, h(y)$$

$$f_\rho = C_2 \left(\frac{x}{2} + y - z \right) g(x)\, h(y)$$

$$b(z) = z$$

$$u(y, z) = z - y$$

$$v(y, z) = +\infty$$

$$\Delta C(z) = \sum_{y=0}^{z} \sum_{x=0}^{z-y} C_1\, g(x)\, h(y)$$

$$+ \sum_{y=0}^{z} \sum_{x=z-y+1}^{\infty} \frac{1}{x} \left[(C_1 + C_2)\left(z - y + \frac{1}{2} \right) - C_2 \right] g(x)\, h(y)$$

$$- \sum_{y=z+1}^{\infty} \sum_{x=0}^{\infty} C_2\, g(x)\, h(y)$$

$$+ \sum_{0}^{z} \sum_{z-y+1}^{z-y+1} \left\{ C_1 \left(z + 1 - y - \frac{x}{2} \right) - \frac{1}{2x} [C_1(z + 1 - y)^2 \right.$$

$$+ C_2(x + y - z - 1)^2] \bigg\} g(x) \, h(y)$$

$$+ \sum_{z+1}^{z+1} \bigg\{ \sum_0^{z-y+1} C_1 \left(z + 1 - y - \frac{x}{2} \right) g(x)$$

$$+ \sum_{z-y+2}^{\infty} \frac{1}{2x} [C_1(z + 1 - y)^2 + C_2(x + y - z - 1)^2] \, g(x)$$

$$- \sum_0^{\infty} C_2 \left(\frac{x}{2} + y - z - 1 \right) g(x) \bigg\} h(y)$$

It will be seen that all except the first three terms reduce to single summations, and in fact, all except the first three terms vanish.

Thus

$$\Delta C(z) = \sum_0^z \sum_0^{z-y} C_1 \, g(x) \, h(y)$$

$$+ \sum_0^z \sum_{z-y+1}^{\infty} \frac{1}{x} \left[(C_1 + C_2) \left(z - y + \frac{1}{2} \right) - C_2 \right] g(x) \, h(y)$$

$$- \sum_{z+1}^{\infty} \sum_0^{\infty} C_2 \, g(x) \, h(y)$$

REFERENCES

Freeman, H., *Mathematics for Actuarial Students*, Cambridge University Press, Cambridge, 1939.

Whittaker, E. T., and G. Robinson, *The Calculus of Observations: a Treatise on Numerical Mathematics*, 2nd ed., Chapter 1, Blackie & Son Ltd., London and Glasgow, 1929.

TWO

Differentiation of integrals

Let

$$F(z) = \int_{a(z)}^{b(z)} f(x, z)\, dx$$

It is not difficult to verify from first principles that, if $f(x, z)$ possesses a continuous derivative with respect to z throughout the region

$$c \leq z \leq d$$

$$a(z) \leq x \leq b(z)$$

and if the derivatives da/dz and db/dz exist, then

(II.1) $$\frac{dF}{dz} = \int_{a(z)}^{b(z)} \frac{\partial f}{\partial z}\, dx + f(b, z)\frac{db}{dz} - f(a, z)\frac{da}{dz}$$

for all values of z in the interval $c \leq z \leq d$.

It is obvious that, if a and b are constants

$$\frac{dF}{dz} = \int_{a}^{b} \frac{\partial f}{\partial z}\, dx$$

and it can be shown that, provided the integral on the right converges, the result is still true when $b = \infty$ or $a = -\infty$.

In operations research, particularly in inventory problems, we often have occasion to differentiate functions $F(z)$ defined by

(II.2) $$F(z) = \int_0^{b(z)} f_1(x, z)dx + \int_{b(z)}^{\infty} f_2(x, z)dx$$

If $f_1(x, z)$ possesses a continuous derivative with respect to z in the region

$$c \leq z \leq d$$

$$0 \leq x \leq b(z)$$

and if $f_2(x, z)$ has a continuous derivative with respect to z in the region

$$c \leq z \leq d$$

$$x \geq b(z)$$

then, using (II.1), we see that

(II.3) $$\frac{dF}{dz} = \int_0^{b(z)} \frac{\partial f_1}{\partial z} dx + \int_{b(z)}^{\infty} \frac{\partial f_2}{\partial z} dx + \frac{db}{dz}[f_1(b, z) - f_2(b, z)]$$

If the expression in brackets in (II.3) is identically zero, then clearly dF/dz may be obtained simply by differentiating the expression (II.2) for $F(z)$ under the integral signs. That is,

(II.4) $$\frac{dF}{dz} = \int_0^{b(z)} \frac{\partial f_1}{\partial z} dx + \int_{b(z)}^{\infty} \frac{\partial f_2}{\partial z} dx$$

provided

(II.5) $$f_1[b(z), z] = f_2[b(z), z]$$

A suggestive way of interpreting (II.4) and (II.5) is to rewrite $F(z)$ as

(II.6) $$F(z) = \int_0^{\infty} f(x, z) \, dx$$

where

(II.7) $$f(x, z) = f_1(x, z) \quad \text{for} \quad 0 \leq x \leq b(z)$$
$$f(x, z) = f_2(x, z) \quad \text{for} \quad b(z) < x < \infty$$

Then dF/dz is given by (II.4) provided the function $f(x, z)$ is a continuous function of x, which possesses a continuous derivative with respect to z except possibly at points on the curve $x = b(z)$.

The result (II.3) can be extended to double integrals by applying it twice, as follows. Let

(II.8)
$$G(z) = \int_{a(z)}^{b(z)} \int_{u(y,z)}^{v(y,z)} f(x, y, z) \, dx \, dy$$

Sufficient conditions for the repeated application of (II.3) are that the derivatives $\partial f/\partial z$, $\partial u/\partial z$, and $\partial v/\partial z$ exist and be continuous with respect to z throughout the region of integration. Then, by writing

$$F(y, z) = \int_u^v f(x, y, z) \, dx$$

we have

$$G(z) = \int_a^b F(y, z) \, dy$$

Then

$$\frac{dG}{dz} = \int_a^b \frac{\partial F}{\partial z} \, dy + \frac{db}{dz} F(b, z) - \frac{da}{dz} F(a, z)$$

The result, which is analogous to (II.1), is

(II.9)
$$\frac{dG}{dz} = \int_a^b \int_u^v \frac{\partial F}{\partial z} \, dx \, dy + \int_a^b \frac{\partial v}{\partial z} f(v, y, z) \, dx$$

$$- \int_a^b \frac{\partial u}{\partial z} f(u, y, z) \, dx + \frac{db}{dz} \int_{u(b,z)}^{v(b,z)} f(x, b, z) \, dx$$

$$- \frac{da}{dz} \int_{u(a,z)}^{v(a,z)} f(x, a, z) \, dx$$

We shall now state without proof the double-integral analog of (II.4) and (II.5). Let a region A of the xy plane be divided into disjoint sub-regions A_i, where $\Sigma A_i = A$; and suppose that for each subregion A_i there corresponds a function $f_i(x, y, z)$. Suppose $F(z)$ is defined by

(II.10)
$$F(z) = \sum_i \int_{A_i} \int f_i(x, y, z) \, dx \, dy$$

Then we may calculate dF/dz by

(II.11)
$$\frac{dF}{dz} = \sum_i \int_{A_i} \int \frac{\partial f_i}{\partial z} \, dx \, dy$$

provided the following two conditions hold:

(a) The boundary of the entire region A does not depend on z.

(b) If A_i and A_j are adjacent subregions, then $f_i(x, y, z)$ equals $f_j(x, y, z)$ at all points (x, y) along the common boundary of A_i and A_j.

Row

operations

Each step in the application of the simplex method (see Chapter Eight) was found to involve the solution of a system of m equations in $n(\geq m)$ unknowns. This was done efficiently, in the simplex tableau, by certain row operations performed on the coefficient matrix. This appendix gives the details of this method for solving systems of linear equations.

First, let us consider a situation where there are as many independent equations as there are unknowns. In such a situation, there will be a unique numerical solution for the system. Consider the system

$$x_1 + x_2 \qquad = 3$$
$$-x_1 + x_2 + 2x_3 = 11$$
$$3x_2 - x_3 = 1$$

A common method of solving such systems is the method of *elimination*. If the second equation is replaced by the sum of the first and second equations, the resulting system is

$$x_1 + x_2 \qquad = 3$$
$$2x_2 + 2x_3 = 14$$
$$3x_2 - x_3 = 1$$

This system will have the same solution as the original system. Continuing, we replace the second equation by the sum of the second equation and twice the third, obtaining

$$x_1 + x_2 \qquad = 3$$
$$8x_2 \qquad = 16$$
$$3x_2 - x_3 = 1$$

Dividing the second equation by 8, we get

$$x_1 + x_2 \qquad = 3$$
$$x_2 \qquad = 2$$
$$3x_2 - x_3 = 1$$

Continuing in this manner, we finally obtain the equivalent system

$$x_1 \qquad = 1$$
$$x_2 \qquad = 2$$
$$x_3 = 5$$

which is also an explicit solution of the original system.

It can be seen that all the operations on *equations* in the elimination method can be considered as operations on *rows* of the following matrix, which represents the original system:

$$\begin{vmatrix} 1 & 1 & 0 & | & 3 \\ -1 & 1 & 2 & | & 11 \\ 0 & 3 & -1 & | & 1 \end{vmatrix}$$

For, if we add the first row to the second, we get

$$\begin{vmatrix} 1 & 1 & 0 & | & 3 \\ 0 & 2 & 2 & | & 14 \\ 0 & 3 & -1 & | & 1 \end{vmatrix}$$

Add twice the third row to the second:

$$\begin{vmatrix} 1 & 1 & 0 & | & 3 \\ 0 & 8 & 0 & | & 16 \\ 0 & 3 & -1 & | & 1 \end{vmatrix}$$

Divide the second row by 8:

$$\begin{vmatrix} 1 & 1 & 0 & 3 \\ 0 & 1 & 0 & 2 \\ 0 & 3 & -1 & 1 \end{vmatrix}$$

Subtract the second row from the first:

$$\begin{vmatrix} 1 & 0 & 0 & 1 \\ 0 & 1 & 0 & 2 \\ 0 & 3 & -1 & 1 \end{vmatrix}$$

Subtract three times the second row from the third:

$$\begin{vmatrix} 1 & 0 & 0 & 1 \\ 0 & 1 & 0 & 2 \\ 0 & 0 & -1 & -5 \end{vmatrix}$$

Multiply the third row by -1:

$$\begin{vmatrix} 1 & 0 & 0 & 1 \\ 0 & 1 & 0 & 2 \\ 0 & 0 & 1 & 5 \end{vmatrix}$$

Re-interpret the matrix as a set of equations:

$$x_1 = 1$$
$$x_2 = 2$$
$$x_3 = 5$$

which is the desired solution.

The essential feature in solution by matrices is that by a succession of row operations of either of the following types:

(a) multiplying or dividing all elements of a row by some constant,
(b) replacing a row by the sum of that row and a multiple of some other row,

we eventually can reach a matrix with ones and zeros in appropriate positions, from which a solution to the original system may be read off.

Now consider a situation where there are more unknowns than equations (as is the case at each iterative step of the simplex method). If there are m *independent* equations in n unknowns, and if $n > m$, we know from algebra that there is no unique numerical solution, but that any designated set of m of the variables can usually be expressed in terms of the remaining $n - m$ variables. The method of elimination, or its matrix analog, may be used exactly as in the case where $m = n$. The following example will illustrate the method.

Example

Given the following system of three equations in five unknowns:

$$\begin{cases} x_1 + 2x_2 + \phantom{x_3 + {}} x_4 = 7 \\ \phantom{x_1 + {}} x_2 + x_3 + x_4 + x_5 = 24 \\ x_1 - 3x_3 + 2x_5 = 8 \end{cases}$$

Solve for x_1, x_3, and x_5 in terms of the remaining variables.

SOLUTION

The matrix representing the original system is:

$$\begin{vmatrix} 1 & 2 & 0 & 1 & 0 & 7 \\ 0 & 1 & 1 & 1 & 1 & 24 \\ 1 & 0 & -3 & 0 & 2 & 8 \end{vmatrix}$$

Subtract row 1 from row 3:

$$\begin{vmatrix} 1 & 2 & 0 & 1 & 0 & 7 \\ 0 & 1 & 1 & 1 & 1 & 24 \\ 0 & -2 & -3 & -1 & 2 & 1 \end{vmatrix}$$

Subtract $(\frac{1}{2})$ (third row) from second row:

$$\begin{vmatrix} 1 & 2 & 0 & 1 & 0 & 7 \\ 0 & 2 & \frac{5}{2} & \frac{3}{2} & 0 & \frac{47}{2} \\ 0 & -2 & -3 & -1 & 2 & 1 \end{vmatrix}$$

Multiply third row by $\frac{1}{2}$:

$$\begin{vmatrix} 1 & 2 & 0 & 1 & 0 & 7 \\ 0 & 2 & \frac{5}{2} & \frac{3}{2} & 0 & \frac{47}{2} \\ 0 & -1 & -\frac{3}{2} & -\frac{1}{2} & 1 & \frac{1}{2} \end{vmatrix}$$

Add $(\frac{3}{5})$ (second row) to third row:

$$\begin{vmatrix} 1 & 2 & 0 & 1 & 0 & 7 \\ 0 & 2 & \frac{5}{2} & \frac{3}{2} & 0 & \frac{47}{2} \\ 0 & \frac{1}{5} & 0 & \frac{2}{5} & 1 & \frac{73}{5} \end{vmatrix}$$

Multiply second row by $\frac{2}{5}$:

$$\left|\begin{array}{ccccc|c} 1 & 2 & 0 & 1 & 0 & 7 \\ 0 & \frac{4}{5} & 1 & \frac{3}{5} & 0 & \frac{47}{5} \\ 0 & \frac{1}{5} & 0 & \frac{2}{5} & 1 & \frac{73}{5} \end{array}\right|$$

Re-interpreting the last matrix as a set of equations, we have

$$x_1 + 2x_2 + \quad x_4 = 7$$
$$\tfrac{4}{5}x_2 + \quad x_3 + \tfrac{3}{5}x_4 = \tfrac{47}{5}$$
$$\tfrac{1}{5}x_2 + \tfrac{2}{5}x_4 + \quad x_5 = \tfrac{73}{5}$$

which yields as a solution to the problem as stated

$$x_1 = 7 \quad - 2x_2 - \quad x_4$$
$$x_3 = \tfrac{47}{5} - \tfrac{4}{5}x_2 - \tfrac{3}{5}x_4$$
$$x_5 = \tfrac{73}{5} - \tfrac{1}{5}x_2 - \tfrac{2}{5}x_4$$

Index